The Life of a Pest

The Life of a Pest

An Ethnography of
Biological Invasion in Mexico

———

Emily Wanderer

UNIVERSITY OF CALIFORNIA PRESS

University of California Press
Oakland, California

Library of Congress Cataloging-in-Publication Data

Names: Wanderer, Emily, author.
Title: The life of a pest : an ethnography of biological invasion in Mexico /
    Emily Wanderer.
Description: Oakland, California : The University of California Press,
    [2020] | Includes bibliographical references and index.
Identifiers: LCCN 2019047767 (print) | LCCN 2019047768 (ebook) |
    ISBN 9780520302624 (cloth) | ISBN 9780520302648 (paperback) |
    ISBN 9780520972537 (ebook)
Subjects: LCSH: Biopolitics—Mexico.
Classification: LCC JA80 .W36 2020 (print) | LCC JA80 (ebook) |
    DDC 333.70972—dc23
LC record available at https://lccn.loc.gov/2019047767
LC ebook record available at https://lccn.loc.gov/2019047768

Manufactured in the United States of America

28 27 26 25 24 23 22 21 20
10 9 8 7 6 5 4 3 2 1

For Nathan

CONTENTS

ILLUSTRATIONS

FIGURES

MAP

ACKNOWLEDGMENTS

This book would not have been possible without the help, mentorship, guidance, and friendship of many people along the way, and it is a pleasure to be able to thank them here. The scientists in Mexico and elsewhere who welcomed me into their laboratories, field sites, and offices made this book possible. They patiently answered my questions and challenged and reshaped my thinking with questions of their own. I am so grateful for their time, expertise, and teaching. In particular, I was assisted by scientists at the Grupo de Ecología y Conservación de Islas, the Instituto Nacional de Enfermedades Respiratorias, AMEXBIO, the Comisón Nacional para el Conocimiento y Uso de la Biodiversidad, the Universidad Nacional Autónoma de México, the Banco Nacional de Germoplasma Vegetal, La Raza hospital, the World Health Organization, the US Department of Health and Human Services, USAID, and the US Department of Defense.

I have been fortunate to work with many brilliant scholars who have shaped my thinking and my writing in countless ways. First, Stefan Helmreich has been an extraordinary advisor. His scholarship inspires me, as does his astonishing generosity with his time and support. David Jones helped guide me through the history of medicine and biology and has encouraged me to think more historically. My scholarship and my teaching have both benefited greatly from his guidance. Jean Jackson shared her impressive knowledge of Latin America with me, and her encouragement has given me confidence. Her keen editing and insistence on engaging and precise writing have significantly improved this work.

The lively intellectual community of the History, Anthropology, and Society (HASTS) program at MIT was a wonderful incubator for this project. Many faculty members at MIT were vital teachers and mentors for me, including Harriet Ritvo, Heather Paxson, Chris Walley, Michael Fischer, Susan Silbey, Manduhai Buyandelger, Erica James, and Natasha Schüll. The graduate student community at HASTS has been an incredible source of support and intellectual sustenance. I thank Amah Edoh, Chihyung Jeon, Amy Johnson, Shreeharsh Kelkar, Nicole Labruto, Teasel Muir-Harmony, Lucas Müller, Tom Özden-Schilling, Canay Özden-Schilling, Rebecca Perry, Sophia Roosth, Shira Shmuely, Alma Steingart, Caterina Scaramelli, Mitali Thakor, Michaela Thompson, and Ben Wilson. Karen Gardner was an essential source of support and assistance in navigating grad school. Fellow members of my writing group—Mary Brazelton, Joy Rankin, and David Singerman—have read many drafts in various stages of organization and have sharpened my thinking tremendously, as well as being a crucial source of support. Lisa Messeri and Rebecca Woods have likewise read and this text and improved it in countless ways; I thank them for both their intellectual engagement and their friendship.

I had my first introduction to the anthropology of science at the University of Chicago, where Joe Masco was an excellent mentor. Karin Knorr Cetina, James Evans, Anwen Tormey, and Elizabeth Campbell were likewise instrumental in my academic formation. I spent a happy year at Bowdoin College, where colleagues both in and out of the Sociology and Anthropology Department contributed to my thinking. In particular, I thank Jenny Baca, Greg Beckett, Monica Brannon, Sakura Christmas, April Strickland, Nancy Riley, and Krista Van Vleet.

I finished the writing and revising of this book while at the University of Pittsburgh. Pitt has been a fantastic place to think and teach, and I thank my colleagues in the Department of Anthropology for making it so, in particular, Joseph Alter, Laura Brown, Heath Cabot, Nicole Constable, Bryan Hanks, Robert Hayden, Gabriella Lukacs, Tomas Matza, Kathleen Musante, Andrew Strathern, and Gabby Yearwood. Students at Pitt have also helped me immeasurably, and working with them has helped me to see things from new perspectives and to clarify my thinking. In particular, I'm grateful to Dafne Lastra Landa and Maria Ryabova for lively conversations and their insightful questions. Colleagues outside the department and at other institutions in Pittsburgh, in particular Nicole Heller, Zach Horton, Ruth Mostern, Abigail Owens, Noah Theriault, and Mari Webel, have shaped my thinking.

I have presented portions of this research in many different settings. Comments, questions, and critiques from a wide array of audiences have made this work better. I would like to thank in particular Michael Dove, John Hartigan, Carlos López Beltrán, Karen-Sue Taussig, Suman Seth, and Sarah Pritchard for their engagement with this project. Mexico City was made more fun by the warm welcome I received there from Ana Kong, Jose María Gómez, Carlos Gallegos, Petra Bühler, and Alejandro Smutny.

Financial support from a number of institutions and foundations was essential to this research. My research in Mexico was supported by a Dissertation Fieldwork

Grant from the Wenner-Gren Foundation and a Doctoral Dissertation Research Improvement Grant from the National Science Foundation. At MIT, I thank the International Science and Technology Initiatives Anthony and Rosina Sun Fellowship and the MIT Center for International Studies for providing support and research funding. A Mellon-ACLS Dissertation Completion Fellowship awarded by the American Council of Learned Societies provided time for writing at an absolutely crucial stage. A Hewlett International Grant from the Center for International Studies at the University of Pittsburgh provided additional support.

Portions of this book have appeared in other forms in "The Axolotl in Global Circuits of Knowledge Production: Producing Multispecies Potentiality," *Cultural Anthropology* 33, no. 4 (2019): 650–79; "Bioseguridad in Mexico: Pursuing Security between Local and Global Biologies," *Medical Anthropology Quarterly* 31, no. 3 (2017): 315–31; and "Biologies of Betrayal: Judas Goats and Sacrificial Mice on the Margins of Mexico," *Biosocieties* 10, no. 1 (2014): 1–23.

Kate Marshall has been a crucial guide throughout this process; I thank her, Enrique Ochoa-Kaup, and the rest of the team at the University of California Press for their editorial work and support. Thanks also to Ben Alexander for his perceptive and sensitive copy-editing.

My family has supported me in every endeavor. I rely on my parents Tom Wanderer and Sara Mannix. They have always encouraged me, and I could not have done this without them. Meghan, Greg, and Stephanie Wanderer are sources of great joy and fun in my life. Members of my extended family—Cathy Smith-Hogan, Thatcher, Brooke, and Whitney Hogan, and Pat Walters—have all been crucial sources of support. My grandmothers Mary Lou Mannix and Joan Wanderer are models for me of generosity and love.

Finally, this book is for Nathan Hogan and Hollis and Greta Hogan-Wanderer. Hollis and Greta make life better; I am inspired by their boundless curiosity and enthusiasm for the world. Nathan has given me confidence and encouraged me through every step of this project. Our adventures together have been spectacular, and I am happy and grateful every day that he is my partner.

Introduction

Living Better in Mexico

VIVIR MEJOR

In 2010, an intriguing symbol was prominent in Mexico: a rainbow-colored rosette accompanied by the words *Vivir Mejor*, or "live better." It adorned buildings, documents, posters, web pages, and T-shirts. Vivir Mejor was a strategy developed by the Mexican government during Felipe Calderón's 2006–12 presidency, and it reflected thinking within the political and scientific establishment about life itself as an object of governance and security. Not a social program, it was instead a way of establishing government priorities for social policies and coordinating programmatic goals. Among other things, Vivir Mejor was intended to improve people's lives through focusing the government's attention on greater access to food, education, health, housing, and other resources. It also articulated the government's commitment to "sustainable human development," that is, to programs that acknowledged that "not only must the disparity between the poor and the rich be corrected, but also the rupture between nature and man."[1]

The human population was the most obvious target of the Vivir Mejor strategy, but, as the call for sustainable development indicated, it is also true that Mexico teems with nonhuman life-forms that tend to go unnoticed by casual observers yet are essential to Mexican conceptions of the nation. These flora and fauna range from microscopic to ecosystemic, from domesticated to wild. They include influenza viruses incorporating genes from swine and avian strains, US-made transgenic maize growing in Oaxacan fields, feral goats ranging across remote islands while wearing radio collars, and salamanders swimming in the canals of Xochimilco in Mexico City. This book is about how these nonhuman life-forms came to be seen

1

as essential to projects of living better and how scientists and the Mexican government made decisions about how to improve and protect life, judging which species belonged and which were alien, which should live and which should die.

The promise to improve life was made by a government suffering a crisis of legitimacy as a result of its battles with drug cartels and the violence and insecurity endemic to some regions of the country. Coverage of this violence in both the national and international press frequently characterized various states and regions as having entirely escaped the control of the federal government. For example, Ciudad Juárez, on the border with the United States in the state of Chihuahua, was notorious as an ungovernable city.[2] Once a thriving border town, in 2008 Juárez had one of the highest murder rates in the world—101 homicides per hundred thousand inhabitants.[3] In 2010, Arnoldo Kraus, a well-known physician and writer, bemoaned the failure of the state to sustain urban life. Writing in the Mexico City daily newspaper *La Jornada*, he called Ciudad Juárez "a dead being that needs life," addressing the urban area itself as a life-form that had lost its vitality and needed tending. Kraus argued that as a result of the growing violence and insecurity, Mexicans were increasingly distrustful and even contemptuous of the country's institutions and were questioning the viability of the rule of law itself.[4]

Many therefore responded cynically to the government's Vivir Mejor slogan. The failure of the state to maintain the health and security of its citizens and cities, let alone improve life, was protested in a line of graffiti that appeared around Mexico City, replacing Calderón's slogan with *Morir Mejor*, or "die better," as seen in the mural reproduced in figure 1. The mural, which depicts a graveyard piled with skulls, bodies, and a decapitated head, was put up in a busy Mexico City square. Meanwhile, protestors hung banners suggesting that in order for Mexicans to live better, Calderón should be removed from office. A drawing by popular cartoonist José Hernández similarly critiqued the slogan, depicting a man bleeding on the ground with his hands tied behind his back. Placed next to a wall painted with the Vivir Mejor graphic, this figure says "Mejor vivir," which might translate as "better simply to be alive." These displays represented the popular viewpoint that under the conditions produced by Calderón's government, rather than striving to live better, Mexican citizens hoped merely to continue living.

Despite these critiques of the failures of government to provide the security necessary for life, the government continued to articulate an objective of better living. And if living better was the ostensible goal of the government, biological research was one mode through which the project and its successes were perceived, measured, and managed. While the state may have intended the subjects of the slogan or injunction "live better" to be the human population of the country, biologists engaging in projects to improve life conceived of the life-forms in question more broadly, drawing in nonhuman populations as essential elements of the

FIGURE 1. Detail of mural in Coyoacán, Mexico City. Source: Author photograph.

nation. Using ethnographic research to examine biosecurity discourse and practice in Mexico, I argue that in these projects biology becomes the focus of security practices, and, as a result, scientists take on new roles in Mexican life. Their research conjoins the political with the biological in what Michel Foucault termed biopolitics.[5]

The shifting roles of Mexican biologists are tied to the centrality of security for the state itself.[6] Recent anthropological analyses have argued that security is only growing in significance as a mode for governing social and political life, particularly in Latin America. Security concerns have been used to legitimize increased state surveillance, as well as the suspension of individual rights and the use of force.[7] Security entails establishing boundaries and borders, marking particular groups as inside or outside; in biosecurity projects, scientists are central to establishing these boundaries, and biology becomes the thread that connects populations and demarcates which life-forms are worth saving or protecting. Security in this context is not only about protecting and optimizing a human population, but also about sustaining and developing biological life more broadly, as scientists move biopolitics and biosecurity beyond the human to include animal, plant, and microbial worlds.

This book examines how contemporary scientists working on human health, conservation, and agriculture identify particular populations as healthy or unhealthy and produce biopolitical apparatuses that incorporate multiple species and sort bodies according to categories of difference that are informed by Mexican history and culture. These projects entail the integration of culture and the natural world, drawing on mestizo and indigenous paradigms for understanding the world in which nature has not been conceptualized as pristine or separate from culture. Guillermo Bonfil Batalla writes of the relationships in Mexico between human life, landscape, flora, and fauna as reciprocal engagements that have produced what he calls a "humanized nature." In addition to these reciprocal relationships, Bonfil Batalla notes that indigenous Mexican languages name and classify the world in different ways than European ones do, linguistic distinctions indicative of the different paradigms on which indigenous knowledge and worldviews are based.[8]

The idea of nature as an autonomous domain separated from culture is a product of Western modernity: culture and nature are analytic categories developed by particular humans to understand the world.[9] Many scholars have examined how the divides between nature and culture, as well as between human and nonhuman, are produced in modern Western culture and science and have analyzed how indigenous paradigms for understanding the world are constructed differently.[10] Donna Haraway suggests thinking in terms of naturecultures to highlight the inseparability and interconnection of these categories.[11] Bodies, for example, are always biosocial: mixed-up hybrids of nature and culture. Marisol de la Cadena's work points to the way that indigenous movements in the Andes have challenged the divisions between nature and culture, rejecting the distinctions between people and nature that have grounded modernity and instead incorporating nonhumans into political and social worlds.[12] Biopolitical and biosecurity practices in Mexico, where nature and culture are not easily distinguished or separated, look different from those in Euro-American places.

Many scientists have made claims about how Mexican biology was shaped by history, culture, and environment in ways that make it distinct and often in need of special protection. Through research on, for example, the links between air and illness or history and viral ecologies, scientists have articulated connections between life-forms and places. As this book will show, biosecurity projects have made invisible entities perceptible and used them as evidence of the biological connections among Mexicans, contributing to ideas of a collective identity based around shared and threatened unseen biology. These projects have assimilated nonhuman life-forms into categories like nationality and ethnicity in distinctively Mexican ways, incorporating and transforming ideas of patrimony; the linkages between people, other life-forms, and places; and *mestizaje*. Mestizaje is the process by which unlike and sometimes incongruous bodies and populations are mixed, generally referring to the mixture of a large number of diverse indigenous groups with European populations and other nonindigenous people. It has become a principal quality of *mexicanidad* and is foundational to ideas of the nation.[13]

Latin Americanists have long interpreted the region as a laboratory for nations and nation-building; this book suggests that a new way of constructing national identity has emerged in Mexico, one that transforms the categories with which we understand human and nonhuman life.

One articulation of the relationship between biology and security in Mexico came in 2011, in an interview with José Ángel Córdova Villalobos, the secretary of health. In this interview, which was published in the journal of the Asociación Mexicana de Bioseguridad (AMEXBIO), a professional organization focused on raising awareness of biosecurity issues in Mexico, Córdova outlined a vision for improving biosecurity and thus the health of the population. He argued that the first step was the construction and improvement of public health laboratories throughout the country to enhance the state's ability to control and diagnose infectious diseases. High-quality labs would allow public health officials to accurately detect influenza, dengue, measles, and other infectious diseases and to formulate rapid responses based on scientific evidence. Supported by centralized national laboratories that could perform DNA sequencing on dangerous microbes, this enhanced laboratory infrastructure would represent an important step towards preparedness by enabling Mexico to diagnose and know the origins of diseases.[14]

Moving beyond the issue of infectious disease, Córdova presented an expansive view of biosecurity, bringing within its ambit any contaminant, pathogen, or organism that might negatively affect Mexican health, including genetically modified organisms, unsafe food, polluted air, compromised water, and infectious disease. He even included climate change. In his assessment, any and all of these issues might be appropriately subject to government intervention in order to produce better living.[15] The popular perception that the government was unable to perform even the most basic functions, like protecting the lives of citizens from violence, did not inhibit government spokespersons like Córdova from articulating an ambitious vision of its role in improving and regulating life. As outlined by Córdova, improving life in Mexico required efforts to protect not only human health, but also the health of nonhuman life-forms and the environment as a whole.

BIOSECURITY VERSUS BIOSEGURIDAD

In the United States, in both public policy and anthropological discourse, the word *biosecurity* has generally referred to practices to protect the health of a population. Its earliest iterations were primarily related to agricultural efforts to protect livestock.[16] Concerns about biosecurity expanded beyond agriculture and became particularly potent in the United States in 2001 when, shortly after the September 11 attacks, letters containing anthrax spores were mailed to the offices of several US senators and media figures. Twenty-two people became infected with anthrax as a result, and five people died.[17] Only the second successful known bioterrorist attack in the United States, the incidents were seen as evidence that the health and safety of US citizens were under imminent threat from new sources of danger.[18] As a result, the US federal government substantially increased funding for research on infectious diseases, particularly those seen as potential biological weapons. These changes were part of a larger trend that Andrew Lakoff has identified as emerging over the past thirty years, in which, as he says, "a new way of thinking about and acting on disease threat had arisen: It was no longer a question only of prevention, but also—and perhaps even more—one of preparedness."[19] Acting in terms of a rationality of preparedness, rather than simply attempting to prevent the emergence of a known risk, the United States continually monitors the population for any potentially emerging disease.[20] The focus is no longer only on prevention, but on preparing for possible threats by developing surveillance infrastructure, identifying systemic vulnerabilities, and preparing systems that can respond to any kind of health or security threat.

While interviewing people about biosecurity discourse and practice in Mexico, I found that they often expressed wide-ranging conceptions of biological security, ideas that echoed Córdova's assessment of the issue and that differed substantially from those dominant in the United States. During a preliminary research trip to Mexico, I gave a poster presentation at AMEXBIO's annual meeting. The audience, composed primarily of scientists from Mexico, was both intrigued by the idea of an anthropologist studying science and insistent that I understand what bioseguridad means in Mexico. As I was instructed, rather than centering on concerns about bioweapons or the misuse of scientific research or materials, biosecurity or biosafety consists of practices to protect life and the environment much more generally.

This broad definition of biosecurity is also apparent in the usage of the term *bioseguridad* in the media. Bioseguridad emerged in Mexican newspapers in mid-1999, when it was deployed in relation to infectious disease (particularly blood-borne pathogens that could contaminate the nation's blood supply) and to genetically modified organisms.[21] In Mexico as elsewhere, biosecurity is a flexible term and concept. This flexibility makes biosecurity discourse particularly convenient, able to encompass and legitimize a wide range of actions concerned with securing life.[22] Use of the term grew in subsequent years, as bioseguridad appeared in conjunction with stories about disease, invasive species that threatened Mexican ecosystems, and biotechnology, particularly genetically modified organisms developed outside Mexico. These security practices are generally concerned with identifying and controlling species out of place; they therefore require definitions of, first, which life-forms are considered native and which are alien, and, second, which human practices foster the continued growth of "good," native species and which facilitate the spread of dangerous, alien species.[23] Defining "native" life-forms requires establishing what is unique and valuable about Mexican biology. By documenting and maintaining the distinctiveness of life-forms in different places, these biosecurity measures are intended to counteract the potentially homogenizing effects of the increasing global circulation of people, animals, plants, and microbes. I define practices of *bioseguridad* as those through which scientists demarcate native or national populations, identify alien life-forms, and seek to mitigate threats to native populations. Through these projects, scientists produce knowledge about Mexican biology (including who or what is included or excluded in these populations). As this knowledge in turn informs political efforts to improve human and ecological health, biosecurity projects become ways in which science and the nation in Mexico are coproduced.[24] These projects were shaped by the historical relationship between science and the nation in Mexico as well as conceptualizations of nature and culture.

Informed by these definitions, this book draws on ethnographic research with scientists to examine the production of biosecurity in a variety of sites: first, by examining how conservationists working in Mexican settings—particularly on islands—alternately protect or exterminate the various life-forms they encounter (chapters 1 and 2); then, how microbiologists and immunologists studying infectious disease in Mexico understand the relationships between environments, bodies, and viral ecologies (chapters 3 and 4); and finally, how ecologists regulating the use of genetically modified organisms (GMOs) establish the ecological identity of a place and make decisions about the significance and potential impact of GMOs (chapter 5). This series of case studies brings together things that are usually seen separately; each case illuminates different aspects of the complex relationship between security, biology, and national identity. How people think about nature and the relationship of people to their environment shape choices about which nonhuman life-forms need protection and which are threats. By bringing together this assortment of interlocutors and research sites, I map the variety of ways that biosecurity projects establish how a shared biological substantiality connects the nation and incorporates human and nonhuman life-forms into political identities. All of these projects entail thinking through the entanglement of human and nonhuman life-forms, making judgments about how people, animals, plants, and microbes have mutually produced one another over time and continue to do so in the present day. While these case studies illustrate quite divergent projects of biosecurity, they all enact an understanding of nature that is not separate from human life and demonstrate how human life in Mexico relies on and fashions nonhuman life-forms.

SCIENCE AND THE NEO-LAMARCKIAN NATION

The founding myths of modern Mexico depict a unified nation emerging from disparate European and indigenous elements. While the precise characteristics of *mexicanidad* are up for debate, nation-building, *indigenista*,[25] and assimilationist projects all draw on ideas of Mexican hybridity represented as a robust, productive form that emerges from the historical interactions of Mexico's heterogenous groups.[26] Debates over the value of mixture and hybridity have often been waged in scientific terms. While European scientists and naturalists in the late nineteenth century claimed that mixing human populations would inevitably lead to degeneracy, people in Latin America produced counterdiscourses that celebrated hybridity. Scientists, intellectuals, and politicians in Mexico disputed European claims that hybridization produced degeneration, arguing instead that mixing human populations, particularly European and indigenous Latin American ones, would have salutary effects.[27] Furthermore, mestizaje was seen as a solution to one of the fundamental challenges of the Mexican state, that of the heterogeneity of the population.[28]

Ideas about mestizaje as a biological and cultural process informed policies and practices regarding daily life, movements of populations, and national identity throughout the history of the Mexican nation.[29] Interest in hybridity was strong after the Mexican Revolution, as scientists promoted racial and cultural mixture as a way to produce a strong nation out of a fragmented colonial history and a heterogeneous population.[30] José Vasconcelos's influential 1925 essay *The Cosmic Race* exemplified the celebration of mestizaje, mythologizing the Mexican population as a superior fusion of races. Vasconcelos presented a utopian fantasy of the emergence of a new "cosmic race" in Latin America. This cosmic race was to be "a mixture of races accomplished according to the laws of social well-being, sympathy, and beauty," which would "lead to the creation of a type infinitely superior to all that have previously existed."[31] Vasconcelos argued that this new type would emerge in Latin America because the region exhibited a greater degree of mixing between races than the United States, Europe, or elsewhere. He drew promiscuously on historic and contemporary scientific theories to make his argument, including Jean-Baptiste Lamarck's theory of inheritance of acquired characteristics, meteorologist Alfred Wegener's theory of continental drift and Pangaea, and Mendelian genetics.

According to Vasconcelos, the "maximum type is not precisely the White, but that new race to which the White himself will have to aspire with the object of conquering the synthesis."[32] In *The Cosmic Race* he transformed European discourse about race, rejecting the idea that hybridization inherently produced degeneracy and arguing instead that through mixing the Mexican population would ascend a hierarchical scale of racial improvement. In this context, indigenous populations were an essential part of the nation. The glorious historical accomplishments of indigenous people were to be celebrated and provide the basis of Latin American civilization. However, it also meant that contemporary indigenous populations should be assimilated into the "cosmic race" through mixing with the rest of the population, rather than retaining distinct identities. For Vasconcelos and others, the future of the nation was in homogeneity, and indigenous populations had no role in the nation as autonomous or culturally separate groups of people.[33] Historical ideologies like that of the emergence of a "cosmic race" powerfully structured ideas of inclusion and exclusion and the treatment of various populations in Latin America. In Mexico, the celebration of mestizaje represented the country as uniquely suited to producing the ideal human population through "constructive miscegenation."

Beyond the emphasis on the value of mixture, this rhetoric also incorporated neo-Lamarckian ideas of heredity, in which the environment was instrumental in shaping the health and vitality of the population, and rejected the idea of sharp boundaries between nature and nurture. In contrast to European notions of the fixity of biological traits, eugenic discourse in Latin America, as well as ideas about race and kinship more generally, emphasized the malleability of biology and its potential for transformation in response to the environment.[34] As Elizabeth Roberts has argued, in contrast to North American representations of human populations as biologically essential groups, for Latin American scientists, populations were formed in relation to the environment and were, correspondingly, malleable and subject to change.[35]

The postrevolutionary state's provision of welfare exemplified these beliefs in the malleability of bodies and biology. For politicians and others, providing medical care served a dual purpose, by both legitimizing the postrevolutionary state and improving the population as a whole.[36] Scientists concerned with population improvement developed child welfare programs, instituted courses in puericulture for women and girls, intervened in food consumption practices, and built schools and playgrounds, all with the idea that managing child development and parenting (particularly mothering) was key to the proper development of productive citizens and the nation as a whole.[37] These programs and medical research emphasized the effect of the social and material environment on germplasm on the grounds that Mendelian genetics was inadequate for understanding patterns of inheritance and development.[38] Eugenic projects informed by these ideas sought to improve the population not only by intervening in reproduction but also by modifying the environment and social behavior.

MANAGING NONHUMAN LIFE

Ideas about mestizaje, the malleability of biology, and neo-Lamarckian ideas of improvement had consequences for the management of the nonhuman world as well.[39] Eugenic projects that sought to manage the environment in order to improve human life highlighted the notion that bodies are produced in and through interactions with the world around them. And, if the human body was shaped by its environment, the environment was also shaped in and through interactions with people. Culture and nature in Mexico, according to those belief systems, were characterized by entanglement, rather than division.

Modern Euro-American thought, in contrast, framed nature as a place apart, untouched by human activity or culture. This pattern is evident, for example, in rhetoric about establishing national parks in the United States. Naturalist John Muir's call for the creation of such sites used dramatic, emotionally charged language to argue for the protection of significant wild places and their maintenance as areas untouched by human activity.[40] In this rendering, nature and culture were in opposition. Conservationists in Europe and the United States frequently contrasted sublime nature with dull, ugly, urban life, reinforcing the divide between humans and nature.[41] The origins and history of national parks in Mexico diverge in instructive ways from parks in the United States. While American parks were justified in terms of preserving pristine nature from destruction by an industrializing society, Mexican parks were not organized around protecting pure nature. Rather, they tended to be sited on land that was perceived as damaged or altered by human activity with the idea of repairing degraded lands for the use of citizens.[42] Conservation in Mexico focused on protecting natural resources in order for them to be used and because of their importance for human health.[43] Forested areas were meant to be properly managed and cultivated, and nature in general was a resource integrated with human life. Emily Wakild points out that scientific experts in the Porfirian period "carefully managed and manicured this new nature just as they shaped the ideal Porfirian citizen."[44] The management of nature and citizens in Mexico City went hand in hand; both were objects of control and improvement, each intended to improve the other.[45] Control over environmental resources, whether trees, water, or other, was both practically significant for the economic development of the nation and symbolically important as a demonstration of the power and legitimacy of the government.[46]

Government efforts to promote conservation by changing the way nature is used and who has access to the land have prompted intense debates. In recent years the state has sought to protect biodiversity by creating biosphere reserves, conservation areas from which people are excluded. These reserves were sites in which the government attempted to articulate a new relationship between the state, citizens, and the natural world, one in which nature was protected by separating it from people, transforming earlier practices. In instituting these reserves, the state took the position that Mexican biology and biodiversity were fragile and valuable entities in need of protection from the damage caused by campesinos. Campesinos critiqued these projects, arguing that they undermined the ejido system of communal land tenure by limiting their access to the land and were a breach of the social contract in which nature was meant to be used as a resource for citizens.[47]

These projects took place alongside a long history of indigenous thought and science which attended to the ways human and nonhuman life mutually made one

another in Mexico. For example, as Roberto González has shown, Zapotec practices
of cultivating maize are based on conceptual foundations distinct from those
deployed in Western science. They attend to the ways maize and human life structure each other, offering an alternative ontology to Euro-American divisions between
culture and nature. In Zapotec perspectives, the earth, rivers, and individual crops
like maize are animate objects and personified.[48] They are entities with which
humans have reciprocal relationships, rather than mere matter. Maize in particular
is noteworthy as a plant-person, one that has a heart and soul and which must be
treated with respect and care. People who behave improperly may find that their
crops fail or their stored maize disappears.[49]

These practices recognize the way both humans and maize rely on one another.
Maize was first domesticated in Mexico, and the various landraces are the result of
a long history of cultivation and trading, one which shaped both human and plant
life.[50] Indigenous Mesoamerican communities' agricultural practices produced a
plant unlike any other grass. In the process of domestication, maize lost its ability to
disperse its own seeds and is now dependent on human intervention for reproduction and survival.[51] As the life cycles of maize and other plants have been shaped by
human activity, human life, including social networks, class, and regional political
culture, has been shaped by people's work to produce plants as commodities.[52] As
chapter 5, "The Bureaucracy of Genetic Modification," analyzes, maize has more
recently been further remade, subject to novel forms of manipulation in the lab,
where scientists have inserted genes from other organisms into its genome.

For many contemporary scientists, ecologists, and conservation experts in
Mexico, ideas of inanimate, pure nature are irrelevant to their work. As one of my
interlocutors noted, "If you are empathetic with the conditions of Mexico, it is very
important that nature provides services and goods to the community. . . It is not
only about nature by itself, but also about nature being used." Nature is configured
as *not* isolated or separate from human life ("nature by itself"); rather, it is connected and integrated with human communities. These conceptual bases have
produced a biosecurity science that diverges from that prevailing approaches to
agricultural biosecurity, which, as Alex Blanchette and others have observed, are
"founded on a fantasy of separation," and are oriented towards isolating human
and animal lives (although the kinds of control and confinement imagined always
exceed what is possible).[53]

This book examines how contemporary scientists in Mexico understand the
interconnections of nature and culture, nonhuman and human. Rather than ideal-
izing separation, these biosecurity practices are an important place in which the
entanglement of human life and politics and nature are made visible and acted
upon. Scientists argue for the need to protect particular populations on the
grounds that the entanglement of Mexican history and life-forms have produced a
unique, "local biology" which needs to be protected and is unaccounted for by

global science.[54] Moving across scales, from ecosystems to microscopic viral life-forms, these case studies represent a range of scientific practices organized around securing and protecting life. They show how some nonhuman life-forms are granted special protection on the basis of their status as unique local biologies, an identity which is often both rooted in a historical understanding of how human and nonhuman life-forms have shaped one another and based on claims of molecular or genetic difference.

COUNTERHISTORY OF THE GLOBAL BIOLOGICAL

Fieldwork in Mexico has revealed the situatedness of technoscientific networks and the stubbornly local nature of scientific research and life-forms. Studying lab practices and what Anna Tsing termed "the sticky materiality of practical encounters" shows how ideas of universal biology are made and reshaped in local experience.[55] The emphasis in biosecurity science on the way that biology is shaped by the particular historical, political, and social context contrasts with modernist notions of the universality of the physical body. These practices underscore the coproduction of the biological and the cultural—both are contingent and both are local.[56]

This focus contrasts with the push within the field of public health to produce global systems of health governance. For the past several decades, the field has emphasized the need to move beyond state-centric and national health projects. Foreign policy and security experts have argued that in the context of increasing globalization, the divide between domestic and foreign health issues has blurred. In particular, the claim has been that globalization has transformed the nature of health risks. They can no longer be limited to one country, but rather, inevitably spread beyond national borders with global effects.[57] Health risks now operate at the scale of the planetary, and countries can no longer operate according to their own immediate self-interest, but should expand the scope of their concerns to think globally. This belief in increased interdependence is apparent in the shift in public health terminology from international health to global health. The change in both terminology and practice reflects an increasing emphasis in the field of public health on the idea of a globally interdependent world system.[58]

The recent case of H1N1 influenza is an instructive example of how, even in the midst of a global epidemic, Mexican scientists produced evidence of material differences in local biologies, made claims for their significance, and located processes like mestizaje at the level of the genome. Despite the evident processes of globalization, they argued, it was important to pay attention to the ways that place and biology are linked. In early March of 2009, patients began arriving at the emergency rooms and clinics of Mexico City, ill not with the usual spring respiratory ailments, but rather a novel strain of H1N1 influenza A, also known as swine flu. Public health surveillance networks documented the emergence of the disease, and officials noted that it seemed to have a relatively high mortality rate and occurred after the end of the usual flu season.[59] As officials and physicians watched, the number of cases rose steadily through the end of March and the beginning of April, and doctors diagnosed patients in a growing number of states as the geographic reach of the disease spread.

In the early weeks, the outbreak dominated political and social action in Mexico. The federal government declared a state of emergency and took measures to contain the disease, shutting down schools, museums, restaurants, and soccer games.[60] The World Health Organization (WHO) also took preemptive action. As global health surveillance networks detected this variant of H1N1 influenza in an increasing number of patients in a growing number of locations around the world, the WHO moved rapidly through the levels of its recently developed pandemic measurement scale. Dr. Margaret Chan, WHO director-general, declared on April 29 that the WHO had decided to raise the level of influenza pandemic alert from phase 4 to phase 5, one step below the highest level on the pandemic scale.[61] Her declaration that the pandemic alert was now at phase 5 indicated that there was human-to-human spread of the virus in at least two countries. The WHO described phase 5 as signifying "that a pandemic is imminent and that the time to finalize the organization, communication, and implementation of the planned mitigation measures is short," and that countries around the globe should take action.[62]

As H1N1 continued to spread, Mexicans focused on controlling the epidemic through monitoring for disease symptoms and testing for presence of the virus. People made public displays of hygienic practices, modeling safe flu behavior like wearing masks and avoiding public gatherings. Elsewhere, responses varied. Other countries engaged in control measures which focused not on unhygienic practices as the source of risk, but on Mexicans and Mexican culture (particularly as represented by and through food) as inherently dangerous. In defiance of WHO advice, some countries quarantined visiting Mexicans, suspended flights from Mexico, and banned imports of Mexican pork.[63] In the United States, a poll conducted by the Harvard School of Public Health for the CDC revealed that a number of Americans were taking swine flu protection into their own hands, engaging in rogue preventative measures not recommended by the CDC. Twenty-five percent of poll respondents said they "avoided air travel or large public gatherings, 16 percent said they avoided people who had recently visited Mexico, and 13 percent said they avoided Mexican restaurants or stores."[64] The conflation of Mexicans and Mexican culture with the virus itself followed historical patterns of response to disease.[65]

One of the challenges of dealing with an epidemic is finding ways to make the contagion visible and thereby subject to control and containment. Confronted with the invisibility of microbes and the absence of obvious signs of disease, people looked for alternate ways to visualize the risk of illness. These tended to depend on historically entrenched narratives of difference and racially located disease.[66] In response to the invisibility of infection, people searched for external markers of potential infection. As H1N1 was strongly identified as emerging from Mexico, markers of Mexican ethnicity or culture such as restaurants or cuisine became pathologized and identified with danger and contamination. While the virus could not be easily identified at border crossings, it was easy to distinguish Mexicans or Mexican planes and turn them away as vectors of contagion.

While the H1N1 outbreak appeared to demonstrate the globalized nature of biol-ogy, responses to the epidemic focused on locating it within particular countries and bodies. This concern with disease as a local issue was reinforced by research by Mexican scientists. On May 11, just two weeks after the WHO declared the H1N1 outbreak a "Public Health Emergency of International Concern," scientists from the National Institute of Genomic Medicine (INMEGEN), one of Mexico's premier scientific institutions, announced that they had concluded a long-term project to produce "a map of the Mexican genome."[67] INMEGEN's mission was to contribute to the health of Mexican people through genomic research and the map of the Mex-ican genome was the product of one of the institute's major initiatives, the Genomic Diversity in the Mexican Population. They convened press conferences to announce their findings, which received extensive media coverage.[68]

The mapping project was structured around both belief in the exceptionality of the Mexican population and fear of exclusion from the benefits of modern medi-cine. The International HapMap Project, the major international project to map human genetic diversity, did not include populations from Latin America.[69] Scien-tists from INMEGEN argued that this exclusion meant that Mexico and other countries in the region would be left out of any potential benefits that might derive from the project.[70] Producing their own map of the Mexican genome was intended to remedy this and was based on the idea that there are significant genetic differ-ences between the Mexican population and the rest of the world that need to be understood. The researchers involved in the project argued that Mexico's sixty Amerindian groups and complex history of genetic admixture made Mexico an ideal country for genomic research, one whose genetic diversity presented chal-lenges, but which also could be "a powerful resource for analyzing the genetic bases of complex diseases."[71] "We know that we come from the indigenous population, or so the story goes, but for scientific work of an international stature, we needed to test it," said Gerardo Jimenez-Sanchez, director of INMEGEN.[72] Jimenez-Sanchez's claims translated mestizaje and collective identity to a molecular and genomic level.

Upon the release of the map of the Mexican genome, Jimenez-Sanchez argued that the Mexican population was unique as a result of its history as a mestizo nation and that this history could now be read in the laboratory on a genomic or molecular level, enacting a form of what Michael Montoya has called "bioethnic conscription," in which biogenetic material is interpreted through and with social and historical understandings.[73] Work at INMEGEN illustrates the traffic between social and political narratives and the practice of genomic science.[74] This research located mestizaje at a new scale, interpreting difference on a molecular level in what I call *biomestizaje*. As Nikolas Rose has argued, as scientists develop new molecular models of life, "biopolitics now addresses human existence at the molecular level: it is waged about molecules, amongst molecules, and where the molecules themselves are at stake."[75] In biomestizaje, the older social category of ethnic identity is translated into a biological substrate that is characterized as uniquely Mexican, one that is produced out of biological inheritances shaped by shared history. Life and potential threats to it are defined on a molecular level, and mestizaje has now become visible in the laboratory.

Jimenez-Sanchez claimed that the genomic map might be particularly valuable in terms of its potential to generate biosecurity. He argued that understanding the genomic composition of a population would accelerate the identification of genetic variations that predisposed people to common diseases and, more immediately significant, that the genomic map INMEGEN had produced might be helpful in understanding why some people are more susceptible to viral infections like H1N1.[76] In its publicity materials, INMEGEN hyped the possible benefits of the research aggressively, asking, "Could genetic differences explain why some people and not others have died of H1N1 Influenza A?" and arguing that the work might one day explain why fatalities from H1N1 occurred almost exclusively in Mexico.[77] These claims identified the human Mexican population as having a unique genetic makeup, one that makes them more or at least differently vulnerable to disease and therefore in need of special biosecurity measures.[78] The outbreak of H1N1 and subsequent responses illustrated a variety of ways in which biology (whether presumed viral or genetic connections) was used to construct collective identity and to make determinations about risk and insecurity.

Historians and philosophers of science Carlos López Beltrán and Francisco Vergara Silva have examined how and why the idea of the Mexican mestizo was taken up by scientists in the twenty-first century. The category of mestizo appeared in lab research in Mexico as a way to classify people and biological materials, demonstrating how cultural categories appear in and are reinforced by scientific research. López Beltrán and Vergara Silva argued that scientists incorporated the idea of mestizaje into their studies of the genomic composition of the nation because it was locally strategic. By characterizing their research as identifying a biological basis for the mestizo and thereby reinforcing preexisting categories of collective identity, scientists drew attention to their research and invested it with significance for the general population.[79] As the publicity surrounding the findings at INMEGEN made clear, molecularizing mestizaje not only gave research more local cachet, it also reinforced ideas about the difference and exceptionality of the population and, crucially, located this difference at the level of the genome. Scientists at INMEGEN called on human genetic information as a source of national identity. Further, they argued this unique identity made Mexicans more vulnerable to certain illnesses (in particular H1N1 influenza) and in need of targeted scientific and medical research, translating their research into security terms.

While this example focuses on the human population of Mexico, the cases in this book will examine the ways both human and nonhuman populations are studied and understood. Bringing together accounts of scientists working on lab safety, urban air quality, viral ecologies, biotechnology and bureaucracy, and island laboratories, this book analyzes the connections between life-forms, human practices, and places that emerge when biology becomes the subject of security practices. My research in Mexico focuses on three main organizations: the Grupo de Ecología y Conservacíon de Islas (GECI), the Departamento de Bioseguridad at the Instituto Nacional de Ecología (INE), and the Instituto Nacional de Enfermedades Respiratorias (INER). At each site, I interviewed and observed scientists, asking how they identify native and alien populations and how they assess which human practices either protect or threaten Mexican populations. I followed individual scientists as they defined the characteristics of native Mexican biologies, developed a repertoire of practices designed to create knowledge about and control over living things, and negotiated global research networks. These projects reveal the importance of place for the production of knowledge.[80] Biosecurity is often made in two canonical places of science, the lab and the field.[81] I also argue for the importance of a third scientific space, the office. The office is distinct from but also entangled with the lab and the field, and is where scientists engage with bureaucratic processes and paperwork and shape the administration of Mexican ecosystems and agriculture.

The first two chapters take place on Isla Guadalupe, a remote Pacific Ocean island, where a group of conservationists study invasive and native species. Chapter 1, "From Degenerates to Regeneration, Convicts to Conservation," delves into the history of Guadalupe as a site for the reconfiguration of human and nonhuman life-forms, first as a refreshment station for whalers, then as a penal colony, and finally as a conservation site. Projects for managing populations on the island are exemplars of multispecies biopolitics, bringing human and nonhuman life-forms into the same frame. Chapter 2, "The Care of the Pest and Animal Betrayals," examines a contemporary project by Grupo de Conservacíon y Ecología de Islas (GECI), a Mexican NGO, to remove invasive mammals from the island. While eradicating animals, scientists engage in what I term "the care of the pest," carefully tending to invaders in order to produce knowledge about their characteristics and social behavior, knowledge that would then be turned against these animals in a "biology of betrayal." On Guadalupe, care and loyalty to the island as a whole entail betraying the goats and mice that are damaging the island's ecosystem. Together, these two chapters examine how scientific voyages and invasive species eradications are used to establish and maintain sovereignty and territorial control over the country's periphery. Further, they explore the consequences for human and animal life of changing perceptions of island ecosystems, from barren wastelands to storehouses of genetic treasures.

Chapter 3, "Acclimatizing Biosecurity," follows microbiologists and immunologists into the lab, analyzing their work to protect life in Mexico from infectious disease and the connections they make between the manipulation and control of microbes and security. While conducting research in bioseguridad, scientists argue for the importance of local biologies, generating tension with global public health projects and regulations premised on the universality of biology. Chapter 4, "Invisible Biologies, Embodied Environments," shows how scientists at INER make the invisible perceptible in the laboratory through studies of air, viral ecologies, HIV, and human genetics and immune systems. The laboratory becomes a key space for articulating the relationship between bodies and environment, as scientists make the claim that human bodies are shaped by environmental contamination and air pollution and are themselves environments that shape viral life-forms. Scientists argue that improving human life requires extending attention both outward to ecosystems and ecological processes and inward to the interactions between human immune systems and viral populations.

The Mexican government prides itself on the country's status as a megadiverse place and as the center of origin for a variety of crops. Plants in Mexico, in particular maize, have long been identified as a national patrimony and crucial resource. The Instituto Nacional de Ecología (National Institute of Ecology or INE) is a key regulatory body for administering and protecting this diversity, charged with assessing the risk genetically modified organisms pose to Mexico's biodiverse ecosystems and agriculture. Chapter 5, "The Bureaucracy of Genetic Modification," follows scientists at INE as they approve or deny applications for the use of GMOs and attempt to manage the ecology of the entire country from their offices in Mexico City. Focusing on the documents and bureaucratic processes of assessing risk and granting or denying permits, this chapter examines how officials interpret the status of ecosystems and the potential threats that GMOs pose to agricultural or wild biota. Making biosecurity in this case is not a field or laboratory science; rather, the office is the key space for the production of scientific knowledge.

The conclusion examines efforts to create a refuge for the endangered axolotl, a species of salamander that is both biologically remarkable and culturally significant. Projects to protect the axolotl are examples of the way biopolitics and biosecurity in Mexico have been extended beyond the regulation of human life and show how understandings and interpretations of history and culture inform the way we think about which life-forms belong in different places. In this and other projects, biologists draw connections between improving human life and the state of the nation and protecting biodiversity more generally. Projects of living better in Mexico seek to remake both human and nonhuman life-forms and undo divides between culture and nature. I conclude by placing these projects, particularly the axolotl refuge, in the context of a larger social movement of Buen Vivir / Vivir Bien that has emerged throughout Latin America in recent decades.

In biosecurity projects, scientists develop practices to protect life and make claims for the importance of biotic substances for the nation. New security practices are based on concepts made significant by scientists—for example, the quality of air and immune systems and the idea of biodiversity—and they have potential effects that reach well beyond the lab. The national populations delineated in these practices include plants and animals, moving biopolitics and biosecurity beyond human life to incorporate a much wider variety of life-forms as essential to the nation. In the process of improving life and producing biosecurity, laboratories become sites for healing the nation, where scientists analyze how place shapes health and reimagine the connections between bodies and environments. Taking their research to the field, scientists also attend to the health of the environment by eliminating life-forms they characterize as destructive to the nation and its biological resources.

In the case studies analyzed in this book, I look at both populations—the included and the excluded—of a developing biosecurity regime. Biosecurity is about regulating circulation and thinking about what belonged in different places and how to manage the travel of life-forms around the globe. Scientists attending to the particularities of place that affect human health and safety produce a counternarrative to that of "the global biological."[82] Rather than a single, uniform biology produced through globalization, scientists reinforce the importance of the local. The knowledge developed about Mexican biology in these projects and the terms on which species are included or excluded demonstrate the ways biological research shapes human practices. At the same time, biological research is culturally shaped, and understandings and interpretations of history and culture inform the way we think about which life-forms belong in different places. Scientists make claims about what life-forms are essential to Mexico and the ways that a shared biology connects the nation, knowledge which then informs political efforts to improve human and ecological health. In the process, biosecurity projects become important sites for producing both science and the nation.

From Degenerates to Regeneration, Convicts to Conservation

ISLAND BIOPOLITICS

Two hundred fifty-six kilometers off the coast of Baja California, in the eastern Pacific, Isla Guadalupe is the westernmost point of the Mexican nation. I went to Guadalupe on a research trip with the Grupo de Ecología y Conservación de Islas, A.C. (GECI), a Mexican nongovernmental organization based in Ensenada, Baja California, a port city one hour south of Tijuana. GECI is an environmental organization dedicated to a comprehensive approach to island conservation, which includes invasive species eradication, native species and ecosystem restoration, environmental education, and public policies. As Alfonso Aguirre-Muñoz, the director of GECI, explained to me, the group's goal is "to comprehensively restore very valuable ecosystems, a priority for the biological diversity of Mexico and the planet, which have been altered by invasive species, with scientific monitoring of the results and the recovery of the ecosystem." GECI is well established within Mexico, where, with the support of the federal government and local fishing communities, it has directed conservation projects on thirty-five groups of islands in all of the Mexican seas: the Pacific Ocean, the Gulf of California, and the Caribbean. As of June 2019, it had eradicated sixty exotic mammal populations on thirty-nine islands. In addition to its work in Mexico, GECI actively collaborates with international partners, working with people, organizations, and governments from Costa Rica, the Dominican Republic, Cuba, Brazil, Ecuador, New Zealand, Australia, the United States, and Canada.[1]

For the past two decades, GECI has been engaged in a long-term, complex research program on Isla Guadalupe, studying the island's ecosystem and working to eradicate invasive mammals, including feral goats, dogs, and cats; to restore soil and vegetation communities: endemic pine, cypress, and palm forests and sage scrub; and to protect seabirds like the albatross, murrelets, petrels, and native terrestrial birds. These projects of restoration ecology include removing invasive species in order to allow plants and ecosystems that had thrived on the island for centuries to return and grow. In addition, GECI engages in the active restoration of native vegetation communities, producing seedlings in a local nursery, dispensing seeds, working on erosion prevention and soil restoration, constructing fences to protect the nesting sites of marine birds from feral cats, applying social attraction techniques to restore the marine bird colonies, and conducting environmental learning and art activities with the local fishing community.

The remoteness of the 26-hectare (64-acre) island meant that it is only tenuously affiliated with the mainland territory, and its connection to and incorporation in the nation are not obvious and cannot be taken for granted (see map 1). As a result, it has been particularly important for Mexico to assert and maintain sovereignty over the territory; territorial control has been accomplished through management of populations, in both social and biological terms.[2] This chapter and the next trace the forms of biopolitics that emerged to classify, manage, protect, and eliminate various forms of life as the island was used as a testing ground, first for experiments in engineering social life and subsequently for ecosystems.

To travel to Guadalupe, Leticia and Flor, two affiliates of GECI, picked me up at my apartment in Ensenada in a car crowded with bags and equipment for the month-long trip.[3] After a quick introduction, I threw my own carefully packed dry bag filled with clothes and supplies into the car and we made our way across town to the harbor, where the M/V *Monasterio*, a 67-meter-long, 988-ton ship used by the Mexican navy as an ocean patrol vessel, was docked. It would take the *Monasterio* eighteen hours to reach Guadalupe. On the dock next to the boat, Leticia, Flor, and I met up with Gabriel, a biologist with GECI's Isla Guadalupe project who would be traveling with us. Already on the island were Adriana and Rafael, two other GECI employees. The six of us would spend the next month living together in the island's biological research station. When we arrived, Gabriel was busy unloading bags of equipment from GECI's van and attending to the myriad other logistical issues that arise when coordinating a long trip to a remote location. In addition to our personal gear (sleeping bags, clothing, laptop computers stocked with bootleg movies and music), we had food, fuel, and scientific supplies—bait for traps, catnip, earrings to mark mice, and sundry other equipment—enough for six people to be self-sufficient for a month and to conduct a series of experiments. As Gabriel lined up the bags for a thorough sniffing by the navy's Belgian shepherds, he simultaneously monitored the arrival of people, organized the equipment, and cracked jokes with the navy personnel.

From the deck I noticed two massive cruise ships, the primary traffic in Ensenada's port. The ships dwarfed the navy boat and in fact towered over everything in

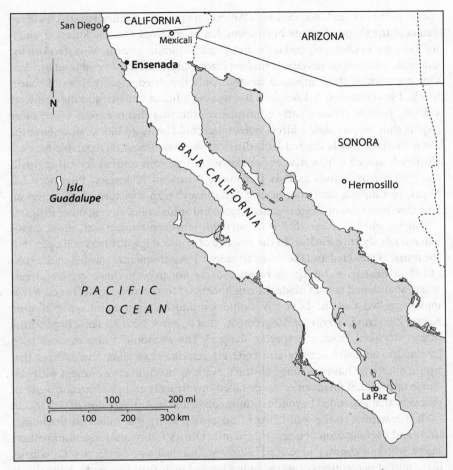

MAP 1. Map of Isla Guadalupe and Baja California. Source: Bill Nelson Cartography.

town. Cruise ships like these periodically shaped life in Ensenada, which was attuned to the coming and going of tourists.[4] Ensenada, like Baja California as a whole, is oriented towards the United States commercially and geographically and culturally set apart from the mainland of Mexico. Fernando Jordán, a journalist who wrote extensively about life on the Baja California peninsula in the 1940s and '50s, referred to it as "the other Mexico," an entity unto itself.[5] On days when ships dock, the streets near the harbor transform for a few hours. The day before our departure, groups of mariachis roamed the town's main street, where a banner welcoming Disney Cruise–goers flapped in the breeze. Most of the stores along the main street cater to tourists, selling generically Mexican souvenirs designed to appeal to the demands and desires of American visitors: ceramics, painted tin orna-ments in the shape of ornate hearts, wooden masks from Oaxaca, knives, T-shirts with slogans in obscenely bad taste, and Mexican jumping beans. Men stand on the sidewalk selling silver jewelry, menacing black whips, and innumerable tchotchkes. One memorable shop appeared to stock only the dried, cleaned jaws of sharp-toothed sea creatures. A downtown bar was often full of tourists, and the staff were working hard to create a party atmosphere, exhorting clientele to have one more tequila shot over a public address system that could be heard blocks away. Near the main tourist street is the red-light district, where the most disreputable bars are clustered, as well as pharmacies popular with American tourists for cheap medi-cine. With names such as Baja Pharmacy, American Pharmacy, Pharmacy Las Vegas, or simply a storefront labeled "Pharmacy" with a picture of an American flag, they tout sales of Viagra, Cialis, Cipro, and amoxicillin, among other drugs.

Nights when a cruise ship is in port contrast dramatically with those nights when no boats have docked. In the absence of cruise ships, the bars still open, but the music is subdued and the decks sit empty. I was frequently warned of the risks of life in Ensenada. My landlady advised me not to walk down certain streets where abandoned houses made the neighborhood less secure. Her fears and warn-ings suggested that the built environment produced a persistent sense of what Austin Zeiderman terms "endangerment," that is, a free-floating sense of potential threat, divorced from any specific danger.[6] The abandoned houses were both havens for unlawful activity and concrete reminders of risks and failures that would otherwise have remained abstract, marking the built environment with evi-dence of personal financial crises or failed investments and producing a sense of precarity that expanded beyond any immediate threat. A perception of risk was in itself threatening to the well-being of Ensenada, a city that relied on the tourist trade and its reputation of being able to offer Disney Cruise passengers and others safety within a country perceived by many Americans as dangerous. Of course, these tourist perceptions captured only a limited picture of Ensenada, a city that is notable for its fishing industry and agriculture (notably vineyards and wine pro-duction), as well as for being the home of a rich cultural scene and a substantial number of academics, scientists, and institutions of higher education.[7]

If Baja California's connection to the Mexican mainland is historically fragile, Guadalupe, where we were heading, is completely detached, a world away (see figure 2). The challenges of a trip to such a distant island are significant. Transpor-tation options are limited to the navy's monthly voyage from Ensenada and the occasional flight made by a two-engine, eight-seat Cessna plane, which brings supplies to the island and returns to Ensenada laden with lobsters caught by mem-bers of the island's fishing cooperative. Even though GECI personnel spend months at a time on Guadalupe and the organization has been working there for years, the remoteness and inaccessibility of the island keep trips from becoming

FIGURE 2. Isla Guadalupe. Source: Author photograph.

routine. Before I went, people at GECI frequently asked if I was "ready for the big adventure" and provided words of advice and warning. This perception of the island as remote and precious is reinforced by the government's designation of Guadalupe as federal property and a "Natural Protected Area" (ANP) because it is "one of the sites of highest biological importance in Mexico."[8]

Despite this isolation, Guadalupe is not an untouched or pristine ecosystem, nor is it an obvious example of "the harmony between man and nature in which man uses natural resources without compromising the environment and without disturbing its equilibrium," as claimed in the management plan established by the Comisión Nacional de Áreas Naturales Protegidas (CONANP), the federal agency in charge of regulating and conserving parks and protected spaces.[9] The plan described Guadalupe as an excellent place to study "the processes of regeneration, succession, and colonization."[10] Guadalupe was a good place to study these processes because, in point of fact, it *had* been radically altered by human activity. People brought animals to the island, intentionally and accidentally, which dramatically changed the ecosystem. Herds of goats introduced by Russian, English, and American sailors pursuing the fur trade multiplied over the years, transforming the once-forested island into a barren, devegetated landscape. They also introduced cats and mice, which proliferated on the island, eating the eggs and young of the seabirds that nested on Guadalupe (more on these animals and their effects in the next chapter). Beyond the invasive animals, humans affected the island ecosystem through rapacious hunting practices that almost exterminated the Guadalupe fur seals and the northern elephant seals that live in the waters around the island. While Guadalupe did not represent a past precisely preserved, GECI argued that it represented a recoverable past, where through careful work it would be possible to restore ecosystems damaged by people in the process of exploiting natural resources.

Aguirre-Muñoz expressed the view that islands play a special role in Mexican identity and imaginings of the nation and that, in order to understand scientific and conservation research in Mexico, one must understand the role and importance of islands.[11] He drew attention to the Mexican coat of arms, which shows an eagle devouring a snake while perched on a nopal cactus growing from a cluster of rocks (see figure 3). The image represents the mythic founding of Tenochtitlán, the center of the Aztec empire, on an island in Lake Texcoco. As the story goes, after years of wandering, the Aztecs encountered an eagle just like the one represented in the shield, which they interpreted as a divine command to build their city on that spot. Tenochtitlán eventually became Mexico City, and the choice of this moment as a national symbol was part of a discourse asserting the centralized identity of the nation, establishing Mexico City as not only the spatial center of the nation, but also its rightful spiritual and governmental center. It puts Aztec identity at the heart of national identity, eliding the presence of Mexico's many other indigenous groups.[12]

In scientific publications on GECI's work, Aguirre-Muñoz has argued that the symbol is multivalent, not only representing Aztec identity and the centrality of Mexico City, but also depicting islands as vital to national identity. He points out that the symbol depicts the founding of the Mexican nation as taking place on an island and that it is thus an example of how islands form "an essential part of Mexican historic identity."[13] In a recent paper on eradications of invasive mammals in Mexico, Aguirre-Muñoz fought to include a 1900 lithograph by J. G. Posada depicting the founding of Tenochtitlán. While the journal editors argued that myth has no place in a scientific publication, Aguirre-Muñoz contended that it is crucial to understanding the history and social context of eradication and restoration projects. Aguirre-Muñoz argued that the GECI's eradication work is a particularly Mexican story, shaped by the mythological, historical, and social place of islands in the nation, and that "it may be inappropriate to suppose that this successful story can act as a model for other regions or countries, because every country or region has its own history and particular cultural, social, or economic setting."[14] Myths and national symbolism are key to understanding how islands are perceived in Mexico; they shape the ways biological and natural resources are managed. In the context of the national symbol, islands are both spaces of nature and deeply Mexi-

FIGURE 3. Mexican coat of arms. Source: Mexican coat of arms vectorized by Alex Covarrubias. Retrieved from Wikipedia.org, http://en.wikipedia.org/wiki/File:Coat_of_arms_of_Mexico.svg

can. Further, in Mexico the majority of the islands are federal property and are seen as patrimony of the nation. National patrimony and inalienable, collective possessions have been central to the legitimization of the nation.[15]

In general, islands have been imagined as utopian spaces where the social and natural order can be rethought. As John Gillis writes, "Remote places seem so much better suited to the preservation of the past . . . and none better than islands, which have become, often despite themselves, a prime repository of pastness" and "ideal venues for time travel to bygone eras."[16] GECI's work to restore past ecosystems exemplifies this sense of islands as a space in which the past was not quite gone and might possibly be recovered. On Guadalupe, this restoration work entailed multispecies projects that sought to orchestrate lives in accordance with categories of value that encompassed both humans and nonhumans.[17]

Islands today, Aguirre-Muñoz argued, are important for Mexico in multiple ways, not only "as ecologically valuable territory," but also as "the basis for a new perspective on Mexico's mainland territory." Guadalupe's management plan proposed that work on Guadalupe could be an example for the nation and claimed that islands are important, not only as unique ecosystems, but also as models for the management of the relationship between nature and society in the rest of Mexico. The island thus was not only a space in which the past could be restored, but was also constructed as a laboratory: a site for the production of generalized knowledge. This meant that the island was often seen as a potential model for the mainland and a place in which the future could be constructed. GECI's restoration projects were not the first time Guadalupe had been held up as a model for life on the mainland; however, the emphasis on the value of Guadalupe's ecosystem and native species was relatively new. This chapter recounts the history of the island to demonstrate how the valuations of different life-forms have risen and fallen over time, as different species and practices are cultivated or eliminated. It examines transformations in the practices by which humans and nonhumans have been managed, valued, and alternately made to thrive or been eliminated as the island was transformed, from a refreshment station for whalers in the nineteenth century to a penal colony and site for social engineering in the 1930s to its role in present-day conservation projects.

WASTELAND

The first recorded sighting of Guadalupe was by Sebastián Vizcaíno in 1602, on a voyage sponsored by the viceroy of New Spain.[19] The purpose of Vizcaíno's voyage was to study and observe the California peninsula and its surroundings. According to Jordán, Vizcaíno was, like Columbus before him, "another foreigner conquered by the magic of California."[20] Since Vizcaíno's first observations of the island, visitors have described it as sterile, inhospitable land. Early visitors saw it as a wasteland—unproductive and unused. When the French admiral Abel du Petit-Thuoars documented the resources and ecology of the island in 1837, he viewed it as little more than a strategic stopping point for galleons traveling to Acapulco from the Philippines.[21] These reports on the island were consequential; like other scientific voyages, they produced representations of the periphery for consumption in the metropole and generated knowledge that enabled the expansion of empire.[22] Europeans on scientific voyages in the eighteenth and nineteenth centuries narrated travel and exploration in ways that supported territorial surveillance, appropriation of resources, and administrative control over the colonies, providing routes to particular kinds of colonial power. As Mary Louise Pratt argues, reports from natural historians that represented landscapes in the colonies as wastelands encoded "non-capitalist landscapes and societies as manifestly in need of the rationalized exploitation that Europeans bring."[23] Natural history as a field supported the extractive attitude of European colonizers. Reports on Guadalupe were no different. The descriptions of the island as a barren wasteland led to efforts to make it productive, leaving undocumented the fragile ecosystem of pine, cypress, juniper, and palm forests, dense chaparral, coastal sage scrub, shrubs and succulent plants, wildflowers, and open fields.[24]

The most transformative of these projects came in the nineteenth century when whalers from Russia, England, and the United States sought to turn the island into a more fruitful refreshment station by importing populations of diverse goats. As the goat population on the island flourished, the island became both a source of goat meat and a center of operation for hunters of the marine mammals that lived in the waters around the island.[25] The whalers' attitudes were exploitative and predatory. Aguirre-Muñoz described the whalers as "hunting whales, sea otters, Guadalupe fur seals, and elephant seals. As many as possible." By the beginning of the twentieth century, aggressive hunting had put in doubt the future of the Guadalupe elephant seal, Guadalupe fur seal, and southern sea otter, all of which had been abundant along the shores of Baja California and the US state of California.[26]

George Hugh Banning, a sailor and writer who traveled to Guadalupe in the early twentieth century, was asked what he hoped to find there. "Nothing," he replied, "and that was the beauty of it."[27] Guadalupe had been described to him as "at best, a mountainous wart sticking out of the sea as a general hindrance to traffic."[28] Upon landing, Banning found Guadalupe to be as deserted as he had hoped; the island was "parched and barren, granting life to not even a patch of cactus." One exception to this sterility was a small patch of pine trees "strangely out of keeping up there in those barren surroundings," which reminded him "of some artificial set implanted by a film director."[29] The pine trees actually had a long history on Guadalupe; what was relatively new was the limited extent of the forest, which had been decimated by the herds of goats roaming the island, which Banning described as, "black goats, white goats, dappled goats and tan; goats by the hundreds and thousands, trampling, bleating regiments of them . . . vast, skirmishing armies of goats.[30]

In 1922 a group of naturalists sponsored by the Mexican federal government, the California Academy of Sciences, the San Diego Society of Natural History, the Scripps Institution for Biological Research, and the National Geographic Society traveled to Guadalupe and other islands in the Pacific to report on the state of marine life, particularly marine mammals (fur seals, elephant seals, and sea otters). The group made observations and took extensive collections of specimens on their trip and, like Banning, noted the large population of goats, describing them as "excessively abundant everywhere and . . . well fed."[31] They were well fed at the expense of the island's forests—stripping the bark from adult trees and eating all the young seedlings, they left an island where no new tree had sprouted for many years. The naturalists conjectured that about one hundred native, endemic species had been rendered extinct by the goats in the fifty years before their visit.[32] In addition to the threatened plant life, several bird species could no longer be found on the island, a disappearance that G. Dallas Hanna, curator of paleontology at the California Academy of Sciences, reflected on with regret. "There is some strange and lonely sadness that comes over us when we think of the last of a species of one of nature's creations having passed its span of existence. Paleontology tells us that hundreds of thousands of species have so passed on in times gone by; nevertheless, when we see one go we feel the loss the same as we do when a dear relative has received a last farewell. The species of birds thus far exterminated on Guadalupe are: Guadalupe Caracara, Guadalupe Flicker, Guadalupe Towhee, and Guadalupe Wren."[33] The extermination of at least the caracara was attributed to efforts to protect the goat population, as soldiers stationed on the island killed them to prevent them from preying on young kids. Cats likewise were problematic: the naturalists noted that "this pest has completely overrun the place," leading to heavy predation on bird populations.[34] Distressed by the state of Guadalupe, they sent a report urging the Mexican government to "protect this relic of a bygone age."[35] President Álvaro Obregón responded to this account of the damage being done to Guadalupe's ecosystem by declaring that the island should be protected, issuing a decree that read as follows:

Considering that the island of Guadalupe of Lower California, and its territorial waters possess natural riches alike in forestry material and in herds, and in game and fish, numbering among its species many of rare occurrence, which species are in danger of extinction, owing to the immoderate exploitation of which they have been the object; That the Federal Government must protect those species which constitute an inexhaustible fount of riches for the Government and the people of Mexico. For that reason, I have considered it well to dictate the following resolution. Article 1. The island of Guadalupe of Lower California, as well as the territorial waters surrounding it, remains reserved for the protection and development of the natural riches which they contain, alike in forestry material and in herds, and in game and fish. Article 2. There be named the technical and administrative personnel necessary for the administration and protection of the said riches.

This decree clearly reflected a belief that Guadalupe was valuable ("an inexhaustible fount of riches") and in need of protection. However, it also demonstrated a disjuncture in beliefs about the value of nature between the federal government and the naturalists who were reporting back from the island. The decree framed Guadalupe as valuable to the extent that it could be made to produce livestock, game, timber, and other commodities. Protecting the island meant exploiting in a more managed and rational way the valuable life-forms it contained—timber, herds, and sea life—and bringing an end to the "immoderate exploitation" which had put these lives at risk. Any land not being intensively exploited or used to support the country's

industrial development was commonly seen as wasteland during the postrevolutionary period.[36] This was at odds with the way the naturalists whose reports had been
the impetus for the decree in the first place understood the significance of these
varied life-forms. For them, rather than at risk, some of the life on Guadalupe was
itself a threat. In this view, the herds of goats were not natural riches of the island or
valuable additions to its ecosystem. Instead, they were damaging pests.[37] The loss of
species and biological diversity that these reports mourned would not be amelio-
rated by the kind of protection that the presidential decree proposed, since making
use of the island for raising livestock was at direct odds with the protection of other
life-forms. Ultimately, however, the protection the decree offered for the Guadalupe
fur seal and the northern elephant seal was crucial for the species' survival.

SOCIAL PARASITES AND PENAL COLONIES

In the 1930s the governor of the Northern Territory of Baja California, Agustín
Olachea Avilés, implemented a scheme intended to make the island multiply productive. He sought both to rationalize the production of animal life on the island
and to reengineer problematic human life through the construction of a model
penal colony. The colony would house "prisoners sentenced as social parasites," primarily indigent people who had been repatriated from the United States to Tijuana
and Mexicali.[38] The island's remote location made it appealing as a place to isolate
individuals deemed dangerous to the social order. Sequestered on Guadalupe, the
general public would not be exposed to their harmful influence, and, in Olachea's
vision, they would learn the more productive labor practices. Olachea presented the
benefits of an island penitentiary on Guadalupe as threefold: isolating the mainland
population from the bad influence of the prisoners, providing prisoners with superior living conditions to the overcrowded and unhygienic mainland jails and an
environment in which they could be remade as productive workers, and solidifying
Mexican control over the territory by developing a permanent settlement. He justified the project in the eugenic terms common in postrevolutionary Mexico, arguing
that the island would permit "regeneration" of prisoners while protecting the Mexican race from degeneration. To nurture this settlement, he planned to commercial-
ize and improve the goats that had been left on Guadalupe by whalers, importing
males of good stock from the mainland.[39] Olachea envisioned Guadalupe as a place
for the improvement and regeneration of both human and animal nature, a multispecies eugenics project.

   While the prisons on Guadalupe were portrayed as a more hygienic alternative
to the overcrowded jails in Ensenada and elsewhere on the mainland and as spaces
in which prisoners might improve their character and lot, in fact, few provisions
were made for the prisoners. They were expected essentially to live outdoors and
to systematically and rationally use "the immense resources of the island," primarily

the goat population, to provide for themselves.[40] Historian Victor Gruel writes that Olachea was ultimately more interested in improving the goat population through strategic breeding than in rehabilitating prisoners on Guadalupe. The nonhumans on the island seemed to offer more potential value than the humans, and Olachea took extraordinary risks with human life, exposing the prisoners to danger and hardship as "a sacrifice for the good of the nation." Prisoners wrote to the mainland, requesting transfers back to the prisons of Ensenada, where, even if they were housed in unhygienic conditions, they might at least receive medical treatment and a respite from forced labor and an unchanging diet of goat meat.[41] Despite Olachea's stated ambitions to make use of the island as a space of reformation, Guadalupe provided few opportunities for prisoners. Rather, they were seen as disposable laborers who might be put to work improving the biocapital of Guadalupe in the form of the goat population.

The use of Guadalupe as a space to reform human populations was not idiosyncratic. Island penal colonies were developed throughout Baja California (and globally). For example, Francisco J. Múgica, governor of the Southern Territory of Baja California from 1941–45, lauded island prison colonies as models of regeneration, "workshops for the poor, irredeemables who within society were harmful for their vices or their evil instincts. In the colony they are docile instruments of labor, raw materials that can be shaped and can assimilate useful knowledge."[42] In the 1951 film *Las Islas Marías*, Pedro Infante, the most famous actor of the Golden Age of Mexican Cinema, played an inmate on an island penal colony.[43] As Infante arrived on the island, the head of the colony delivered a speech spelling out the human engineering principles behind island penal colonies. "Here begins a new life. It will depend on you to make it your regeneration through work. For those who come prepared to comply with the discipline of the prison and achieve your rehabilitation, it will not be difficult to adapt to the life of settlers on the island. But for those who are inclined to rancor and rebellion, and who try to cause problems for our community, life in prison will be hard. And you'd better learn that only repentance will keep this island from becoming your grave." Penal colonies were meant to be doubly transformative. Prisoners by their work transformed island wastelands into agriculturally productive spaces, as well as remaking themselves into productive members of society.

The Guadalupe prison was developed in concert with an ongoing campaign of *mexicanización*, an effort to populate all areas of Baja California to protect Mexican sovereignty from the grasping United States. Colonizing Guadalupe was meant to ensure that this former refuge for pirates and foreign smugglers was being made productive for Mexico.[44] It also affirmed that the outlying territory was properly Mexican. The 1848 Treaty of Guadalupe Hidalgo, which ceded approximately 55 percent of Mexico's territory to the United States (land which today constitutes all or part of Arizona, California, Colorado, Kansas, Oklahoma, Nevada, New Mexico,

Texas, Utah, and Wyoming), continued to trouble the Mexican government, sharpening fears not only that foreigners would exploit and misappropriate natural resources, but also that Mexico might lose sovereignty over outlying territories. Baja California seemed especially vulnerable, as a place disconnected from the mainland in which foreign companies dominated commercial development and government-granted land concessions.[45]

These fears were sharpened and made more tangible by more recent losses of island territories, in particular the 1931 loss of Clipperton Island to France. A brief detour through the history of Clipperton is instructive for its illustration of islands' potential as sites of transformation and of the fragility of sovereignty over distant locales. A tiny, remote island 1,080 kilometers southwest of Mexico in the Pacific Ocean, Clipperton has an ecosystem dominated by voracious land crabs and seabirds. Currently uninhabited, the island in the past has periodically played host to various human residents, including a colony established in 1897 as a way of solidifying Mexican sovereignty and subsequently a phosphate (seabird guano) mining operation and accompanying settlement. The island's residents were essentially abandoned during the Mexican Revolution. Without supplies or contact with the mainland, the small colony experienced multiple disasters. The group suffered from scurvy, and all the men, with the exception of the lighthouse keeper Victoriano Álvarez, drowned in an accident. Isolated from and abandoned by people on the mainland, Álvarez declared himself king, brutally ruling the island and raping the remaining women and girls for two years until one of them killed him with a hammer. The survivors were rescued shortly afterwards by the USS *Yorkmen*, but after the disastrous termination of the colony, Mexico's hold on the island was tenuous.[46] In international arbitration, King Victor Emmanuel III of Italy determined that Mexico's claim to the land was "not supported by any manifestation of her sovereignty over the island," and awarded the territory to France, which claimed to have made the first documented landing and geographical surveys of the island in 1858.[47] The island continues to be French territory today.[48]

The well-known, dramatic story of the colony's denouement might well have served as an illustration of the potential of islands as spaces in which the social order could be radically reconfigured, in which a lighthouse keeper might become a king. On Clipperton, the rules of ordinary human conduct were suspended and people tried out new roles. Disconnected from the mainland, all islands are potentially compelling sites of dramatic transformations. The story of Clipperton and its loss was also a reminder of the importance of maintaining vigilance over outlying territories and the potential tenuousness of land claims on places like Guadalupe, reminders that may have made the prison colony appear essential not only as a mode of discipline for the prisoners but also as a means of maintaining the island as Mexican.

BIOLOGICAL CEMETERIES AND THE VALUE
OF BIODIVERSITY

After the failure of the prison colony on Guadalupe, concerns about protecting the island's biodiverse life-forms began to take precedence among people engaged in managing island life. Returning to Jordán's account of the island from the 1950s is instructive. After visiting Guadalupe, he lamented the damage done by invasive species, calling the island a "biological cemetery." He regretted the loss of life-forms on the island, from the diminished elephant seal population to the many species of flora and fauna endemic to the island that had disappeared as a result of anthropogenic activities. Beyond the hunting of elephant seals, Jordán pointed to the introduction of invasive species, particularly the goat, as the source of Guadalupe's diminishment. Ecologists in 2000 likewise were concerned about invasive species, but they did not see the island either as a wasteland that needed to be made productive or as an irredeemable biological cemetery. Instead, it was a fragile, threatened paradise, a space in which human and nonhuman lives needed to be managed together to produce particular economic and ecological futures.

Part of GECI's work is to produce representations of islands like Guadalupe for the vast majority of people who are unable to visit them. These include photographs in scientific papers, heavily illustrated government reports, films, and didactic materials such as field guides and children's games. One person describes the videos that GECI produces as its calling card, which she shares liberally with people she meets as she travels in order to explain and promote GECI's work. Through aesthetically appealing images of seals, albatrosses feeding their young, blue-footed boobies, and white sandy beaches with palm trees, they sell the importance of these islands through their charismatic species and reinforce the idea of the value of the islands as sources of biodiversity, natural capital, and resources for the nation. Sentiment helps promote the importance of the islands; the images, often of mother birds or mammals caring for their young, are touching. These pictures, which demonstrate the beauty and liveliness of the island's nonhuman populations, differ markedly from those produced on earlier scientific voyages in which Guadalupe was represented as barren and reinforce the importance of conservation work and value of the islands.

The contemporary work of GECI on Guadalupe demonstrates the particularities of more-than-human biopolitics in a place where conservation and invasive species eradication are *not* about protecting pristine nature, but rather about conservation that is adaptive and connected to the social. *The National Strategy for the Conservation and Sustainable Development of the Mexican Island Territory*, a federal strategy document integrated by GECI, highlights the importance of the islands to the nation, positioning them as "valuable national patrimony" in terms of the important marine resources they offer and because they are "an irreplaceable natural capital in terms of biodiversity."[49] The document goes on to note the importance of assimilating the islands into the nation because of the wealth of resources they house, stating, "It is imperative that as a Nation, Mexico incorporate the islands, which are certainly an integral part of the territory, and recognize them as a cornerstone of national development."[50] Conservation in this case is not reductively focused on preserving a pristine wilderness or eliminating human impacts. Instead, it is about nature being used in a sustainable way.

This position resonates with attitudes towards conservation and land protection in Mexico that reach back to the postrevolutionary period, when the government began establishing parks as a way to conserve resources for the nation's future generations. As described in the introduction, the establishment of parks and early conservation efforts in Mexico focused on restoring degraded environments. The first parks in Mexico tended to protect forests and areas that were easily accessible for public enjoyment, places that had immediately apparent economic, recreational, and biological value.[51] While Guadalupe differs from the parks that were established in the postrevolutionary period because it is not accessible to the general public, GECI's work echoes early conservation efforts in that it focuses on repairing a damaged ecosystem and does not require excluding human activity. This stands in contrast to the biopolitics governing life and territory in places like the Galápagos, where international NGOs historically managed life in accordance with Euro-American models of "pristine" nature, calling for the exclusion of humans to protect nonhuman life and ecosystems from contamination.[52] This model of "fortress conservation," which presumes that the best way to protect biodiversity is by excluding human populations and that the presence of local residents will always result in environmental destruction and degradation, has been deployed globally with significant consequences.[53] Despite its remoteness, the scientists who work on island conservation on Guadalupe do not conceive of it as a space of pristine nature, or as one from which humans need to be eliminated. Rather, GECI's strategies for protecting nature involve collaborating with island residents, particularly members of the fishing co-op that has long been located on the island, as well as with the government, to protect biodiversity. Rather than seeking to separate nature and culture, the island is seen as a place where both natural and certain cultural forms can thrive, and a place where particular forms of social life can and should be respected and cultivated.

EJIDOS GONE TO SEA: HUMAN LIFE ON THE ISLAND

The ship was a microcosm of the island's social worlds. Present on the *Monasterio* were representatives of the three primary human groups currently populating the island: conservationists, the military, and members of the island's fishing co-op, the Sociedad Cooperativa de Producción Pesquera de Participación Estatal

Abuloneros y Langosteros. In addition to the GECI personnel, on board was a crew of sailors in the Mexican navy, outfitted in tan and dark brown camouflage, tall boots, and caps. They milled restlessly on the deck, guns strapped to their backs, until they gradually began to make themselves comfortable, unrolling sleeping mats and bags, unpacking portable DVD players, and generally preparing for the eighteen-hour boat ride ahead of us. On another island a soldier had told me that the first thing he learned in the navy was to sleep whenever and wherever he could; this crew seemed to have learned that lesson as well. Even before the boat had left the dock, soldiers were sprawled out on the deck, sleeping. They were being posted to the island as part of a permanent navy deployment there, one that was meant both to protect the island and to maintain Mexico's sovereignty over it. The presence of the naval forces indicated the importance of the island to Mexico and also something about the role of the Mexican navy. Aguirre-Muñoz explained the NGO's relationship with the navy to me, stating that "it's a mutual learning process." Scientists and the military were both increasingly attuned to each other's concerns. He noted, "We understand more all the time about the value of sovereignty, and the island is an open border. It's very critical and very vulnerable. On the other hand, they understand that it is not only about having the flag or the garrison, these physical things, but also the quality of the nature there, and that they can make a difference for the country together with environmental conservation." The navy donates supplies, labor, and the use of boats to GECI. According to Aguirre-Muñoz, they are "committed to conserve not only the territory, but the quality of the territory." Our ride out to the island was material proof of the navy's support for GECI's project.

One officer explained to me that, in contrast to the United States, where the military is primarily associated with armed conflict and international security, for Mexico, international conflicts are much less frequent. The job of the military is, in his words, "subir al país," or lift up the country, and the job of the navy specifically is to protect human life at sea and on the beaches, islands, and reefs of Mexico. Maintaining sovereignty over the island has been significant for a number of reasons. Modern island territories provide their possessors with extensive benefits, namely with sovereignty over the waters two hundred nautical miles from their coasts, in the form of an exclusive economic zone (EEZ). Within its EEZ a country has exclusive rights to the use of marine resources, including fishing and drilling, making island territories quite valuable. To maintain sovereignty and to protect the nation, sailors are sent around the country to supervise fishing and diving and to protect the sea, animals, and plant life. Improving and lifting up the country means sending military forces out to its most remote reaches to protect not only human life, but nonhuman life-forms as well.

Also accompanying us on the boat were families from the Isla Guadalupe fishing cooperative, which has held exclusive rights to fish the waters around

Guadalupe for over fifty years.[54] The families set up tents on the deck of the boat and busied themselves securing the household items they were transporting to Guadalupe, a wide range of materials including mattresses, cribs, bicycles, stoves, pillows, tires, PVC pipe, and bags and boxes of miscellaneous items. Members of GECI referred to it as the equivalent of an "ejido gone to sea," the oceanic equivalent of the system of communal land tenure that was enshrined in the 1917 constitution produced after the Mexican Revolution. Aguirre-Muñoz described it to me as "the equivalent of the social ownership of land that was linked to Emiliano Zapatas's 'land and freedom,' which was half of the Mexican Revolution; the other half of which was Francisco Madero's liberal democracy following the US model . . . . In the case of the sea and the islands, that thing of land and freedom was constructed as a fisherman co-op, more or less like the Soviet model or the equivalent to the kibbutz in Israel—a community that has common access to natural resources and limited entry." Even as the system of ejidos was dismantled as part of the neoliberal economic policies of the 1990s, the fishing cooperative on Isla Guadalupe (and other fishing cooperatives) held on.

Protecting nature on the islands is not about isolating it from people. Rather, it is about simultaneously protecting both nature and particular social forms. The national strategy document articulates the idea that the islands, despite the failure of the penal colony experiment, can and should be places in which human lives play an important role and the historic rights of communities are respected and reinforced. The presence of the fishing cooperative reinforces views of Guadalupe as a link to both an ecological and a social past. Guadalupe is a contemporary example of the ways islands can be both models of and exceptions to legal and social order, through the continued existence of an institution that is idealized but has primarily been relegated to the past on the mainland.[55] While GECI's projects seek to remove plants and animals and return the ecosystem of the island to its state before the arrival of humans, they do not attempt to isolate the island from people. Rather than calling for the co-op to be dismantled and human presence eliminated, GECI collaborates with members of the co-op and works to support it as an essential part of island life and sustainable development that cements national links between nature, place, and territory. The cooperative is particularly valued as a historical social form that uses nature to produce equitable income distribution for local residents in contrast to neoliberal management and industrial development schemes that tend to concentrate wealth in the hands of a limited number of people.

GECI scientists work to support and maintain the co-op through their integral approach to conservation, work which includes enhancing the possibilities for children on Isla Guadalupe. GECI has worked with the co-op to build a secondary school with computers and a satellite internet facility so that children can get an education on the island, rather than needing to be sent to the mainland to live with grandparents or other family. They have also sought to ensure the cooperative's support for their efforts, working with the children of co-op members to clean garbage off the island, as well as conducting educational campaigns and activities to learn together to value and appreciate the common environment. Aguirre-Muñoz observed that conservation cannot come solely from externally imposed and enforced regulations, but also requires an internal change in people working together in the same territory, noting that as well as a government that enforces regulations and the rule of law, "we all need the good citizen attitude, which is self-regulated."

GECI's efforts with regard to labor practices go beyond supporting the cooperative. They consider conservation itself as not only about protecting nonhuman lives, but also producing new career and economic opportunities for people on the islands. The development of conservation projects has made the islands into spaces where new forms of labor are in demand and in which people can be trained and prepared to work as scientists. As the national strategy document states, "In addition to the traditional work of fishing that occurs from the islands, the environmental conservation in these territories in Mexico generates growing, sustainable employment of high quality for Mexican technicians and scientists. In addition to restoring and caring for a natural patrimony of Mexico that is of unmatched value, these activities are part of a specialized niche of a new and rich knowledge economy, related to research, development, and high-level education in the theme of conservation of islands, extraordinary labs for ecological research and the modeling of the sustainable use of natural resources."[56]

Aguirre-Muñoz told me that many of the members of the co-op were "starting to feel that the daughters, even more than the sons, could have an option being biologists. Half of the persons here [at GECI] are women." Aguirre-Muñoz argued that the strong representation of women among GECI's workforce, particularly as project directors, has powerful effects on the residents of the islands where they work. He observed that "they go to places and the fishermen in the co-ops look at them working in very efficient ways with lots of ability. They are very capable people, jumping from the *panga* to the boat, measuring places, taking the birds, putting on the bands, using the GPS, driving a four-wheel-drive vehicle, things that they really value, because [the fishermen] see that they are doing different things than making the flour tortillas for the burritos for breakfast. And I think that they are starting to understand that could be something interesting and options for their daughters." Fishermen had started to ask if it was okay if their daughters helped GECI with their work on bird populations during vacations and in the summertime. By producing alternative careers that will allow families to remain rooted in the islands, GECI's work is transformative not only for island ecosystems, but also for the way people on the island envision futures for themselves and their families.

GECI conservationists, in this case, position themselves in opposition to scientists from the United States. In early collaborations on work on Isla Guadalupe, some of the American scientists involved proposed negotiating for the fishermen to leave the island, so that marine mammals, particularly sea otters, could return to the island. The sea otters in particular feed on the resources that divers and fishermen use for their economic livelihood. They could be in direct competition. In this framing, in which original and untouched biodiversity is elevated, it becomes convenient to limit human presence. This has not been GECI's approach. Aguirre-Muñoz explained that for GECI it is very important to consider humans and biodiversity together. "We mean that it is not only about the seabirds, or the turtles, but that it is a very wide and encompassing approach that links the human interest with the conservation of nature. . . . Another perspective coming from the north is less humanistic. Sometimes nature gets a very high privilege in front of the local community or the humanistic perspective." He clarified that while some scientists in the United States had prioritized things like the return of the sea otter, focusing on the sea otter meant neglecting other important values: "first of all, the life of a community, and then the importance of another value, which is sovereignty, which is not only having the Mexican flag on an island and a garrison or something like a navy base, but *also* to develop sustainable economic activities. To have a permanent population that has sustainable economic activity. So this is, as you can see, sovereignty and economy, and the survival of a local community, together with biodiversity." Concerns around sovereignty echo the policy of mexicanización, which shaped earlier strategies of territorial and population management. While American scientists considered the possibility of removing a human population in order to produce a pristine, untouched nature and to secure nonhuman lives, GECI scientists, along with the Mexican government and the local cooperative, envisioned an alternative approach, in which humans and some nonhumans could thrive on the island. Encouraging particular human populations was a way to maintain the territory as Mexican. In this ranking and prioritizing of lives, the return of the sea . otter was not more valuable than the success of the fishing cooperative.

On our trip out to the island, Flor, Leticia, and I explored the ship together, ending up in the galley where a soldier passed us plates of food. Over dinner, we speculated on what we would find on Guadalupe; it would be the first time there for all three of us. Flor, a perpetually cheerful student in her twenties, was volunteering on this trip while completing her undergraduate degree. She was optimistic that her volunteer work might lead to future employment as a biologist and steady work after several years of odd jobs. Her family life had been difficult and she had drifted, unfocused, from one job to another. Working for GECI gave her an opportunity to do work that she found more engaging, something that made use of her academic studies at Universidad Autónoma de Baja California (UABC). Even so, she almost turned down the chance to come to Guadalupe. GECI's projects and its approach to protecting ecosystems often require killing animals, particularly invasive mammals. After Gabriel offered her the position she hesitated, unsure whether she wanted or was emotionally equipped to spend a month trapping and killing cats and mice. Although she told herself that killing animals was ultimately for the good of the entire ecosystem, she was not sure this rationalization would make it any easier for her to kill. She decided to come after Gabriel reassured her that this trip would not be focused on eradication. Gabriel told me that he is also troubled by the eradication work, but he tries to reframe it as not killing a cat or a goat, but saving a population of seabirds or a forest of cedars. This sentiment was common, and I heard from many people that eradications were the worst part of the job. One GECI employee told me that she wanted to be a biologist because, like everyone in her family, she was an *animalero*, that is, someone who likes animals. Invasive species eradications forced her to consider what it meant to be an animal lover and to decide that loving animals sometimes meant killing them.

Leticia also found the decision to work in the field a difficult one, primarily because of the isolation it entailed. Leticia had been hired on as a contract employee, a step up from volunteering, but still without the security that permanent employees received after completing a trial period. Like Gabriel and Flor, she attended UABC, where she became friends with several current GECI employees. As a student she had been passionate about ecological fieldwork, volunteering for a pair of herpetologists each weekend and traveling with them twice a year from San Diego to La Paz, looking for snakes. She loved these trips to the field and stopped going only when she became pregnant with her now eight-year-old daughter. She was gradually getting back into work as a biologist. This trip to Guadalupe was her second in the field after spending three months the previous summer working to restore seabird populations. Her happiness at getting a chance to do fieldwork was tempered by sadness at leaving her daughter for months at a time.

While we searched the ship for dinner, Gabriel continued to organize our gear and make friends with everyone on the boat. He was unfailingly cheerful and friendly, qualities that were vital to the success of the work. Conducting research required not only scientific ability, but also the skills to manage the emotions of the people involved, to stay on friendly terms with the navy officers and the members of the island's fishing cooperative, and to engage their continued support of the project. Supervising a crew of people on a remote island is not easy, from dealing with the logistics and practical matters to ensuring that everyone gets along, but Gabriel kept everything running smoothly, equally adept at managing people, plants, animals, and trip logistics. In the face of the challenges of working in the field, he was calm and unflappable, entertaining the crew with jokes and an encyclopedic knowledge of Mexican tunes. Even as he worked to keep everyone in good spirits, he had an eye on the details of the trip, carefully checking each box of supplies and its location on the ship, ensuring that everything was directed to the proper place.

Gabriel had wanted to be an oceanographer since childhood. Growing up in a landlocked city, the ocean had seemed like another world, remote and mysterious.

He pursued his studies in oceanography and received a master's in marine ecology. While he was a student, the ocean was both an object of study and a source of sustenance. Relying on a small scholarship for his living expenses, he foraged for mussels along the rocky coast when he ran out of money for food. His research focused on marine mammals, tracking the travels of whales from Baja California to Alaska. Gabriel followed a similar migratory path himself, moving north to Alaska, where he worked in a cannery on a tourist visa. He spent two years in Alaska, processing salmon, until he grew sick of fish and the job and returned south to Mexico.

As a biologist working on the Isla Guadalupe project, he spent half the year on the island. The rest of the year he worked on GECI projects on other islands, or in the office in Ensenada. While he loved working on Guadalupe, the demanding travel schedule meant that he had to sacrifice having a regular home life in Ensenada. Many of Gabriel's closest friends were his fellow GECI employees—they had interests in common and shared a lifestyle that few other people in Ensenada understood. Frequently in the field, isolated from everyone but other members of the group, they developed close relationships with one another. On the rare occasions they were back in Ensenada, they tended to spend both their working hours and their leisure time together. People within the organization shared apartments and occasionally dated each other. Over lunch one day, Gabriel mused about the connections between ecologists, saying, "We're like a tribe." He jokingly suggested initiation rites that could be used to mark a new member of the tribe of ecologists, signs that someone was ready to go work on the islands: "You need to carry a cooler by yourself and be able to walk between three launch boats without tripping." He noted that their shared language and experiences in the field made it easy for ecologists to converse and understand one another. For a group that left their families and friends behind to work in remote areas, these common skills, understandings, and histories helped them feel connected with their colleagues.

They also envisioned connections for this group that went beyond the social, suggesting that the hours spent in close proximity on remote islands had also produced a kind of shared biology, a microbial connection among the group. Over a pizza in Ensenada, Carolina and Luis, two ecologists who had worked for GECI for a long time, told me that everyone in the group shared a special strain of bacteria, spread through the close contact that came with living together and sharing food and drinks. Luis told me, "Out on the islands, you share." This sharing extended to the nonhuman life-forms that inhabit human bodies. He went on to joke, "We all share the same bacteria, and new people come and add their own bacteria and it gets incorporated into the GECI strain." Water bottles were referred to as "bacteria water" as they were passed around the group. Out at restaurants, they often ordered one dessert to share, which everyone ate with the same fork. I joined the group for dinner one night, and after we had shared a plate of dulce de leche crepes, someone announced to me, "*Now* you're part of the group. This is your baptism." The isolation of the islands produced both unique and vulnerable ecosystems and new human relationships. Set down with few resources, they were isolated from mainstream social life and forced to rely on one another. Along the way, they developed rituals and routines that marked inclusion and exclusion from the group, and came to think of themselves as not only connected through shared history, but also drawn together by a shared biology.

Fishermen, military personnel, and scientists all spent a long night sharing the ship's crowded deck until the early morning light roused everyone. By the time the sun was up, we had crossed most of the 240 kilometers to Guadalupe. Shortly before we reached the island, someone spotted a large, expensive motorboat of the kind that generally belonged to tourists, which caught the attention of the naval officers on board. Guadalupe has earned a certain notoriety after being promoted on the Discovery Channel's shark week programming in the United States as "the sharkiest place on earth."[57] The island's inaccessibility by mass transport makes shark-seeing trips quite expensive. Most of the boats sail from San Diego, carrying tourists from around the globe, and while they are permitted to sail in the waters around the island, Isla Guadalupe itself is off limits to the general public—only authorized members of the navy, the fishing cooperative, and biologists (primarily from GECI, which has developed and operates a biological station there) working on conservation projects may land. However, since the navy only rarely patrols these waters and the island's navy personnel generally remain on one end of the large island, unauthorized boats or small planes occasionally land. Gabriel pointed out that without much official presence, Americans sometimes did not even realize they had arrived in another country, a reminder of the tenuousness of mainland regulations in remote regions. In this case, however, the official presence was impossible to ignore, as a crew of eight jumped from the ship into a launch boat to interrogate the boaters and to remind everyone that this was Mexican sovereign territory.

While the navy completed its inspection of the boat, I joined my companions in looking for signs of land. We finally made out a smudge on the horizon under the grey clouds and pale blue sky. As the sky brightened, we saw a group of starkly silhouetted, steep-sided islets and then our destination, Isla Guadalupe. Gabriel, accustomed by years of work to arrivals and departures from Guadalupe, was busy organizing our gear for disembarking (see figure 4), but Leticia, Flor, and I were exhilarated by our first glimpse of the island, snapping pictures as it came into sight. From the sea, I looked for biological treasures and a flourishing ecosystem, trying to match up the pictures of Guadalupe teeming with wildlife that I had seen in reports on the island with the grey cliffs ahead of me. Scanning the steep cliffs, I sought signs of life: traces left by goats or even just vegetation, but from a distance the rocky coasts appeared stark and uninhabited.

FIGURE 4. Unloading the *Monasterio*. Source: Author photograph.

"Living better" on Guadalupe has always meant thinking about human and nonhuman lives together, calibrating and administering populations of goats, marine mammals, fish, sea otters, fur trade hunters, prisoners, co-op members, and scientists, although the nature of these management practices has changed over the years. Biorisks or threats are not universal or objective; rather, they are cultural products, dependent on the values, concerns, and rationalities of the community.[58] As constructivist theorists of risk have highlighted, the choices that we make of risks to focus on reflect culturally specific ideas and ways of seeing the world.[59] Valuations of life have not remained constant; as the island has been variously interpreted as a wasteland in need of human improvement and a storehouse of biodiversity, different populations and social forms have been encouraged and protected. The island has been not only a place for cultivating animal life; both human and animal populations have been jointly remade. Just as the island might be improved by human activity, humans might be improved by the island, whether they were criminals being rehabilitated or mainland residents who might be edified by the cooperative economic practices of the island's fishermen.

The island is now valued for its ecosystem, as well as its potential to maintain social forms that are linked to past ideals of Mexican sociality and economics, in which an alternative to neoliberal uses of natural resources may thrive. The next chapter will detail GECI's project to eliminate invasive species, work which represents a transformation in the selection of threats on which to focus attention and, indeed, what threats are even visible as risks. As the place of islands in the Mexican imagination shifted and they became valued as storehouses of biodiversity and biological resources for the nation, animals like goats that had been nurtured are reinterpreted as destructive pests. Contemporary practices of conservation reveal the way Guadalupe is envisioned as a natural laboratory, but *not* one in which a pristine nature might be isolated from human contamination. Rather, Guadalupe is a place that can produce generalizable knowledge, including about how humans and nonhumans could live together.

2

The Care of the Pest and
Animal Betrayals

ISLAND LABORATORIES

While Guadalupe had a history as a space for transforming human populations, this was not GECI's primary concern. The island was more crucially a site for restoring a valuable ecosystem by remaking and transforming nonhuman life, for producing biopolitics and biosecurity beyond the human, and for human engagement with nature. A key demonstration of this came in 2007, when a cohort of goats led hunters to their fellow herd members, revealing their hiding places in the island's inaccessible cliffs. By identifying the location of their conspecifics, these goats made it possible for hunters to complete the eradication of the entire goat population of Guadalupe. These turncoat goats had been dubbed "Judas goats," when the technique was developed by technicians who specialized in eradications in the United States, Australia, and New Zealand. The name casts their actions as a betrayal of their fellows. More than just a biblical allusion, the name also borrows from slaughterhouse terminology; the original Judas goats were goats deployed in stockyards to bring sheep from their pens to be slaughtered. After a period of apprenticeship as kids, Judas goats would lead generations of sheep to slaughter.[1] On Guadalupe, hunters sterilized and tagged goats with radio transmitters. These transmitters would allow them to follow the goats, and made them key instruments in GECI's project to rid the island of invasive species. Goats had been one of the most destructive of the invasives on the island, and their removal was a crucial step in the effort to restore the island ecosystem to an earlier state.[2] While the goats were the most visible of the alien species on the island, they were not the only ones. The fields also hid a substantial population of field mice that proliferated after arriving as shipboard stowaways. In this chapter, I will tell the tale of how mice and goats were managed and eradicated.

DISCOURSE AND PRACTICE

Anthropological writing on invasive species has primarily addressed the question of discourse and definitions, looking at how scientists and others identify organisms as native or invasive. The way groups categorize, define, and make distinctions about biological entities can reflect how they think about nature and culture, as well as human and nonhuman agency.[3] These categorizations are shaped by political, economic, and social concerns.[4] More specifically, social scientists have argued that the rhetoric about invasive species is informed by fears about the movement of capital, commodities, and people, and related fears of outsiders taking over a country or contaminating a previously pure environment.[5]

Definitions of exotic, invasive, and native species in Mexico and elsewhere focus on potential harms to biodiversity, the economy, and public health.[6] The language used to describe the threats posed by invasives is striking. In 2010, representatives of federal agencies, universities, and NGOs, including GECI, produced the *National Strategy on Invasive Species*. The strategy was an important planning document that defined some of the key terms related to invasive species. It identified native species as "those naturally found in a region as a result of a long process of adaptation to existing environmental conditions," while alien species, on the other hand, were species occurring outside of their past or present natural range. Invasive species are a special subset of alien species that are distinguished both for their capacity to establish long-term populations in an area and the threat that they pose to the health of native life-forms and the Mexican economy.[7]

In recent publications by the Secretaría de Medio Ambiente y Recursos Naturales (the Secretary of the Environment and Natural Resources, or SEMARNAT), the Instituto Nacional de Ecología (the National Institute of Ecology, or INE), and the Comisión Nacional para el Conocimiento y Uso de la Biodiversidad (the National Commission for the Knowledge and Use of Biodiversity, or CONABIO), invasive species were categorized as the principal threat to biodiversity on islands in Mexico and "one of the greatest contemporary threats of global dimensions" more generally.[8] This threat to biodiversity and the environment in turn is described as having significant social effects. For example, Ana Lilia González Martínez, a specialist on invasive species at CONABIO, argued that the invasive pez diablo both disrupted ecosystems and destroyed communities. In this accounting, by displacing native fish with greater commercial value, the pez diablo led to the separation of families as the diminished returns from fishing meant men migrated to the United States in search of economic opportunity, leaving women to take over the work of fishing. As families were divided, according to González, "the social network begins to disintegrate." With the arrival of the fish, delinquency and security problems grew, "all as a consequence of an invasive species."[9]

Invasive species are released in Mexico, according to Martín Vargas Prieto, the director of the Direction General of Wildlife in SEMARNAT, "because in this country there is not a culture or sense that alien species should be in strict confinement and not released into the environment on a whim." This comment suggests that the problem of invasive species is one that is produced on the level of individual actors and that it might be remedied by the development of a collective awareness of the value of native plant and animal populations. Painting the movement of alien species as whimsical and capricious, it overlooks the ways in which the movement of species is rarely traceable to a single individual. Invasive species are often the product of the travel and movement attendant on global capitalism, as cargo may unintentionally include invasive hitchhikers. Alternately, as was the case of the goats on Guadalupe, alien species may be released intentionally for economic reasons, rather than due to individual caprice.

According to the *National Strategy for the Conservation and Sustainable Development of Mexican Islands*, invasive animals in 2008 were "growing out of control," while *Animales exóticos en México: Una amenaza para la biodiversidad*, a report by the National Commission for Knowledge and Study of Biodiversity, characterized them as catastrophic and one of the "four horsemen of the apocalypse."[10] This rhetoric was echoed in newspaper accounts of invasive species in which they were described as aggressive and insatiable, with high rates of reproduction and potentially devastating effects on local ecosystems.[11] One exemplary article described the invasive pez diablo as a "very devilish" fish (true to its name), a "dangerous predator" with a "voracious appetite." Like other invasive species, the pez diablo was described as having destructiveness written in its biology, "genetically programmed to eat everything it can."[12] This kind of rhetoric naturalizes certain species as inherently problematic, erasing the ways in which invasive species only become destructive when they move or are moved into new ecological niches.

In *El Universal*, a Mexican daily newspaper, Esteban Moctezuma Barragán described Mexico itself as "threatened." Mexico, of course, is threatened from all directions, but Moctezuma clarified that he was not writing "about lawlessness, or the power vacuum. Nor narcotrafficking or organized crime." He did not "refer to the fragility of economic growth, nor the devaluation of the dollar, the growth in poverty, related to the insolvency of the pension system, nor the desertification of the national territory."[13] While these threats to the state are of concern in Mexico, Moctezuma wanted to draw the reader's attention to another threat to the Mexican nation: the palomilla del nopal, an insect that could "kill, devastate, and otherwise impact our biodiversity." The palomilla del nopal, or *Cactoblastis cactorum*, eats nopal cactuses. As Moctezuma writes, the nopal is a "symbol of our country, an economic foundation for the countryside, a delicious dish, a product recommended for good health and an inspiration for our art and culture."[14] The "voracious" palomilla del nopal threatened to end all of that. CONABIO and other organizations are carefully tracking the advance of the palomilla on Mexican borders, estimating that every year it is 158 kilometers closer, and that once it arrives "it will have a terrible effect on desert and semi-desert areas."[15] Moctezuma's writing elevates the insect, equating it with a variety of problems that threaten the stability of the nation.

Perhaps in response to language that depicts invasive species as an existential threat to the nation as a whole, descriptions of programs to control invasive plants and animals often describe the engagement of conservationists with invaders as a war, using explicitly military language. Invasive species are "in the cross hairs" of conservationists who are battling against them, making use of SWAT teams, sharpshooters, and "a combination of brute force, high-tech gadgetry, and cutting edge science."[16] These campaigns employ "professional killers" with .223-caliber rifles and "hollow-point ammo good for blowing baseball-size holes in flesh," in order to attack the enemy.[17] They have "military-style planning and hardware" and divide conservation areas into "kill zones."[18] Articles about invasive species deploy powerful imagery and language to represent the destruction wrought by these species, characterizing them as threats to national security by way of threats to the ecosystem. Conserving nature and protecting the environment thus become a national issue. Nature belongs to and makes up local communities, regions, and ultimately the nation.

While this powerful discourse may motivate action against invasive species, in what follows I suggest that social scientific analyses of alien and invasive species eradication programs would benefit from closer attention to *how species meet* in these encounters.[19] By looking at *practice* in addition to discourse, I argue that we can discern new kinds of animal-human and animal-animal connections in the making in invasive species research. While the dominant narrative about invasive species in Mexico is of a battle against voracious invaders that are destroying both the ecosystem and the social structure of the country, in practice, confrontations with invasive species do not necessarily take the form of a battle. This narrative conceals the range of relationships between scientists and invasive species.

Animals are not mere symbols in invasive species politics, but are actors entangled with humans.[20] On Guadalupe, biologists deal with unwanted invaders, problem animals. Working alongside these scientists as a participant-observer, I saw them engaging in the care of the pest, carefully tending to exotic invaders in order to produce knowledge about their characteristics and social behavior, knowledge that would then be turned against these animals in what I will term a *biology of betrayal*. There were multiple betrayals at work on Guadalupe, and these betrayals took different forms. A betrayal can be a conscious decision, but in addition to intentional violations of trust, betrayals can be accidental exposures. In the case of goat eradications, while goats did not intentionally assist scientists with the destruction of their fellow herd members, they did betray their existence and make their extermination possible. While the goats betrayed one another, they were also betrayed by the scientists who worked with and cared for them until the time came to destroy the herd. These betrayals are the counterpart or consequence of the scientists' larger loyalties. On Guadalupe, care for the island as a whole entailed betraying the goats and mice that were damaging the island's ecosystem. Scientists first tended to and learned about the goats and mice, developing individualized relationships with the animals that were different from those produced in laboratories, where scientists are trained to see the animals they use as standardized tools.[21]

On Guadalupe, people destroyed in order to preserve, eliminating invasive species in the service of what Aldo Leopold termed "the health of the land," that is, the ecosystem's ability to sustain itself.[22] While the goats had been of practical use for people on the island as a food source, attention to the total processes of an ecosystem meant that scientists had to eliminate certain organisms for the greater health of the island. Ecosystem restoration on Guadalupe was GECI's most long-standing project, one of many years' duration. While historically practices of ecosystem regeneration focused on restoring the productivity of the land, even if that meant planting exotic species, GECI's efforts to restore vegetation focused on the return of native plants through the construction of a nursery and greenhouse that has produced tens of thousands of seedlings of forest and scrub native species.[23] Their efforts to restore the ecosystem extended to work to improve the soil to create conditions to favor the return of native vegetation communities. This labor to garden wild areas and to improve on nature through the addition of new plants was intended to facilitate the ecosystem's regeneration after the removal of the goat population.[24]

Goats and mice on Guadalupe, their histories, the changes they have brought to the landscape, and their transforming relationships with humans are useful subjects for thinking about what Jake Kosek calls "the consequential materiality of nature," the agency of nonhuman actors, and differences in interspecies relationships over time.[25] Eben Kirksey and Stefan Helmreich chart the emergence of anthropological writing in which nonhuman life of all sorts appears "alongside humans in the realm of *bios*, with legibly biographical and political lives." These works examine "the host of organisms whose lives and deaths are linked to human social worlds."[26] A close look at the practice of invasive species eradications and the care of the pest highlights how lives of nonhuman animals shift between *bios* and *zoe*, as they are at one minute individuals with names and personalities toward which scientists feel responsibility and at the next are pests to be eradicated.[27] While the previous chapter analyzed the management of human populations on the island, this one draws on ethnographic fieldwork to detail the management of nonhuman life, particularly how animals were incorporated into scientific practice. Telling the story of eradication in practice on Guadalupe permits me to ask about the particular organisms at issue: goats and mice. I track how these creatures were variously enlisted into consumption, laboratory, and field practices, adding here to literature in the history of science and science studies that examines the role and status of animals in laboratory-based scientific research. Guadalupe was variously configured as a feedlot and slaughterhouse, field site for ecological research, and laboratory, configurations which had consequences for the relationships between human and nonhuman actors. These metaphoric constructions of the island shaped human engagements with animals in important ways as animals were variously understood as meat, wild creatures, or lab instruments according to whether the island was a source of food, an ecosystem to be protected, or an experimental place.

GUADALUPE TODAY

When we finally arrived at the island and disembarked from the *Monasterio*, Rafael, a GECI employee, was waiting for us in a bright yellow pickup truck. After two months on the island, Rafael was happy to see some new faces. Near the dock, Guadalupe fur seals frolicked on nearby rocks, sunning themselves and diving into the sea. Guadalupe fur seals are one of the island's endemic species; they had previously been distributed across a wider range, but hunters from Russia, England, and the United States had brutally hunted them to extinction everywhere else. The history of the seal population on Guadalupe was fraught as well; they had twice been hunted almost to extinction, and at one low point only fourteen remained. Now protected, the population had grown beyond the carrying capacity of the island, and fur seals were slowly returning to other parts of their former range, a natural experiment in regeneration and return.

Once we had loaded the trucks with equipment, we began the long, bumpy trip to GECI's biological station on the northern end of the island. Gabriel acted as a tour guide to the island, pointing out the sights as we jostled our way along a dusty road. We were surrounded by dry fields of silvery-gold grass that Flor joked looked like the island's grey hair. Guadalupe is a semidesert, and we had arrived at the end of the dry season when everything on the island looked parched and sunbaked. The rolling fields were punctuated by high, barren, rocky peaks. We drove past the nesting grounds of the Laysan albatross, empty now, but which would begin to fill up in a month with some two hundred albatrosses. For most of the year the birds remain at sea, touching down on land only during the breeding season. Large seabirds, with a wingspan of six feet or more, they make an impressive sight on the island. Gabriel was well acquainted with the breeding pairs on the island and their offspring, noting that "every albatross that comes to Guadalupe has a first name and a last name." The birds are monogamous, and each pair returns to build a nest at the same site year after year, over the course of their long life spans. The oldest known banded bird in the world is a Laysan albatross named Wisdom, who at 65 years old continues to raise healthy chicks.[28] The population on Guadalupe was slowly increasing as more birds survived to return and mate; however, a number of factors hindered its growth, including feral cats that preyed on albatross eggs and chicks. Gabriel worried about how to communicate the precariousness of the albatross population to residents and visitors.

After three hours of bouncing along the dirt road, we turned down a driveway lined with ten-foot-tall evergreens and arrived at the biological station that GECI had gradually been developing since 2003. Perched on one of the island's high points, the station was adjacent to a small forest of young cypress trees. The cypress trees were native to the island, and the forest was a sign of the island's progress towards regeneration and an example of the kinds of life-forms that could flourish after the eradication of goats. Beyond the forest was grassland that stretched out to cliffs that dropped down to the ocean. As we arrived, Adriana, an ecologist with GECI who had worked on Guadalupe for a long time, came out of the kitchen building, smiling and welcoming us to the island. She showed us around the camp, one of GECI's more comfortable and well-established field sites. The kitchen was in the oldest building, constructed long ago out of cypress trees that had survived the goats' depredations to grow to full size. We spent most of our time as a group there, hanging out, sharing meals, preparing for the day's work, and analyzing data. The kitchen was also a haven for the island's mice, which scampered boldly across the floor and up the walls. Shortly after we arrived we heard the snap of a live trap being triggered. The traps were part of a half-hearted effort to limit the reign of mice over the building. Adriana grabbed the trap and effortlessly extracted a squirming mouse, demonstrating as she did how to handle it and how to identify its sex before releasing it outdoors. I only half paid attention, unaware of how much this activity would dominate our days on the island.

In addition to the kitchen, there were six small buildings with bedrooms for scientists and other visitors, each building named after an island animal—albatross, junco (a small sparrow endemic to Guadalupe), and chivo (goat). Rafael's stories, which were full of animal characters, mystified me at first. "The junco told me this," he would say, or "the junco and the chivo were monitoring the cat population." Only gradually did I realize that some of the frequent visitors to Guadalupe had been nicknamed after the cabin they slept in and that the junco and the chivo were GECI employees, known by other names back in Ensenada. Along with the dormitories, GECI had built a dry latrine, showers, a garage, workshop, office, and a large meeting room. The station is supplied with power from solar panels and wind turbines. Occasionally on cloudy or still days the station ran out of power, but usually there was enough energy to run laptops and lights at night and in the early morning. Even with the limited satellite internet available, the station felt isolated and disconnected from the rest of the world.

JUDAS GOATS

In 1919, British naturalist Frederic W. Jones was mesmerized by the unloading of several hundred wild goats onto the municipal pier at San Diego. Hoisted by their horns from the deck of the Gryme, "each bunch of cud-chewers presented a sorry spectacle as they dangled in midair, with no apparent destination or clue on which to base hope for a much needed relief and their bulging glassy eyes seemed about ready to burst from their sockets."[29] Intrigued by the dramatic arrival of the goats, Jones tracked them to their origin point on Isla Guadalupe. "Following the precedent of Adam and Eve—after many years, Billie and Nannie Goat are said to have settled on Guadalupe Island and their descendants of Billies and Nannies, through many generations, have in all probability, numbered into the millions by this time."[30] At this time, before the development of the penal colony, goatherds were making systematic use of the goats, trapping them in corrals when they came to drink from the island's spring and shipping them to San Diego, where they would be sent on to the slaughterhouses and meatpacking companies of Los Angeles. Guadalupe and its sparse vegetation were being made productive resources as a feedlot for wild goats.

Jones found the masses of goats to be for the most part indistinguishable, with the exception of one noteworthy goat named Monte Cristo, who had once been corralled by the herders but leapt from a San Diego–bound boat and swam back to Guadalupe, where he devoted his "career to the furtherance of the highest interests of his fellow goats." A sociable animal, he thwarted the efforts of the herding gangs, marshaling the other goats, watching for the appearance of boats and keeping goats away from the spring where they might be trapped, until he was finally captured himself. Jones admiringly wrote that even in captivity "he remained obdurate and still possessed his indomitable will." Jones asserted that in his photograph Monte Cristo "appears quite resigned, although, were his inner consciousness exposed and expression given to his thoughts there might be revealed, the words made immortal by our old friend, Patrick Henry: 'Give me liberty or give me death.'"[31]

Monte Cristo's behavior, as fanciful as Jones's narrative of it was, is indicative of characteristics of goat sociality and agency that became important for GECI. While Monte Cristo was a hero for Jones, rescuing his fellow goats, by 2004 GECI would seek to use the very kind of goat sociality that Monte Cristo demonstrated against the goats themselves. In June of that year, GECI began an eradication project, an effort to eliminate every goat from Guadalupe so that native life-forms, particularly plants and forests and the terrestrial birds that used them as habitat, would regenerate. Mammals are the most frequent targets of eradication efforts internationally and are often thought to be the primary causes of extinction and ecosystem changes on islands.[32] For island conservationists, the goats were no longer heroes, nor were they useful sources of food. Instead, they were invasive species in need of eradication. As the island began to be seen as important as a repository of biodiversity and a site of remarkable natural beauty, the economic and food value of the goats lessened in significance. Recuperating the native plant and bird populations of Guadalupe for their aesthetic, ecological, and genetic value became more important than making use of the island as grazing land for goats. Shifting priorities in Mexico changed the way that people framed and understood the landscape and determined the fate of the goats.

The goats left on Guadalupe had indeed been transformative and significant agents of ecological change. Gabriel told me that when they first started their work, "the island was full of goats . . . goats that were here because European boats would bring the goats to have a food supply. But the fur trade hunters stopped coming back to the island because they exterminated the population of fur seals, but the goats stayed. There started to be more goats all the time, and more goats, and more goats, and for some people they were convenient."

Left by hunters of marine mammals to their own devices, the goat population grew and the goats consumed much of the island's vegetation, reducing the size of the forest of cypress, cedar, and pine trees unique to the island. One scientist high-lighted the dramatic nature of this change, noting that "it was quite a collapse—it was close to extinction," with only eighty-five hectares left out of an original forest of eight thousand hectares.

The few people who visited Guadalupe remembered when goats were plentiful, and the island figured both historically and in present-day Ensenada as a feedlot and proto-slaughterhouse, where meat goats descended from the population left on the island by fur trade hunters in the nineteenth century were free for the taking. When we had been on the island for two weeks, a pilot arrived in a small Cesna with the call sign TGW, which he told us stood for Tengo Ganas de Whiskey (I Want Whiskey), and an insignia of a goat with two long, curved horns painted in white on the tail. We met him at the landing strip, an old, paved runway with a dotted white line painted down the middle, eagerly awaiting his arrival since he was bringing important research supplies. The pilot asked Adriana how work was going, and commented that whenever he came to Guadalupe, people wanted to know if he would bring them back a goat to Ensenada for a barbecue. Adriana laughed, but later she sighed over his comment. This was one of the challenges for the goat eradication project. People had gotten used to making use of the goats on the island and to bringing them back for parties on the mainland. Guadalupe was legendary—you could go there, get a goat, free! And people did not want to give that up. Her comment reflects a moment of shifting priorities for people who man-aged the island, as its value in terms of food production had been overshadowed by its ecological value.

The idea of eliminating goats was not immediately popular with everyone; however, while co-op fishermen were initially hesitant, they ultimately agreed on the value of restoring the island ecosystem. Over the course of a century, goats had become part of the landscape of Guadalupe and the social life of nearby residents. For some time, people had come to the island from Oaxaca to acquire dry and salted goat meat to use in chito, a traditional Mixteca Baja dish. While GECI looked back to prewhaler times, doing archaeology of the island to establish the "original" or preinvasion conditions, in the historical memory of the people on the island and in Ensenada, goats and Guadalupe were intertwined and meant to be together. Animal life in contemporary agriculture is typically rigidly organized from the moment of often highly technologized breeding up to the death of the animal and the conversion of the carcass into meat. Animals in these cases are deindividualized units of meat that need to be moved with maximum efficiency and invisibility to their final destination as food. This was not the case on Guadalupe, where the island's remoteness conveniently minimized human interaction with the animals, keeping them and their slaughter on the margins of human experience. However, it also meant that the goats were always feral and meat production was never highly organized or particularly efficient.

Despite the inefficiency of Guadalupe as feedlot and slaughterhouse, Adriana recalled that "there was opposition on all sides" to the eradication. She clarified that people did not frame their protest in terms of animal rights, but rather as a waste of a valuable resource: "There were still a lot of people that came to take goat meat. . . . It makes more sense to buy a goat in Ensenada, but people didn't see that because they say, 'Okay, on the island they are free, and it's nothing more than a question of going and grabbing one, no?'" So the opposition was more in the sense that this was a resource people wanted to use. People were not so concerned that the goats would be killed, but rather that a valuable renewable resource that they were accustomed to making use of would be used up and wasted. Adriana explained:

> There were always animals on the island. When people took goats, they left females or young behind because yes, they wanted to use them, but also to leave some to sustain the population on the island. They weren't going to finish off the population, they thought it was important to maintain it. And there are some people who still believe that the goats are an important genetic resource because the animals are very resilient and they have adapted to the environment. They think the goats were like a new breed, and they said, "you have to protect it, care for it, how can you eradicate it?" Everything along those lines. Everything. And there were other people who wanted all the goats to be moved off the island for people to make use of, so that the resource wasn't wasted. But at the end we explained to them that there was no way to do it; it was very, very expensive to take animals from here and also very dangerous.

On the island as feedlot and slaughterhouse, the goats were generally not individualized (with the exception of the rare character like Monte Cristo) beyond the most general characteristics of sex, age, and breed. A 1998 report on the problems of food production in Mexico and the importance of conserving domestic animal diversity in Mexico called for the preservation of the twenty autochthonous species of domestic animals identified by the Food and Agriculture Organization of the United Nations.[33] The feral goats of Isla Guadalupe were named as one of Mexico's two native breeds of goats. The identification of the goats as a native breed initially posed a problem for eradication projects. A preeradication report on the state of the island's vegetation noted that some of the federal agencies with authority over the island were resistant to the eradication project because they considered the goats a positive addition to the island, and "a valuable resource with unique genetic characteristics (a breed of goats specifically adapted for difficult conditions), that could be exported and used for human populations that needed alternative sources of food."[34] Despite claims for their value based on breed characteristics, Adriana argued that it was obvious that the goats needed to be eliminated. "You saw the island, and you realized, even if you didn't know the island before and weren't a specialist, you saw old trees falling, you saw the island totally bare where there used to be grass, the damage had an emotional impact. Anyone who came to the island could see that something is happening. And that you have to rescue what's left." Adriana's commentary about the emotional impact and the need to rescue the island is a typical example of the way that scientists on Guadalupe were simultaneously engaged in observing and caring for the island as well as exterminating. The act of eliminating the goats was part of her work of caring for the island as a whole, of thinking ecologically.

ISLANDS AS LABORATORIES

Not long after we arrived, Adriana explained to me why conservationists focus on islands: "Islands are incredible opportunities because it's a little piece of land, and whatever you do, you'll be able to see the difference right away." She went on to say:

> They are sites where one can see conservation in action, one can see the effects immediately, and one can see how the island responds. Islands are often described as being laboratories. For example, Guadalupe is an enormous island, but the ecosystem is relatively simple because there aren't any mammals—it just has birds and invertebrates. You know more or less what you should do, that you should remove some things. Because of its simplicity, it's easy to have an image of what it used to be like, and where you want it to get to. You want to try to move these species, and make a difference in the islands. In this island particularly, since it is the most isolated in Mexico.

Raised in Tijuana, Adriana was one of GECI's first employees, hired by Aguirre-Muñoz for a temporary position on Guadalupe. After her first stay on the island, Aguirre-Muñoz offered her a permanent position, and she has been working for

GECI ever since. In 2010, her trips to the island became less frequent. She had moved to New Zealand to study for her doctorate on a scholarship from the federal government, and now she was returning to Guadalupe to collect data for her dissertation research on invasive species. Adriana was only one of several GECI employees studying in New Zealand. As an island nation with an ecosystem protected from contact with other landmasses, New Zealand has a high percentage of endemic species and few native mammals. Its biodiversity is considered to be exceptional and highly vulnerable. In addition, agriculture is a major part of the New Zealand economy, making biosecurity and crop protection of major interest. In response, New Zealand has developed some of the world's most sophisticated techniques to detect and eradicate invasive species, and it was this history that attracted the attention of people at GECI, who hired hunters and consultants from New Zealand, imported tools, and borrowed protocols for invasive species eradications. GECI employees often traveled to New Zealand for education and training, with the goal of bringing useful knowledge back to Mexico. New Zealanders likewise make the trip to Mexico to learn from the new approaches and techniques developed by Mexican scientists.

Gabriel reinforced Adriana's remarks about the value of islands, telling me:

> It's like a gigantic laboratory. The fact that we are geographically isolated allows us to observe in a set environment processes of adaptation and evolution. Charles Darwin had his vision of evolution on an island, precisely because it's a zone where you see adaptation so clearly, and above all on the oceanic islands, because they're so far from the continent. We have geographic isolation that triggers all these evolutionary processes and generates adaptations, changes, and differences. You can see the evolutionary processes on an island. It's very positive. The other thing that's not as positive, and you need to know how to manage it, is the fragility of the ecosystem. Guadalupe is very fragile, and because conditions here are unique, what disappears here is not going to turn up somewhere else. Guadalupe has a very specific equilibrium, because it is relatively small and it doesn't have constant inputs from the exterior, inputs of species or genetic inputs. . . . Evolutionary time is very long, and the processes of adaptation take a long time and are not solved from one day to the next. All this makes the island very fragile, very sensitive to changes, like the introduction of animals, pollution, changes in the topography, in the communities, in the climate, in the hydrology. All these man-made changes can very quickly have effects. That is, it's very slow to make all these species, and it's very quick to kill them . . . Ultimately this is part of the wealth of the island, this fragility. It's like observing a beautiful flower, with very delicate petals. The island is something very beautiful, it's something very different, but it is something that is very, very delicate, very fragile, and because of this it's very important not to disturb it with tourist development, with pollution, with invasive species, with the abuse of the resources, with the exploitation or overexploitation of resources.

The isolation, limited access, and relatively simple ecosystems of many islands give scientists a degree of control that is impossible on the mainland. Scientists are free to experiment with the ecosystem and act as if the island is, as Kohler described the ideal laboratory, "a world apart from the world."[35] Gabriel and Adriana articulated a view of island ecosystems as precious and endangered, a transformation from historical views of the island as a barren wasteland that must be made productive through human enhancements like Olachea's efforts to cultivate the goat population. Instead, the goat population was a threat to life that needed to be eliminated. While in these moments they represented the island as a laboratory, this was not the only way the space was interpreted and deployed.

GECI planned to eradicate the goats from the island first by replicating herders' earlier method of corralling the goats at the spring. However, while corralling the goats is an efficient way to gather a large group for shipment on the hoof to the mainland or for slaughter, it is ineffective as an eradication method since not all goats will come to the corrals of their own volition. In addition, the characteristics of goats that made them appealing to sailors as food sources and that made them such successful invaders also made them difficult to eradicate. They have a low metabolism, thrive on a wide variety of plants, and have efficient digestion, low water requirements, and a high reproductive rate. In order to effectively eradicate them, GECI needed to learn about and make use of goat tendencies and goat behavior.

On an early reconnaissance trip, Adriana followed José Antonio, a professional hunter who had worked for GECI for many years, as he tracked goats on Guadalupe. "Back then there were still goats, many goats," she said. "So he placed traps, and I went with him and watched how he placed them. I started to get interested in the knowledge that you have to have of the animal that you are eventually going to eradicate. To know how to control them." Learning about the goats was key to developing effective eradication strategies, strategies that would make use of goat behavior in order to eliminate them. In order to kill, they had to understand the goats, know how they lived, where they went, what their behaviors were. And ultimately, they found that they could not ever sufficiently know or track the goats well enough to hunt them all. Goats know things that we do not. They can sense each other and locate each other more efficiently than humans ever could.

To take advantage of goats' capabilities, GECI drew on techniques developed and refined in the United States, Australia, and New Zealand, among other places. They captured and sterilized forty goats before equipping them with radio collars and sending them off into the island backcountry to seek out their companions. Through these collars, GECI recruited goats into their eradication plan, turning them into biological instruments that would betray their fellow herd members and remaking the island from a field site into a laboratory. Scientists and conservationists have debated use of radio tags because of their capacity to alter human interactions with wilderness; however, on Guadalupe scientists lauded this transformation.[36] Working with hunters from New Zealand in a helicopter hired by GECI and deployed to Isla Guadalupe by a special Mexican navy vessel, GECI hunted the remaining goats that were hiding in Guadalupe's inaccessible cliffs, canyons, and caves. "In this case it was critical to work together with the National Protected Areas Commission, and, maybe even more important, with the Mexican navy," Aguirre pointed out to me. "The island is very far away from the continent, so you need to navigate for one day or so to get there. It's not easy to get there with a helicopter, it's an oceanic flight. And you needed a helicopter to get rid of the goats." The cliffs on the island are up to a kilometer high, and the terrain is very rough, making ground hunting impossible.

The Judas goat technique used by GECI was first developed in the 1980s by conservationists in Hawaii, where small remnant bands of feral goats were stymie-ing efforts to eradicate the population. Ecologists Dan Taylor and Larry Katahira observed that the feral goats that evaded eradication efforts maintained social groups and fixed home ranges, and that goats found other goats far more success-fully than even experienced human hunters.[37] Studies of both domestic and feral goats showed that solitary goats have a strong drive to locate other goats, a social behavior that is extremely consistent.[38] Taylor and Katahira adapted goats' gre-garious nature as a tool to eliminate the remaining population, releasing radio-collared individuals into the backcountry. In these programs, experienced trackers followed the Judas goats as they led them to the remaining goats, tracking them quietly while remaining downwind and out of sight.[39] Trackers observed the goats for a few minutes before withdrawing to avoid detection and radioing their posi-tion to waiting helicopters and snipers. Taylor and Katahira described the goats' response to the sound of an approaching helicopter, noting that "they usually sought refuge in earth cracks, caves, gullies, under shrubs or trees, or they fled across open terrain. Observers directed the helicopter to hiding places or escape routes, and could thus confine the goats or keep fleeing goats in a group. Shooters in the air and on the ground consequently had the advantage of clear targets and safe shots."[40] All goats except for the Judas goat were killed, while the Judas goat was spared so that it would search out other goats and the process of tracking and hunting was repeated until Judas goats encountered only other Judas goats, and the eradication of goats was complete.[41] Occasionally, even after the feral goats had been eradicated, a few radio-collared Judas goats were kept around as biological detection devices, monitoring tools used to confirm the successful eradication or to detect any remaining individuals. If any new feral goats appeared, the Judas goats would find them and betray their presence.

Although all goats are social, female goats are generally used as Judas goats because they are more efficient at locating herds, and they quickly "betray the loca-tions of male admirers."[42] Their efficiency is hindered, however, because female Judas goats "are often pregnant at the time of deployment or become impregnated in the field; pregnant females leave associated goats to give birth, causing downtime of Judas goat operation."[43] To avoid downtime of their field operatives, Judas goat projects often used sterilized female goats, while later projects went further, sterilizing "'Super Judas' nannies, implanted with hormones to draw billies."[44] These "Super Judas" goats are also known as Mata Hari goats.[45] Like Mata Hari, an exotic dancer and spy for Germany during World War I, these goats will both seduce and betray their fellows. Not all animals are suitable for these kinds of tracking and hunting projects. Programs to develop Judas pigs have failed; lacking the gregarious nature of goats, pigs fail to seek each other out.[46] Judas goats are particularly useful for the final stages of an eradication operation, when the density of goats on an island is low, making other forms of hunting less efficient. Human hunters frequently become frustrated when tasked with hunting work that has low rates of success, and goats are notoriously difficult targets.[47] For example, during an eradication project on the Galápagos, guards complained that the bullets from their .22-caliber rifles simply bounced off the tough hides of the billy goats. Exasperated guards were reported to resort to chasing the goats down and killing them with knives. The persistence of goat populations generated both irritation and creativity among the people working to eliminate them. In the Galápagos, biologists and park officials mused over beer about the effectiveness of introducing rabies, swine fever, foot-and-mouth disease, anthrax, or rinderpest to the islands as agents of biological control.[48] While the idea of releasing some kind of fatal, contagious disease held appeal for the frustrated officials, ultimately on the Galápagos as on Guadalupe it was judged to be less risky and more effective to rely on Judas goats.

As GECI developed their plans for eradication, they saw characteristics of goats beyond their efficiency at converting forage into meat. Goats were no longer meat on hooves, but wild animals in the field over which humans lacked control. As GECI focused on eliminating every goat, the goats appeared less predictable and more individualized. Successful eradications require not only understanding of goats as a species, but also knowledge of individual goats and their movement patterns.[49] Particular Judas goats were noted as especially effective at locating other goats. In the original Judas goat experiment, scientists reported that the "most successful animals were release #5 at Hi-lina Pali, release #4 at Polio Keawe Pali, and 2 Mauana Loa releases."[50] While scientists sought to learn about goats, they also worked to prevent goats from becoming educated. The use of original Judas goats in slaughterhouses exploited the ability of goats to learn from each other how to execute a task. This aptitude was a hindrance to eradication efforts, since an educated goat was much more difficult to kill. Goats learned quickly to be wary of hunters, becoming highly sensitive to the sound of hunters and looking for and avoiding their tracks and traces.[51] Since goats rapidly learned and became watchful, it was important for eradication projects to move and kill quickly.[52] In a report on a feral goat eradication campaign on Santiago Island in the Galápagos, the authors noted that it was essential to minimize chances that a goat might escape during the hunting process, "to prevent a naïve population from learning to avoid hunting methods."[53] Animals at low densities are difficult to detect, even with the use of Judas goats, and goats that have learned to be distrustful of humans increase costs and the probability of eradication failure.[54]

In the process of executing a Judas goat project, scientists learned from and about goats, incorporating them into the project as scientific instruments, while simultaneously engaging with goats as wild animals whose behavior cannot be controlled, animals whose capacity to learn and to thwart scientific goals is something to be reckoned with. In this way, eradications are an unusual contact zone between humans and goats, producing cross-species interactions and intraspecies betrayals. While eradication projects are often described as wars between people and animals, goats here are seen as collaborators and willing betrayers of their fellow goats. The choice of "Judas goat" as a name is judgmental, labeling goats doing goat things as betrayers, making a conscious choice to sell out their fellow goats to save their own skins, a reversal of Monte Cristo's heroic rescues. It frames these encounters in a particular way, one that attributes to goats an evil kind of agency, fitting with goats' traditional symbolic association with the devil and treachery.

GECI neither originated the term *Judas goat* nor used terms like *Mata Hari*. Aguirre argued that it was an unfortunate metaphor, and he objected to it, along with the term *betrayal*, on the grounds that they inappropriately stigmatized animals and did not properly reflect the compassion and attention to animal suffering that GECI scientists brought to their work and which was demonstrated in my observations of scientists in the field, where their careful attention to and respect for all life was obvious. Aguirre argued that even the use of the word *killing* was inappropriate to describe what they did: instead, at GECI they used the term *scarify* so as not to suggest a lack of compassion for animal life and suffering. To understand GECI's approach, he suggested that I read Pope Francis's encyclical letter *Laudato Si*, which is a call to all people to take action in a time of ecological crisis and, as Aguirre points out, highlights "the need to ask for forgiveness to nature, and act in a responsible way and proportionally to the damage that we already have done." On Guadalupe, the Judas goat program ended successfully for the conservationists in 2007, after they eradicated approximately ten thousand feral goats. With the eradication of the goats, seedlings of native and endemic species that had been absent for more than one hundred years began to grow again, and plant species that had been thought long extinct began to reappear.[55]

COMMEMORATING THE DEAD ON GUADALUPE

As Halloween approached, Rafael began to talk of holding a Halloween party. He mused on the costumes we could put together using the minimal supplies we had and suggested that he might dress up as a junco. Halloween has long been a subject of debate in Mexico, decried as a "fiesta gringa" invented by business to promote

FIGURE 5. Day of the Dead altar on Guadalupe. Source: Author photograph.

consumption and an example of the insidious penetration of American capital and interests into the country.[56] Ultimately, despite our planning and anticipation, Halloween came and went with no celebration. Two days later we did celebrate Día de Muertos (Day of the Dead), building an altar in the kitchen by draping a blue cloth over a table and festooning it with decorations (see figure 5). According to Rafael, our altar represented the first time that people from GECI had celebrated Día de Muertos on the island. Claudio Lomnitz observes that Day of the Dead is "an officially promoted identitarian ritual," one that became especially important on the Baja California peninsula as way of affirming connection with the mainland, and renouncing US influence, an invented tradition that binds the nation together.[57] Our altar was a mishmash of island materials as we tried to replicate mainland Day of the Dead celebrations using what we had at hand. Rafael taught Flor and me how to make roses out of tissue paper, and Adriana and Leticia decorated the altar with cypress seeds, dried grasses, flowers, and seedlings from the greenhouse where GECI was raising native plants. We supplemented these decorations with bottles of homemade wine, canisters of instant coffee, tea, and tuna fish. We wrote names of our dead relatives on strips of cardboard and taped them to the altar. Flor wrote out the lyrics to her recently deceased grandmother's favorite song, and Gabriel printed pictures of three workers from CONANP who had died on the island nine months earlier in an accident in their all-terrain vehicle.

Lomnitz argues that death itself is the sign of the Mexican nation, noting that "the management of death, and indeed the ability to kill, are cornerstones of state sovereignty."[58] The management of death and thereby life on the island was a key move in establishing sovereignty. However, the targets of biopolitics in this case were not human subjects but animal bodies. On Guadalupe, distinctions were made among species of wild animals, and in order to optimize and multiply the life of some animals, others were killed. Invasive species were eradicated so that native species could live. While some deaths on the island were commemorated, eradications were not. Some goat skulls were scattered around the biological station, but despite the presence of goat remains, their deaths were not remarked on or regretted.

SACRIFICIAL MICE

Although the goats were gone, GECI's work on the island was not finished; rather, the attention of the group had shifted to the next animal. After a week on the island, our days had taken on a rhythm. We woke at 5:00 to drive across the island to the field site where we spent our days monitoring the mouse population. As the sun came up, Adriana interpreted the scenery around us, pointing out which species were invasive and which were native. She knew the island best after years of working as the project manager, and she saw the landscape in terms of its history and its future. The grasses that covered the hills next to the road were all invasive, mostly European, although some had come all the way from Australia. While she showed us the species that are problematic on Guadalupe, she added that the traffic has gone both ways. Mexican species have also traveled around the world, invading other countries. The presence of the nopal cactus in Australia is a notorious example. While the cactus is beloved in Mexico as a plant, as food for the insects used in the production of cochineal, and as an important part of the cuisine, it is a plague in Australia.[59] Adriana noted that despite the destructive power of invasive species, controlling the travel of plants and animals across borders receives relatively little attention. Efforts to manage the movement of nonhuman life-forms across borders tend to focus on the microbial scale, particularly on disease.

Adriana explained to me the dramatic transformation she had seen over the years she had been on the island:

> I've seen the island before and after the goats. I'm very moved to see that the island has this capacity of regenerating all these life-forms. It was lacking a lot, and there is still a lot to do, because yes, there still is damage, and it needs help to recuperate, but for me, it's very obvious what happens . . . when you do nothing more than remove the viper, in this case the predator. The plants, sometimes it's so easy to do it. It's just a question of removing the threat. . . . I didn't think that the island, no one thought that the island would respond so quickly.

While we were now surrounded by lush fields of invasive grasses, when the goats were here there was almost no vegetation—they consumed everything. Deep gullies still cut through the landscape, the result of erosion that occurred when rain fell on the deforested landscape. Adriana imagined a future that would develop as the ecology continued to transform. "As the little trees start to grow and form shade, the grass won't grow anymore. I think that little by little, a community called chaparral will develop." She went on to describe what chaparral would look like, explaining, "It's trees of two meters, like the one alongside the dormitories . . . With plants of this size, with the shade they create, the grass won't grow. So I think that eventually, after many years, that's where we're going to be."

After jostling along the dirt road for an hour, we arrived at the meadow where yesterday we had placed sixty-four traps to catch mice. On this morning we worked in teams of three to process the traps placed the night before. We used Sherman traps, thin metal boxes designed to catch live mice. Each trap was filled with handfuls of a soft material called estopa and a generous pinch of dry oats: bedding and food for a mouse for the night. We lined up the traps in squares of eight by eight, placing them in regularly spaced intervals in each quadrant. Leticia always placed the first row, labeled A, because it reminded her of her daughter Alejandra.

Gabriel, Flor, and I worked together. We processed mice methodically, but very slowly, and Flor dubbed us Team Turtle, while Leticia, Rafael, and Adriana, the efficient and speedy workers, were Team Hare. We snapped on latex gloves and gathered the traps, carrying stacks of them to the center of the quadrant, where we worked, surrounded by metal boxes. It was quiet except for the scrabbling of nails and teeth against metal, as the mice gnawed at the metal doors of the traps, fighting to escape. They occasionally managed to chew a hole through the metal and escape, fleeing into the field. The boxes emitted a pungent odor, which I realized after several days in the field was the smell of mouse urine. Each day the odor became more noxious, as we reused the bedding in the traps.

In the field, we made difficult judgments about the life and death of animals. At an earlier field site, Gabriel and I watched as baby turtles emerged from their nests, struggling to break free from their shells, and then dig themselves out of the sand. As they emerged from the nest, the orange and purple land crabs that buried themselves in the sand across the island swarmed, grabbing the turtles and eating the soft parts of their bodies. The turtles that made it past the claws of the crabs were picked up by frigate birds as they reached the sea. I asked Gabriel why they let the crabs eat the turtles, and he said, "If the crabs were an invasive species, we'd kill them. But they are from here. We'll kill the mice on the island, but not the crabs." The destruction of turtle life by the crabs was thus judged appropriate and necessary, on the basis of the crabs' equal claim to indigenous status.

However, we did not kill the mice on Guadalupe, even though they were unwanted pests and GECI's goal was to eliminate invasive species. Gabriel explained to me that we were in the midst of an experiment that required that the mice live. By tracking how many previously caught and marked mice were recaptured each day and using a program developed by researchers in New Zealand, GECI could develop an estimate of the size of the population. Repeating this experiment at different times of the year allowed them to track annual variation, and understand how shifts in food availability and predator population affected the mouse population size. The capture/recapture experiment also recorded how mice moved around the quadrant, data that would allow GECI to better understand population dynamics and individual activity. The data that we collected from these carefully tended mice would enable GECI to plan and time subsequent eradications.

Eradication efforts tend to focus on larger species first, since they are easier to eradicate and it is easier to prevent their reintroduction. One pregnant mouse hitching a ride on a ship can undo years of eradication work, but it is less likely that larger animals such as cats or goats would be accidentally reintroduced. Larger, topographically complex islands like Guadalupe also make eradication work more difficult—there are more spaces for the animals to hide, and therefore more chances for them to escape the eradication. One of the crucial questions for GECI was what would happen to the mouse population if the island's cat population were removed.[60] The cats are on Guadalupe as the result of a failed effort at biological control. They were initially brought to the island to keep the mouse population in check, only to become a worse pest than the mice, eating eggs and baby seabirds. When the mouse population is low, cat predation on birds increases. While GECI scientists argue that removing the cat population is an important next step in restoring the island, they are also concerned that by removing the cats they could inadvertently do more damage to the ecosystem. Without predators, the mouse population could explode, and mice are also destructive: they eat the eggs of nesting seabirds and the seeds of native plants.

Our monitoring now was to establish what kind of predator-prey relationship exists between mice and cats. Does cat predation control the size of the mouse population? Would reducing the number of cats allow the number of mice to grow?

Or does the size of the mouse population depend on the availability of food for the mice? This project was designed to characterize the relationship between these two populations. Half of our quadrants were located in fenced areas; cats could not enter, but predatory birds and other native predators continued to have access. The other areas were open, accessible to cats. GECI had been monitoring the cat population for five years and mice for almost as long. Their research had shown that the size of the cat population depends on the size of the mouse population, although cats' relatively slower reproduction rate meant that changes in the mouse population size were not immediately reflected in the cat population. The mouse population, on the other hand, responded almost immediately to environmental conditions. If it rained, there would be a corresponding increase in grass and seeds, and shortly after that there would be more mice and, eventually, more cats.

Gabriel began processing the first trap, shaking the contents into a ziplock bag. A clump of bedding fell out, followed by a mouse. He looked thoughtfully at the trap, feeling the weight, and shook it again. A second and then a third mouse fell into the bag. He sealed the bag and grabbed one mouse through the bag, pressing its whiskers and nose into the corner. Holding it by the loose skin at the back of the neck, he extracted it from the bag. Gabriel manipulated the mice expertly, rarely suffering bites. When I expressed admiration for Gabriel's technique with the mice, he told me he used to be disgusted by them. He described himself as an oceanographer masquerading as a biologist, and asserted that he was most comfortable and interested in sea mammals—mice were outside of his area of expertise and training. Flipping the mouse upside down, he observed that it was female, not currently pregnant, and weighed it, while Flor recorded the data. As Gabriel held the mouse with a firm but not tight grip on its scruff, I pulled out a pair of pincers and a rectangular metal tag a few millimeters long. Each tag was engraved with a three-digit number, which I read to Flor before placing the tag on the mouse's ear and clamping the pincers shut, locking the tag in place. I then colored the mouse's belly and tail with a green permanent marker. Gabriel joked that I would think that GECI's primary goal was to make animals more beautiful by giving them earrings and decorating them with colored markers. Once the mouse was fully documented and marked, Gabriel returned it to the trap in which it was caught. Once we had processed all sixty-four traps, we released each mouse in the spot where it had been captured.

When Gabriel grabbed the next mouse from the bag, we saw the glint of a metal tag in its ear. Flor noted the number and returned the mouse to the trap. This was our third day in this quadrant, and some of the mice we encountered were being captured for a second or third time. Flor grabbed the next trap, shaking out a fat little mouse (see figure 6). She remarked on how plump he was, and how he nonchalantly continued to eat an oat even as she grabbed the scruff of his neck. "You're my favorite, fatty!" she exclaimed, "I'll remember your number always." She held

FIGURE 6. Portrait of Fatty the mouse.
Source: Author photograph.

him up next to her face, and I took their picture together. At this stage, even though mice were destructive invaders, we were engaged in caring for them in order to produce data. Alongside that careful scientific work, we developed more individualized relationships with the mice.

Even as we acknowledged that mice were harmful to island ecosystems, we developed an attachment and affection for them. While handling hundreds of mice, we still distinguished among them and found their signature characteristics, jokingly attributing human qualities to our mousy friends. When they squeaked, we referred to it as singing or crying. Over in Team Hare, Adriana and Leticia kept up a steady stream of chatter. "Behave yourself! Don't you bite! My, aren't you fat. And this one is quite a crybaby." If a mouse cried or squeaked a lot while being handled, they joked that it was surely male. Leticia picked up a particularly big-eared mouse to put an earring in and exclaimed, "My, what beautiful ears you have! And they're going to be more beautiful now." She complimented the next, remarking "what a nice white belly you have." Every so often Adriana held a mouse up to Leticia's face and told her to give it kisses.

We had been catching and releasing mice for a few days, and while I had grown more comfortable handling mice and piercing ears, I still lagged behind Gabriel in skill level. As I manipulated and measured the mice, I was frequently bitten, a consequence of holding the scruff too loosely, leaving the mouse enough flexibility to twist around and bite my hand. After a particularly stinging bite—mouse teeth, while not particularly sharp, can still deliver a painful pinch—I grabbed a mouse too tightly. Its eyes bulged, and before I had time to loosen my grip, the mouse died. I was shaken that I had inadvertently strangled an animal and that it happened so quickly and easily.

When a mouse died in the course of our work, Gabriel usually gave its chest a few thumps or a massage to try to revive it before we buried it in a grave near where we were working. One particularly cold morning, Leticia and I were working together when I opened a trap and found that the bedding inside was cold and wet with dew, with a mouse so still I took it for dead. However, Leticia was more optimistic and determined to revive the mouse. After we processed it, checked its sex and weight, she placed it in her wool hat. Dubbing the hat "the incubator," she tucked it inside her jacket, keeping the mouse cozy as we carried on with work. Emptying the rest of the traps, we found three more immobile, frigid mice. Each one was added to the incubator, and by the end of the morning all four had warmed up. Having returned them to life, she released them.

We had conflicting feelings about mice, and it felt strange to be working with such care and effort to handle them and keep them healthy at the same time that their presence on the island was judged a destructive one. We all confessed to feeling challenged by various aspects of work in the field. For Flor, it was the mice in the buildings in the biological station—all she could think about was mice running over the dishes. I admitted that I was disgusted beyond reason by earwigs, particularly the flying variety that lived on Guadalupe. Gabriel asked, "even more than cockroaches?" trying to establish a scale of horrifying insects. He also told me that earwigs can crawl into your ears and eat your eardrum, which, true or not, was the thing that occupied my thoughts as I settled into bed at night after picking the earwigs off my mattress and pillow.

Unlike the goats, the mice had no defenders. No one outside of GECI suggested that they had any value or that they contributed anything positive to the island. As Karen Rader notes, we do not weigh the fate of all animals equally. The ethical yardstick by which animal experimentation and use is measured is variable. While dogs and cats are seen as pets and companions, mice have "been hangers-onto human culture for thousands of years, so their cultural identity as undesirable pests derived first and foremost from that relationship."[61] As a result, she writes, few people have strong emotional attachments to mice or a great deal of concern about their fate.

We paused our mouse processing to eat lunch on the side of the road, bundled up in jackets against the cold. Rafael took a look at us and laughed, "We look like we're waiting for a coyote to take us to the US." As we finished lunch, Rafael pointed out a cave entrance between the road and one of the quadrants where we had been working. The entrance was deceptive, a narrow crevice in the ground that, once you squeezed through it, opened into a large cavern. In the cave we found a cache of goat bones, including a headless carcass. The dry air had mummified it, leaving leathery skin stretched tight over its ribs. Although the goats had been eradicated, their traces remained on the island: this carcass, the bleached horns and skulls that are littered over the island, and the memories people on the island have of goats.

After lunch, we headed back to activate the traps for another night of mouse catching. We threw oats and estopa into each trap and set it up at its designated point in the quadrant. As we walked through the fields, we heard the snap of the traps behind us as mice entered them almost immediately after they were deposited. We placed the traps in the evening, finishing as the sun began to set, and we started work early in the morning so that the mice would not be left baking in the metal boxes in the heat of the day. Our schedule and work were arranged around carefully tending to these invasive creatures, thinking of their health and handling them with the utmost care. While talk of invasive species is about eradication, elimination, prevention, and whether things do or do not belong, the day-to-day work is of caring for the animals that are here. Producing knowledge about this population, whatever its history or fate on the island, involved caring for the mice that were there now.

The mice slipped in and out of pest status, crossing borders back and forth between being our friends and our enemies, between *bios* and *zoe*. One minute they were matter out of place, destructive eaters of bird eggs, invaders of an island paradise, and disgusting trespassers in our living space. The next they were model animals for our research that we tended to carefully, identified, and were affectionate with. Once they were made experimental subjects, they became useful and valuable. We had an emotional relationship to our Guadalupe mice that exceeded the ordinary connections between humans and mice.

Eva Hayward writes of the way animal bodies "carry forms of domination, communion, and activation into the folds of being. As we look for multispecies manifestations we must not ignore the repercussions that these unions have for all actors." She notes that, in trying to make sense of the corals she is working with, she aids in their death; "this species-sensing is not easily refused by the animals."[62] Likewise, our care of the mice is nonoptional for them. We interact with them and they leave their marks on us in the form of bites, torn gloves, chewed-through traps, and soiled bedding. But ultimately, we choose the terms of our engagement with them. Making mice into experimental models requires caring for them, learning how to optimize their life in the laboratory.[63] Our traps disciplined the mice to be model animals for our experiment, which would produce the knowledge necessary for future eradications.

At the same time, these mice were not quite laboratory animals. While the earrings and markings turned them into measuring devices and instruments for us, they remained distinct from lab mice, which are raised under carefully controlled conditions and are bred to be standardized, easily exchangeable for one another and to have characteristics suited for particular kinds of experiments. Furthermore, lab mice are not generally valued for their ability to produce knowledge about mice themselves; rather, they are interesting for the way they can be made to speak to other biological systems.[64] Here on Guadalupe, now configured as a field site, we did not seek to alter the mice's behavior. Instead, our goal was to enlist the mice as collaborators so that we could describe and map their wild patterns of behavior.

When we finished our mouse work, Flor, Gabriel, and I sat in the truck bed, riding back to the biological station. The sun had set and it had become quite cold, leaving us shivering under a pile of coats, looking up at the stars. Flor marveled at the clarity of the sky, asking if it was clearer here than on San Pedro Mártir, the island where the main observatory in Baja California is located. Gabriel agreed that the sky was remarkably clear, something confirmed by a group of astronomers from the Universidad Nacional Autónoma de México who had recently traveled to Guadalupe. According to Gabriel, they were so impressed with the environment on the island that they hoped to establish a permanent observing station. The title of their presentation sounded like science fiction to Gabriel: "A voyage through time to search for the origins of the universe." Guadalupe was a site for both biological time travel, where eradicating animals can lead to the restoration of a historical ecosystem, and, perhaps in the future, astronomical time travel.

Discourse about invasive species is revealing. The emotionally heightened rhetoric that people use when they talk about alien species, representing them as sources of existential threat and risk, demonstrates the ways in which they think about nativeness and purity, about insiders and outsiders. However, this discourse, while effective in mobilizing action, does not capture the complex ways in which humans and animals engage in the field. Looking at conservation practices in Mexico demonstrates the ways in which invasive species become visible as a threat. Within the context of a single island, the meaning of animal life and cross-species relationships transformed as human priorities changed, remaking the island from slaughterhouse to field site to laboratory. Thinking about the island within the national context of Mexican biodiversity and ecosystem health, rather than its potential for producing meat for the local population, led scientists to a reinterpretation of the value of animal lives. This interpretation went counter to the various ways that other people, who did not see biodiversity as an essential or obvious resource, used and relied on these ostensibly threatening animals. For scientists at GECI, the project was about preserving the island for Mexico—not just as a piece of property that significantly extended the boundaries of the nation, but also as a place with a particular ecosystem.

As people began to think about the importance of the island in new contexts and on new scales, slaughter for conservation replaced slaughter for food. Scientists transformed the island from feedlot to laboratory, along the way incorporating animals into their scientific practice. Animals are a normal feature of many biology laboratories, where they are carefully tended up to the moment of their sacrifice so that they may produce information about biology more broadly. In laboratory-based research, model organisms such as mice and *Drosophila* have become key elements of the material culture of biology, shaped by and shaping the lab.[65] Animals transform as they enter the laboratory where they are domesticated, standardized, and commoditized. Scientists selectively breed animals so that their characteristics are known and regularized, and intervene in their lives until they resemble instruments and are part of the lab apparatus. At the same time, laboratory ecologies are constructed around the particularities of their biology.[66] Kohler argues that "laboratory organisms should be treated as constructed artifacts, no less than physical instruments, and as tools for investigation rather than as objects to be investigated."[67] Michael Lynch writes of "sacrificing" animals in the laboratory, a process by which scientists transform animals from "naturalistic" animals of everyday experience into "analytic" objects, or legible data.[68] As tools and data, model organisms in experimental systems are not treated as individuals. Rather, they stand in for human biology, or shed light on more generalized biological processes.

As much as the island was made to resemble a laboratory, however, in experiments on Guadalupe, where animals remade the landscape and where animals betrayed one another, the multispecies relationships produced differed significantly from those between scientists and model organisms in ordinary laboratories. The animals on Guadalupe diverged from the "furry test tubes" that experimental organisms in the laboratory resemble.[69] Crossing the terrain between lab and field, scientists from GECI moved from intervening and experimenting with the ecosystem and producing data and results generalizable to the world at large to describing and mapping Guadalupe as a unique ecosystem. While the laboratory is an epistemically advantageous space because it allows scientists to isolate the phenomena of interest from the rest of the world, the field site enables scientists to study events or objects of interest in the messy and unruly context in which they are usually found.[70] Field sites are located in areas where the ecosystem presents characteristics of interest to the scientist, in this case a high concentration of imperiled endemic species. As a result, field practices are designed to minimize disruption and to observe what is already present. In this context, the animals of Guadalupe were less research tools than subjects of research themselves. While animals in the agricultural system and in the laboratory are subject to intensive interventions in breeding, mobility, habitat, and diet, in the field animals are subject to fewer interventions and controls. Rather than easily manipulable, accessible, and standardized, they are interesting for their autonomy and their ability to act independently of human control. In the field, animals are less predictable and more individualized than in the laboratory.

In these encounters, animals were instruments as well as recipients of individualized care and attention. Goats and mice on Guadalupe were both loved and betrayed as scientists engaged in simultaneously seeing and caring for the island

and exterminating, a far more complex relationship than simply annihilating a threat. These interactions represent an alternative multispecies relationship, one that is darker than the stories of companion species, interspecies communications, connectivities, or practices of living together that have been characterized in other multispecies ethnographies. GECI's conservation projects are exemplars of work that move conservation beyond nature/culture divides. Built on rigorous science and an empathetic concern for social life, they show how protecting biodiversity requires thinking about human and nonhuman lives together. The remarkable success of GECI in its projects is a lesson for life in the Anthropocene, a moment in which human activity has inevitably changed the very geological processes of the earth and, by extension, all life on it. Living in the Anthropocene, we need to rethink philosophies that prioritize conserving only pristine, untouched nature, and instead look for models of conservation, like those produced by GECI, that seek to sustain biodiversity in disturbed landscapes in collaboration with local institutions and communities.

3

Acclimatizing Biosecurity

On a sunny summer day in 2010, I took a green and white Mexico City microbus to the Instituto Nacional de Enfermedades Respiratorias (the National Institute for Respiratory Diseases, or INER) in the southern neighborhood of Tlalpan (see figure 7). The microbus was crowded with other people traveling to INER—nurses and technicians wearing white coats with "Instituto Nacional de Enfermedades Respiratorias" embroidered in blue script over their chest and patients laboriously carting oxygen tanks. INER is the oldest hospital in Mexico City's "hospital zone," a cluster of hospitals and research institutes seventeen kilometers south of the city center. In addition to INER, there are hospitals dedicated to cardiology, mental health, nutrition, and pediatrics.

As the microbus entered the zone, we drove past a sculpture of a giant footprint inscribed with the message "Welcome to solid ground." Because Mexico City was constructed on the former site of Lake Texcoco, most of the city rests on lake bed sediment that is heavily saturated with water. The sediment has gradually subsided over the years, producing sinking, tilting buildings. In addition, the softness of the soil amplifies the seismic waves from the relatively frequent earthquakes, intensifying their power. In contrast, the hospital zone is located in the foothills of the mountains surrounding Mexico City, where the subsurface is solid rock. The sign welcoming us to solid ground signaled that we had left behind the danger posed by earthquakes.

I was going to INER to meet with Edgar Sevilla, a microbiologist who had been deeply affected by the outbreak of H1N1 influenza described in the introduction.

FIGURE 7. El Instituto Nacional de Enfermedades Respiratorias. Source: Author photograph.

For Sevilla, the disease was both a major public health event and a validation of his fears. A few weeks before the outbreak, he and a few colleagues had founded the Mexican Biosafety Organization (AMEXBIO). A professional organization devoted to raising awareness of biological security and safety issues, AMEXBIO's goal was to address the risks associated with infectious disease, genetically modified organisms, and invasive species. Anxious that Mexico was failing to manage biological risk adequately, Sevilla and his colleagues had started the organization to promote "a risk management culture that would help prevent adverse impacts to public health, animal health, and the environment."[1] News reports tracking the spread of H1N1 made the nation aware of the dangers of infectious disease and put the biosecurity issues the fledgling organization focused on in the spotlight. Further, the rapid movement of the disease around the world, through human and nonhuman vectors, made manifest the global interconnection of living things and the permeability of national borders. In the context of the outbreak, the difficulties of monitoring and controlling the movement of corporeal beings like humans and animals, let alone insubstantial viruses, became clear. For some observers, the disease conjured a recognition of the existence of a global biological community, as the spread of illness demonstrated how seemingly unconnected places like a swine farm in rural Mexico and a Beijing hotel might link up.[2]

The idea of a global biological community is one that has been taken up in public health rhetoric and practice. Public health projects have increasingly shifted from nation-by-nation efforts to fight disease to approaches that seek to manage health on a global scale, addressing what Bruce Braun has termed "the global biological."[3] For example, in 2005 the World Health Organization ratified a new set of International Health Regulations (IHR) which represented an effort to produce global regulations and health practices. The IHR 2005 are legally binding regulations that call for all member states to enhance certain public health capacities, specifically those related to detection, assessment, and response to public health emergencies. The WHO emphasizes that these detection and surveillance resources should be directed primarily to events with the potential to cause the spread of disease internationally and interfere with international traffic.[4] Biocontainment laboratories constructed in Mexico enabled the country to comply with the IHR 2005, providing detection and surveillance resources and becoming part of the global network of laboratories called for by the WHO in order to produce global epidemic response capabilities. However, for reasons this chapter will explore, the development of a global network of laboratories has proven difficult.

CAN BIOSECURITY GO GLOBAL?

While Sevilla and other organizers of AMEXBIO were concerned with protecting life in Mexico, others framed the problem differently, seeking to establish and institute regulations globally in order to protect the security of life in the United States. Ren Salerno and Jennifer Gaudioso, staff scientists at Sandia National Laboratory in the United States, attended AMEXBIO's second annual meeting in Puebla in 2011. They were deeply concerned with the development of biosecurity in Mexico and the question of whether biosecurity could "go global."[5] In a report on their work, Salerno said, "Even now, anywhere around the world, someone can build a laboratory to work with the most dangerous pathogens and be subject to no construction standards, no operating standards, and no safety or security standards." Andrew Weber, the US assistant secretary of defense for nuclear, chemical, and biological defense programs, discussed the work on biosecurity being done at Sandia, noting, "An outbreak anywhere, deliberate or natural, is a threat everywhere. It's not something we can just deal with within our own borders."[6] These statements frame global public health and scientific research as integral to the security of the United States, highlighting US fears about global biological interconnections. They situate security issues at a global level, one that requires systems of global governance and response. These statements reflect a growing perception among US and WHO officials that state-centric health and security projects are no longer effective.

Weber argued that national borders have become less relevant, suggesting that since US insecurity can come from an outbreak anywhere, the United States needs to extend its influence outside its own borders. The Sandia team envisioned tracking both microbes and scientists throughout the world. Their trip to the AMEXBIO conference was part of an effort to work with scientists globally to establish systems to inventory, control, and monitor access to dangerous pathogens used in research.[7] Their ultimate goal was to produce a global public health network that would be capable of responding to the new hazards and risks that globalization represented for the United States.

The network anticipated by the scientists from Sandia draws on American political impulses to govern life through what Melinda Cooper describes as "speculative *preemption*."[8] She argues that responses to biological and military risk in the United States are characterized by fears of "our absolute, uninsurable exposure to an uncertain future, our coimplication in events that recognize no sovereign boundaries."[9] Traveling outside the borders of the United States, Sandia scientists attempted to preempt the possibility of scientists elsewhere intentionally or accidentally producing harmful effects that could expose the United States (and the rest of the globe) to catastrophic consequences and to produce a monitoring system that reflected their perception of the global nature of health risks.

CONTESTING THE GLOBAL BIOLOGICAL

These public health efforts to manage the global biological are in tension with the logics of security. While public health projects seek to treat the biological as a global system, security projects are attentive to variations in life-forms in different places. Biosecurity projects grid out global space to secure life while still enabling freedom and movement.[10] The local institutions, infrastructures, and practices that I examined were oriented towards characterizing the human and microbial life in Mexico in order to protect it. They sought to protect the diversity of life-forms by regulating and controlling the global circulation of biology (through monitoring the movements of viruses, plants, animals, and genomes, as well as scientific practices).[11] Carlo Caduff describes scientists who work on biosecurity as "biologist[s] of context" who "consider the pathogenic agent in its biological milieu, emphasizing its relationships."[12] Life-forms like invasive species are not inherently risky, dangerous, or threatening; it is only within particular contexts and relationships that they become so. Likewise, as this chapter will show, the risk posed by pathogenic agents varies in different milieus. The idea of biology as relational has been taken up by a variety of analysts.[13] Alex Nading, for example, describes the production of a relational knowledge of life in Nicaraguan campaigns to control dengue. While he describes global health as "centered on a compulsion to redraw the lines between people, bugs, and viruses, often in the name of 'biosecurity,'" the practice of mosquito eradication demonstrates the interconnection of people, other life-forms, and the built environment.[14] In Mexico, biosecurity research likewise draws on a history of concern with the importance of relationships and context for producing life. Nature was not treated as pristine or separate from human practices; rather, scientists structured their lab work around their knowledge of the entanglements and interconnections of nature and culture.

The expansion of global projects designed to produce security generated conflict in Mexico between international expectations and local implementations. While public health programs like the IHR 2005 and the Sandia project were premised on the universality of biology, scientists in Mexico emphasized malleability of biology. Lab practices, which highlighted the importance of local biologies, were at odds with these programs.[15] Sevilla and his colleagues at AMEXBIO argued that protecting life in Mexico required attention to how history, politics, and environment had shaped biological substance; the way biomestizaje shaped life-forms had consequences for security and research practice in Mexico. Attention to the plasticity and malleability of life-forms and their interactions with the environment complicated projects of global health. In daily practice, scientists' struggle to translate international expectations and regulations challenged the idea of the global biological and made local difference tangible. The difficulties that scientists encountered in developing bioseguridad and translating research principles to Mexico brought into focus the ways both lab practices and the materiality of life itself are place-dependent. The experiences of scientists in the lab made it evident that local differences in bodies, culture, regulations, and infrastructure had consequences for scientific practice, making it difficult for biosecurity to become a global project. As a result, even as organizations like the WHO sought to implement global systems of governance, the nation continued to be an important organizing concept, and scientists in Mexico challenged the idea of a global biological.

Implementing biosecurity projects and programs in Mexico revealed the national specificity of scientific practices, even those that were part of global regulatory and health systems. Differences in the Mexican environment, expertise, economy, and regulatory system made it difficult to transplant practices from elsewhere. To borrow a term from natural history, these practices needed to be acclimatized in order to thrive in Mexico. I draw on the idea of acclimatization in reference to the history of projects to bring life-forms to new places across the globe. These efforts were a frequent feature of nineteenth-century colonial botany and zoology, attempts by Europeans to remake the world's biogeography to suit their economic, aesthetic, and imperial aims, and they represent the efforts of scientists to assert control over the natural world and to make possible the transfer of organisms or ecosystems from one place to another.[16] As Harriet Ritvo has pointed out, however, acclimatization projects rarely proceed according to plan.[17] Similarly, efforts to transplant modes of biosecurity or safety culture rarely go smoothly. The efforts to implement these plans and the challenges that they faced reveal previously unobserved or unconsidered differences between places, as well as undercutting the supposed universality of scientific practice and culture.

Recent work by anthropologists has demonstrated the contingent nature of biomedicine. For example, Elizabeth Roberts observes that reality in Ecuador is shaped by "specific sets of relational contingencies, connections, and constraints." This Ecuadorian reality has important consequences for both the practice of biomedicine and biological organisms themselves.[18] Julie Livingston frames the responses of scientists and other biomedical professionals to these varying realities and contingencies as "improvisation," writing that "improvisation is a defining feature of biomedicine in Africa. Biomedicine is a global system of knowledge and practice, but it is a highly contextualized pursuit."[19] Doctors tailor their practice of biomedicine to suit their specific situations, and clinical practice is marked by improvisation. Research in Mexico demonstrates similar improvisations, but I argue that contextualization is not an aftereffect or unintended aspect of biosecurity research. While organizations like the WHO sought to implement global systems of regulation, scientists in Mexico confronted a biological that refused to be global, remaining idiosyncratically local. Contextualization and improvisation were means through which scientists understood and made visible how biologies differ around the globe. This is not to say that Mexico and other developing countries are the only places in which improvisation in biosecurity research is shaped by the place in which science happens; globally, science is equally the outcome of such improvisations and is not choreographed in advance or rigidly bound by rules. This research demonstrates how biology and understandings of it are entangled with the environment, as people, animals, microbes, climate, and scientific practices all shape one another.

In this chapter, I analyze how efforts to manage the global biological played out in Mexico, particularly how scientists sought to protect biological life in Mexico by safely conducting research on infectious disease. This meant being attuned to how the plasticity of biology meant that life in Mexico varied from other places and adjusting scientific practices accordingly. Scientists at INER and AMEXBIO argued that the differences they found in local microbial ecologies, human immune systems, and political and regulatory systems had consequences for the risks of conducting research, as well as treating and preventing disease. They countered the idea of universal or globalized biology that animated many public health projects by attending to the elements of place that produced biomestizaje and affected human health and safety. By analyzing laboratory work, meetings, training sessions, and risk management workshops, as well as AMEXBIO-related events, I show how and why scientists made claims about local differences in regulations, infrastructure, bodies, and culture. I begin with responses to the H1N1 epidemic and the varying ways that people in Mexico perceived and responded to the risk of infectious disease and envisioned threats to security. I then provide empirical accounts of the design of a high-security lab and the training of scientists to work with infectious organisms, analyzing how scientists made manifest differences in regulations and bodies and how they reinterpreted regulations established elsewhere in order to safely conduct research. Finally, I report on AMEXBIO's annual meeting, focusing on the promotion of "safety culture" and the use of the concept of culture in infectious disease research.

"WE WERE COMPLETELY OFF GUARD"

I had contacted Edgar Sevilla early in my fieldwork because of his central role at AMEXBIO, of which he was not only a founding member but also the president, and he invited me to meet with him at INER. AMEXBIO did not have its own offices or any paid staff. Sevilla had taken on the role of president in addition to his full-time position as a microbiologist at INER and his responsibilities teaching and training students at nearby universities and hospitals. When I arrived at INER, I found the institute less than welcoming to the general population. Patients seeking urgent care entered a waiting room watched over by gun-toting security guards. Explaining the guards and the weaponry, a scientist solemnly reminded me that the most common source of danger or injury to hospital personnel was not from exposure to disease, but from outbursts by violent patients. Next to the emergency room was the entrance to the main research, surgery, and clinical care area. Here as well, INER was carefully defended against unauthorized visitors. Multiple security guards checked the identification of people entering and inspected the cars of those leaving the institute. On the other side of this barrier, separated from the commotion of the busy street, was an open, green campus. Dozens of cats prowled the lawns and sunned themselves on the warm cars in the parking lot, convening in a noisy group in the afternoon when a nurse appeared with a bag of cat food. They apparently preferred being fed to hunting for themselves and did little to solve INER's ongoing mouse problem.

I met Sevilla near the entrance to the institute. Sevilla was a slightly built, dark-haired man in his thirties and an animated speaker. Like most of the scientists at INER, Sevilla generally dressed casually in T-shirts and jeans. While we walked across the hospital's lawn and down the corridor to his office, he recounted what life had been like at the hospital during the previous year's H1N1 outbreak, gesturing emphatically at the emergency room and clinic that had been full of people with the flu. His English was peppered with the occasional British slang, traces of his time in the United Kingdom, where he had gone for graduate training after growing up in Mexico City.

Sevilla introduced me to the crew of microbiologists and immunologists with whom he shared an office before we sat down in a quiet corner to discuss the effects of H1N1 on Mexico and his efforts to raise awareness about biosafety.

Returning to the subject of influenza, he told me that for scientists in Mexico, "everything is going to be before and after H1N1. Everything. First of all, in our case, in terms of biosafety, now people don't look at you like you're mental, 'why should I wear any protection' . . . People now understand that they have to protect themselves. They're more aware of the risk they could have. I have said before H1N1, the only people wearing respiratory protection were those in direct contact with tuberculosis patients. The others were not wearing anything." At the time of the outbreak, leaders of public agencies acknowledged that it had taken them by surprise and that the lack of adequate lab facilities prevented states from responding quickly.[20] This lack of preparedness was confirmation for Sevilla and AMEX-BIO's other founders of the importance and timeliness of their mission. Sevilla noted that the country "got caught off guard because our preparedness plan for an influenza pandemic was divided into six stages according to what the WHO had drafted. Originally it was Stage 1, well, there are one-off cases somewhere in Southeast Asia. Stage 2, there is some transmission, very local, controlled, nothing's happening, *in Southeast Asia*. . . . Stage 3, whatever; Stage 4, was like, some cases getting to the US; Stage 5 was some cases getting into Mexico." By that time, according to the plan, Mexico would have gotten information from the CDC and the WHO about the nature of the pandemic, the clinical progress of the disease, and treatment recommendations. The plan noted only that "in the event that the pandemic does not begin in Asia, the phases of the pandemic in Mexico will be adapted."[21] Planning was oriented towards the scenario that was envisioned as most likely: a bird flu originating in Asia. Other possibilities were neglected.

In general, prior to the outbreak of H1N1, public discourse was focused on avian influenza as the most likely threat. Reporting on influenza in *La Jornada*, José Antonio Román noted that according to the then–secretary of health, Julio Frenk Mora, Mexico's federal government was taking the threat of *avian* influenza very seriously and was prepared for an outbreak of the H5N1 virus.[22] The UN's Food and Agriculture Organization called on Latin America to remain vigilant against avian influenza, even though the region had not yet been affected by H5N1.[23] The Inter-American Development Bank warned that in addition to the cost to human health, an outbreak of avian influenza would have significant economic consequences, noting that many Latin American countries were vulnerable to global epidemics because of their weak sanitary control systems. According to this report, Mexico's plan for pandemic response and its investment in a vaccine against avian influenza and stockpile of antiviral drugs made it more prepared than most places in Latin America.[24] But as Sevilla pointed out, the outbreak of 2009 did not look like the ones that people had prepared for or predicted. "No. It started here. And no one knew. Nothing. Nothing. No one . . . we were completely off guard."

Instead of avian influenza from Asia, which would have given doctors and public health officials in the Americas plenty of time to prepare and respond, what happened instead was an outbreak of swine influenza from within Mexico itself. In our first conversation, Sevilla was animated as he emphasized the urgency of the situation to me. As president of AMEXBIO, he was often in the position of trying to convince his fellow scientists, the public, and funding agencies of the importance of what, prior to H1N1, had been an overlooked issue. Even though I had come to Mexico already interested in the development of biosecurity, Sevilla sought to further persuade me of its importance and neglect in Mexico. He seemed both practiced in his pitch about the need for a Mexican biosafety organization and genuine in his concern and frustration about the country's vulnerability.

The surprising outbreak provoked a strong response in Mexico, where public gathering places were closed and a national debate began over public health, sources of risk and insecurity, and how to protect Mexican life. AMEXBIO's take on the outbreak was just one of the many responses to H1N1 influenza that emerged in its wake. In the aftermath of the epidemic, stories about H1N1 and its origins circulated through Mexico. These narratives identified particular sites or activities as risky, and people suggested different approaches to managing the risks of infectious disease.[25] Influenza experts called on Mexican authorities to investigate the country's hog farms and determine whether the infections had indeed originated there. Smithfield Farms, a United States–based industrial agricultural firm that operates several giant hog farms in the area where the first cases of H1N1 in Mexico were diagnosed, was frequently identified as a likely culprit. Journalists in Mexico condemned the farms as "pig cities surrounded by seas of shit and waste that grow where environmental regulations are weak and the authorities are permissive."[26] While critics were obviously concerned about the potential for an epidemic disease to emerge from the farm, disease was also a proxy for a broader critique of the way of life that the farms represented. The analyses that attributed the emergence of swine flu to Smithfield Farms used the H1N1 outbreak as a means to condemn industrial agriculture, the neoliberal reforms that weakened regulations, and human patterns of consumption. In these stories, swine flu was an industrial accident along the lines of Bhopal and Chernobyl and the disease a by-product of the processes of hog farming. In story after story, journalists reported on industrial agriculture as an alien phenomenon, one that globalization and trade agreements like the North American Free Trade Agreement (NAFTA) had brought to Mexico.

Mexican government officials worked to personally protect and recuperate industrial pig farming and the resulting pork products. In an effort to limit the economic damage from the pork bans and to forestall consumer demands for increased regulation, officials attempted to demonstrate that Mexican pork, as currently produced, was perfectly safe. To display his confidence in the pork industry, then president Felipe Calderón traveled to his home state to eat carnitas, "a typical Michoacán dish."[27] This public display of pork eating was meant to demonstrate not only the safety of pork, but also the Mexicanness of pork as an essential element of traditional cuisine. The president's trip was reinforced by similar journeys of other officials who traveled throughout the country eating pork and encouraging other Mexicans to do so as well.[28] H1N1 and the subsequent efforts to recuperate pigs made visible the connections of nonhuman life-forms to particular places and their inclusion in biopolitics.

H1N1 first became marked as a Mexican virus, one which shaped treatment of Mexicans globally. Then, as the government and SAGARPA sought to recuperate the reputation of pigs, pigs became marked and celebrated as particularly Mexican, practices which countered the conception of a global biological. While the fears of problems with industrial agriculture and desire to demonstrate the safety of Mexican pigs as a food source led to the nationwide displays of officials eating pork, people also identified other sources of risk. They thought about sources of risk and interventions at the level of the molecule, the individual, the lab, the nation, and the globe, and different groups configured biosecurity risks at different scales. Threats, and how to respond to them, appeared differently and called for different interventions at the level of the laboratory than they did at a global scale.

ANTICIPATORY INFRASTRUCTURES

Prior to the H1N1 outbreak, Mexico had begun building a national network of biosecurity labs and intelligence units intended to "allow the timely detection of potentially harmful risks to the population" and to permit the government "to respond to an epidemiological threat before it can put national security, the working class, or productive activities at risk."[29] Mexico's national plan for development called for these labs as a "shield against epidemiological threats."[30] The plan cited the risks of economic globalization and the corresponding "increase in the intensity of the exchange of goods and services, as well as the transit of people," as both a source of national economic development and a threat since "this increases considerably the population's exposure to external epidemic risks, like SARS or avian flu," diseases which "represent latent threats against the conditions of stability and security that business, industry, and regional development require to prosper."[31] Public health officials touted this network in Mexico's national plans for combating bioterror and pandemic flu, presenting these labs as protecting Mexican health by enabling the rapid testing, identification, and response to disease. These arguments position labs as a tool for national security and health and cast the risks of disease as particular kinds of dangers. They may be global in scope, but they can be solved through local, even micro, manipulations. In the face of porous global borders and the growing challenges of containment, the sociocultural form of the lab promises control at a microbial level and reduces the scale of intervention. Rather than reshaping social practices in the name of safety, lab proponents argue that security can be produced through manipulation of microbes.[32]

INER has been a key location in the development of biosecurity practices in Mexico and the home of one of Mexico's most sophisticated biosecurity laboratories. A national institute of health, INER is dedicated to conducting research to improve the respiratory health of the Mexican population. In addition to its research mission, it provides clinical care for patients with the most challenging and complex conditions and for indigent patients with no health insurance and no other access to hospitals. In general, it is one of the best-equipped hospitals in the country for the treatment of respiratory ailments. As a result, during the H1N1 outbreak of 2009, very sick patients flooded the hospital. INER is also home to one of Mexico's most advanced clinics for the treatment and research of HIV, the Centro de Investigación en Enfermedades Infecciosas (the Center for Research on Infectious Diseases or CIENI). Doctors at INER began the HIV clinic because patients were arriving at the hospital with opportunistic infections like pneumonia that were the result of undiagnosed HIV.

The labs at CIENI are divided into spaces for clinical work and basic research, and are well equipped with polymerase chain reaction (PCR) machines used in sequencing and analyzing DNA, robots for automated specimen processing, and other equipment for analyzing samples and making diagnoses. As I admired the equipment on an early visit to the lab, Sevilla pointed out a sophisticated flow cytometry machine that can track seventeen parameters. Flow cytometers are machines designed to characterize cell populations. They pass thousands of cells per second through a laser beam; as each cell passes through the laser, it refracts the light, scattering it at all angles. Cells of different sizes, granularity, and structure produce different light patterns that are recorded by detectors, and these measurements are then documented in graphs called scatter plots showing the different types of cells in the sample. Highly sophisticated flow cytometry machines, like the one at CIENI, are able to track more parameters through the use of fluorescent molecules like fluorophore-labeled antibodies, which bind to specific molecules on the cell surface. The cytometer measures the different levels of fluorescence that cells emit when they pass through the laser. Cells can be tagged with multiple different fluorophores, producing a more fine-grained analysis of the composition of the cell population.

At the time that CIENI acquired its seventeen-parameter flow cytometry machine, there were only ten similar machines in the United States, making it an unusual piece of equipment and a point of pride for the center. Although the lab equipment was a substantial investment, Sevilla pointed out that the expenditures did not end with building and equipping the lab. The day-to-day costs of running experiments are high as well. The lab needs to be supplied with reagents and other materials that can be quite expensive; for example, in 2009 fluorescent tags for PCR reactions could cost $500 for a set. Some of the more sophisticated machines represent improvements because they can run many reactions with very little material, improving efficiency and decreasing costs.

CIENI is also particularly noteworthy because it is home to one of the few Biosecurity Level 3 labs in the country. BSL3 labs are high-security labs designed to allow scientists to work with pathogens that can cause serious or lethal illness and can be transmitted via aerosols, that is, through tiny particles suspended in the air. Aerosols can be created when an infected person coughs, sneezes, or exhales. They are also incidentally created in the course of standard lab procedures, such as the use of centrifuges. Several weeks into the H1N1 outbreak, these labs rose in prominence when Calderón made a highly publicized visit to a BSL3. Trailed by photographers, he talked with scientists and observed the lab space where epidemiological samples from all over the country were being processed. During the visit, Calderón learned how scientists identified the presence of the virus, observed the new equipment purchased by Mexico for this purpose, and urged the lab staff to keep up its intense pace of work.[33] The center's promotional materials touted the lab as "constructed and equipped for the correct management, research, and diagnosis of infectious agents of high priority in national and international public health . . . To our knowledge, there does not exist another laboratory in Mexico that has the characteristics required to correctly manage these pathogens."[34] The specialized nature of the lab was apparent in the restrictions on who could access the facility. While I was able to observe work in most of the microbiology labs immediately after arriving, entering the BSL3 was more challenging. I had previously been trained to work safely in a BSL3 lab while conducting ethnographic fieldwork on biosecurity in Chicago. This fieldwork became essential for access to the lab in Mexico—only after the biosafety officer at the lab in Chicago had sent a document certifying that I had completed training was I able to enter and observe work in the lab.

I interviewed Chema, the scientist who oversaw lab design and construction, several times. His schedule was packed with meetings with contractors and scientists as CIENI moved forward with the process of designing a new facility for attending patients, and he kindly met with me for conversations during the rare pauses in his schedule. These interviews would inevitably be interrupted by someone with an urgent question about a procedure or an architectural drawing or an order that needed to be placed. Describing the BSL3 construction process, Chema told me, "I designed the lab. For good or bad, but I did. So yeah, I designed the lab. But I hadn't any kind of experience. But I was the one that was interested, the one who had the background to know what was at that point biosafety, what we'd like to do with our lab, what we'd like to innovate at that point . . . We started to build it, and I was involved in the entire process of building and selecting the equipment." He pointed out that his role in lab construction meant that he was deeply involved in decision-making. While he had no prior experience in working in or designing BSL3 labs, neither did anyone else at INER. Chema learned about bioseguridad in the process of designing the lab, becoming one of INER's resident experts on the subject. His expertise in bioseguridad was in high demand, slowing progress on his own research and on the completion of his doctorate. The design and construction of the lab and Chema's ad hoc development of expertise were indications of the improvisations that went into bringing bioseguridad to Mexico.

He and his colleagues designed their lab with an eye toward international regulations and collaborations, building a facility that exceeded their needs for their current research. The lab was constructed to meet the US National Institutes of Health's (NIH) standards, described in the publication *Biosafety in Microbiological and Biomedical Laboratories*, with the goal of making research conducted there eligible for NIH funding and to facilitate collaborations with United States–based researchers. As he took me on a tour of the lab, Sevilla boasted about how well equipped it was while also pointing out aspects of the lab that were unfinished or incomplete. In the vestibule leading to the lab, Sevilla pointed to a spigot approximately six feet off the ground. It was a hookup for a shower, but, as he noted, it lacked a showerhead or handles to turn the water on. The showerhead was a gesture to the future, a display of potential security infrastructure. Constructed to comply with NIH standards for BSL3 labs working on higher-risk organisms in the hope that the lab might be inserted into global networks of research and funding, the shower was currently unused and nonfunctional.

I asked Chema why the showers were unfinished, and he explained that they were not currently using the showers "because of our risk assessment, because with HIV you don't need to shower out. But if we started to work on something that you need to shower out, we are capable of it." He elaborated that since it was the only BSL3 lab at INER, they needed to be prepared for any kind of future research that might be needed, and "we have the money to do that [invest in preparations for the future] at this point . . . It's important because Manuel [the head of the lab] is innovating, so we have equipment that not even entire institutes in Mexico or even the States have in the same building." While researchers in the lab were primarily studying HIV, which is not transmitted via aerosols and does not require a BSL3 environment, the lab was constructed in anticipation of the future. The currently unneeded infrastructure was a symbol of an investment in security and preparedness. By constructing a sophisticated biosecurity laboratory, Mexican scientists hoped to claim for themselves the ability to participate in international scientific networks on equal terms. They intended to challenge international scientific hegemony and stake a claim for Mexico as a place where scientific facts can be made.

IDENTIFYING DEFICIENCIES

Despite national and global ambitions for these biocontainment labs, during the H1N1 outbreak Mexican scientific resources were insufficient to identify and diagnose influenza strains. The labs lacked the reagents that would allow them to characterize this specific strain. The molecular diagnostics that were accessible and in common use in labs in Mexico failed to detect H1N1 or even the fact that patients were infected with an influenza virus. Sevilla recounted his memories of this distressing situation. "So, you would have people who had clinical signs of flu, but when they were tested it came up negative." Samples from sick patients were tested for all kinds of respiratory viruses, including influenza A, influenza B, respiratory syncytial virus, coronavirus, and arenavirus, without positive results. As a result, Sevilla told me, officials had to send samples to the Public Health Agency of Canada or the CDC in the United States for diagnostic testing. He noted, "We sent the materials, it took one week to get the result. We sent them to Winnipeg, and to Atlanta, I think, to the CDC."[35] The bottleneck that developed as the labs in Winnipeg and Georgia were overwhelmed with both national samples and those from Mexico meant that flu cases went unconfirmed and Mexican authorities were unable quickly to assess the size and spread of the outbreak. Not until several weeks after the outbreak did Mexican public health officials acquire the reagents to test for swine flu and begin to run their own diagnostic tests in laboratories in Mexico City and Veracruz, rather than relying on Canadian and American scientists.[36]

Journalists cited the failure of Mexico's scientific infrastructure to respond quickly to the disease as evidence of the inadequacy of governmental support for scientific research in Mexico. Liliana Alcántara, writing for El Universal, argued that H1N1 caught Mexico unprepared, lacking the equipment and the materials required for disease detection, as well as the capacity to produce vaccines.[37] Javier Flores, a reporter for La Jornada, argued that H1N1 made it clear that Mexico was scientifically several decades behind the Global North. According to Flores, the great lesson from swine flu was that Mexican science was weak. Although the country had constructed an extensive epidemiological surveillance system, Mexico continued to be dependent on foreign science and technology and "the significant weaknesses that we demonstrate in science and technology make us dependent on foreigners, and foreign experts will have the last word on the origin of the pandemic and how to prevent it in the future."[38] The political failure to develop science and technology was a threat to health and sovereignty. The reliance on external laboratories during the H1N1 outbreak was seen as clear evidence of Mexico's disadvantage and a warning to invest in science and technology. The influenza case seemed to recapitulate a long history of resources being extracted from Mexico for the creation of value elsewhere, as raw materials (in the form of samples) were sent out of the country for analysis. Mexico's position in the scientific network that produces information and value out of nature remained unclear. Were they inside or outside of global scientific practices? Participants or subjects? The lack of national capacity for scientific research became a point of contention as a result of H1N1.

Alcántara's complaint was about Mexico's failure to think about disease in terms of preparedness or to ready the country's infrastructure for this kind of emergency.

Alcántara read H1N1 as evidence of Mexico's neglect of preparedness activities and a lack of governmental foresight. She quoted José Santos, a specialist in infectious diseases, who argued that the epidemic was "an alarm bell to invest more in science and technology, because otherwise we will always be behind."[39] While Mexico had not prepared for H1N1, Santos argued that the country's experience of the epidemic should shape its future actions. It was not too late for Mexico to begin preparing for future biological emergencies.

However, not everyone saw H1N1 as a serious incident indicating major problems within the country and requiring a response from the Mexican government. People suspicious of the government argued that H1N1 was a pretext being exploited by the government in order to prevent political change and to distract the population from their dissatisfaction with Calderón. While I was transcribing interviews at home one afternoon, Juan, a young artist and writer who lived next door, stopped by to chat. He asked me about my work, and when I mentioned H1N1, he told me that he was skeptical about the aggressive government actions in response to the pandemic. In particular, he critiqued the suspension of any public gatherings. He viewed the action cynically, as a move by the unpopular Calderón to cripple a nascent movement protesting his presidency. His theorizing about the invention of influenza was in line with the rumors that spread around the country. A columnist for *El Universal* reported on the laundry list of conspiracy theories: "The government says more than it knows, the government says less than it knows, the media exaggerates, the media minimizes, the military will take over the supermarkets, Calderón invented influenza to win elections, the legislators invented influenza to get the drug dealing law approved, the United States invented influenza as an excuse to send soldiers in to Mexican territory, the IMF invented influenza so that Mexico would go into more debt, the leaders of the G-7 designed influenza to revive the global economy."[40]

For the less conspiracy-minded, H1N1 was most noteworthy for scaring people away from popular vacation spots, which responded by lowering their rates for those brave enough to travel in the face of an epidemic. The international tourist trade in Mexico came to a halt, and despite the Mexican government's call for people to stay home, resorts in Cancun, the Riviera Maya, and Baja California began advertising vacation packages at steep discounts for adventurous travelers from within the country. Sevilla told me that the people who took advantage of the low rates came back raving about the empty beaches and that "there was no one around. It was empty, you could enjoy everything."

MEASURING AND EVALUATING RISK

For the personnel at INER, of course, H1N1 was not cause for a vacation, but rather a reason to examine their own security and risk management practices. One Monday morning, María, a member of INER's Department of Biological Engineering, stood in the front of the classroom as a few stragglers entered the already crowded space. She was preparing to deliver the introductory lecture at a five-day training workshop organized by the institute's biosafety committee on the evaluation and control of risk in infectious disease research. It was clear that there were more attendees than the organizers had expected; in response, they hastily rearranged the desks and began searching for more chairs. At this first meeting, María promised the participants in the surprisingly popular workshop that they would gain the tools for identifying, evaluating, and controlling biorisks in their own labs. As María talked, a photographer documented her and the attentive students. Over the course of the training sessions, I learned about the mundane challenges of developing biosecurity research capacity and the rationalities that structured risk management.

The workshop was part of a broader national project to generate bioseguridad, but it was also attuned to the specific needs of scientists at INER. The goal was to inculcate in the participants a way of thinking about and managing biological risk, to produce them as members of a "safety culture," a concept I will return to later. Over the course of five sessions, María, Sevilla, and others provided us with a variety of tools with which to assess our risk. We spent mornings charting possible dangers and threats, creating "fault trees" that showed where our procedures could go wrong and answering questions like "Is your lab clean?" in bioRAM, the biological risk assessment program produced in 2010 by Sandia National Laboratories. Along the way, both students and instructors acknowledged the complexity of assessing the dangers of lab work. We could only guess at what microbes samples from patients might contain and thus how best to handle them. Assessments of issues like lab cleanliness were likewise difficult to make. What was the standard? The risk assessment tools took for granted that there was a universal understanding of what "cleanliness" was.

Furthermore, actually putting into practice the methods of microbial control that we were learning was often challenging, from remembering how to put on and remove personal protective equipment to moving properly in the lab in order to control the airflow and prevent contamination. Our security in the lab would depend on how well we executed the procedures we planned at the workshop. However, even as participants sought to rigorously plan their research procedures, lab work always consists of improvisation.[41] Scientists must respond to unique lab conditions, making safety and security measures harder to establish in advance. In the event that something goes wrong, like an accidental jab with a contaminated needle or a broken vial containing a microbial culture, it is difficult to remain calm and to remember how to follow procedures that one may never have implemented before. Despite these complexities, at the end of the training exercises we had produced neat charts that identified the likelihood of failure in our lab and the consequences of that failure as low, medium, or high. The charts were models of clarity, providing precise quantifications of risk levels. As Sevilla noted, "people love to see numbers." The charts, imperfect and arbitrary though they were, made risk appear measured, calculable, and tangible.[42] They provided us with a sense of mastery of the risks of lab work, even as we acknowledged their flaws.

The process of producing these quantifications of risk made clear that our calculations were based not just on an assessment of the microbe we were working with or the procedure we were doing, but that microbe in relation to the place where we were working. Our instructors repeatedly reminded us that risk analysis was site-specific, depending on the infrastructure, equipment, the laws and regulatory system governing the lab, the local microbial ecology, and the social and biological characteristics of the lab workers.

For example, one could not count on lab equipment to be the same everywhere. Equipment to work with pathogens at INER had been imported from the United States, and while the United States had standards and regulations about how biosafety equipment should function and be maintained, Mexico had no equivalent laws. Marta, one of the scientists overseeing work in the BSL3, explained to me the regulations governing security and safety practices in the lab.

Emily: What are you doing to prepare for future outbreaks?

Marta: Since then [H1N1] we have been preparing the lab to be a reference lab.

Emily: What does that mean?

Marta: Well, to start, all the labs must have the NIH [US National Institutes of Health], all the NIH guidelines.

Emily: Is that like the BMBL [Biosafety in Microbiological and Biomedical Laboratories, produced jointly by the NIH and the CDC]?

Marta: Yes. So what we did is remodel the BSL3 to be in order with this guide. And that was the first thing we did. We made a shower and the anteroom. We also redid the lab spaces for work; that was the first thing we did after the outbreak. . . . I think it needs to be evaluated by the CDC, or the WHO, the World Health Organization. That would be the next step.

Emily: They come here and review it?

Marta: Yes.

Emily: In terms of BSL3, those are the regulations you use?

Marta: Yes, we use World Health Organization and CDC guidelines because there are no guidelines in Mexico. . . . It's just that biosafety is still not well constituted in Mexico. So we're also one of the premier labs, we and one of the centers in Veracruz, so that's a contribution. We started with the engineering, guided by the BMBL, and developed an organizational manual, and right now we're just writing protocols, SOPs [Standard Operating Procedures]. We've been trained by Emory University.

However, translating United States regulations was not a straightforward matter. When students in the class asked how they could ascertain whether their equipment was functioning properly, Sevilla sighed: "We have a problem. There are no regulations in Mexico. There are only the regulations of the United States." Sevilla later explained to me the problems that this caused, noting that often there are Mexican companies that claim they can service biosafety equipment, but lacking regulations about how equipment should be maintained and serviced, he said, "Perhaps we're being deceived." Sevilla told me that while Mexico needed guidelines for research on infectious diseases, the United States, which has a plethora of often-contradictory guidelines issued by different organizations, was not a good model for research regulation.[43]

LOCAL BIOLOGIES, LOCAL RISKS

In addition to differences in equipment and regulations, scientists drew on their understanding of the malleability of biology and its relation to the environment to structure their lab practices and interpret research risks. Differences in local biologies mean that the public health implications of pathogens vary. In thinking about the risks of conducting research, scientists concerned with bioseguridad refer to the health of the population in the area surrounding the lab. While teaching risk assessment practices, Sevilla noted, "It's not the same when a Mexican is exposed to Salmonella as when someone from Finland is exposed to it, because we're used to being in contact with it all the time." Exposure to Salmonella can provide immunity against subsequent infections, so the consequences of exposure to the pathogen are different for people who have previously been infected than for people who have no prior exposure.[44] The risk of working with organisms depended on the immunological characteristics of the scientists and on the local ecology of pathogens. Sevilla elaborated: "Salmonella might be a risk in the US, where people would be extremely concerned about it. But here, where it's pretty widespread, people are exposed all the time; it wouldn't have as big an effect on the population, who have developed some resistance, nor would it be as noticed, because outbreaks of Salmonella happen all the time. Of course, there are some more virulent strains of Salmonella that are of greater concern."

Salmonella outbreaks in the United States, on the other hand, tend to draw intense investigation, media attention, and product recalls. In addition to these geographic variations in pathogen ecology, there are variations in the immune systems of the population, produced by differences in the material environment, such as typical diet or exercise practices. Sevilla argued that the general immune state of the Mexican population had an important bearing on the risk of working in a biocontainment lab.[45] In particular, he cited the high incidence of diabetes in Mexico as affecting risk assessments.[46] In the risk management workshop, we learned that lab workers with diabetes have depressed immune systems and are more prone to infection.[47] The body of the scientist is far from universal, and as a result lab practices need to be reconfigured.

In a training session I attended on biocontainment work in the United States, one scientist put it this way: "Working with dangerous pathogens can be emotionally stressful. You want to feel safe." She went on to ask, "Do you trust your colleagues?" In this formulation, safety and risk management required managing emotional states and establishing trust between colleagues. In Mexico, scientists paid attention to the ways these emotional states might be somatized and affect the immune system. Francisco, the director of a lab studying pathogenic fungi, told me that immunocompromised people face higher risks when working with pathogens. I expected him to elaborate on the higher risks that accompany diseases that depress the immune system, but Francisco extended the possibility of being immunocompromised to a much wider category of persons: "Your immune system might get depressed if you fight with your girlfriend—or if you are sad, it's certain that you're going to get infected. It's better to work on the computer than with microbes in these cases." Francisco drew attention to the connections between mind and body, which mean that emotional vulnerability can translate to physical vulnerability to microbes. Both formal research programs and lab practices at INER respond to the particularities of human immune systems and microbial life around the lab.

BIOSEGURIDAD WITH MINIMAL RESOURCES

In August 2011, at AMEXBIO's second annual meeting in Puebla Mexico, tensions between the implementation of global systems and the local particularities of biological research emerged as organizers and the approximately one hundred attendees grappled with the question of how to produce bioseguridad in Mexico. Topics of concern included infectious disease, genetically modified organisms, and animal health. Puebla is the fourth largest city in Mexico, but it is tranquil compared to Mexico City, home of many of the conference attendees. AMEXBIO had arranged for walking tours through the cobblestoned streets of downtown Puebla, and at the end of the first day of the conference scientists ambled through the city, snacking on the sweets that Puebla is known for and admiring the well-preserved cathedrals decorated with locally made tiles. The photogenic city center made a dramatic contrast with the industrial outskirts of the city, where colonial architecture gave way to factories. The conference itself was held in the William O. Jenkins Center, a recent addition to the city. On the edge of the historic downtown, the upscale convention center was located in a converted textile factory, the old equipment removed and replaced with up-to-date amenities for meetings. While the buildings referenced Puebla's recent industrial history as an important producer of textiles, the name of the convention center hearkened back to revolutionary times and to the political and commercial entanglements of Mexico and the United States.

William O. Jenkins, the center's namesake, was an American businessman who made a fortune in Mexico—*Time* called him a "mysterious buccaneer-businessman who has built the biggest personal fortune in Mexico."[48] In addition to his monetary success in Mexico, he served as United States consul in Puebla during the Mexican Revolution.[49] Jenkins's history in Mexico was checkered, making the choice to name the conference center after him somewhat surprising. Tensions between the United States and Mexico were high during his tenure as consul in 1919. At the time, Mexico had recently reclaimed all subsoil resources as patrimony of the nation, to the dismay of Americans in Mexico. The conflict between the two countries escalated when Jenkins was abducted in Puebla. He was released after paying part of his ransom, only to be arrested and charged with colluding in his own abduction by the Mexican government. Outrage in the United States reached such a level that war with Mexico seemed possible and was only averted when Jenkins was eventually freed.[50]

The complicated connections between the United States and Mexico that Jenkins represented lived on in contemporary Puebla. The AMEXBIO meeting itself was the product of these interconnections—it was initiated and planned by Mexican scientists, while the US Department of State's Biosecurity Engagement Program provided funding. The Biosecurity Engagement Program was an effort to monitor biosecurity projects and research around the globe. By providing funding and training to scientists, the Biosecurity Engagement Program hoped to gain access to and information about biological research and laboratories around the globe. Along with their financial support, they sent representatives to Puebla to observe the meeting.

I had come to Puebla from Mexico City, where I was living with a thirty-two-year-old Mexican musician and nonprofit start-up entrepreneur named Ana. She had welcomed me into her apartment near Plaza Iztaccihuatl in the trendy neighborhood of Condesa. The apartment was home to a rotating cast of roommates, including Ana's cousin, an engineering student working as a waiter for the summer, as well as a Paraguayan filmmaker editing his latest script. Ana did not hide her incredulity that I was in Mexico to study biosecurity. "Biosecurity? We don't have any biosecurity in Mexico. We can't even drink the water here," she informed me shortly after I had arrived in Mexico. Alarmed by my naïveté, she proceeded to warn me about traveling on the metro and the metrobus, the two primary forms of public transportation in Mexico City. Rather than cautioning me about pickpockets or potential harassment (a problem so widespread that both the metro and the metrobus have special cars designated exclusively for women and children), she warned me about public transportation's poor reputation for protecting the health of its passengers. She told me that UNAM, the country's premier university, had done a study showing that public transportation was very "dirty," contaminated with microbes that could make one sick, and how I must be very careful to wash my hands after riding. After our conversation, I was sensitized to the microbial life around me on the metro and I began to notice the tools deployed against microbes, like the heavily used hand sanitizers at the metro exits.

Ana continued to alert me to the microbial presences around us, showing me how to wash fresh fruit in water treated with iodine to make it safe to eat. She railed against the Mexican government and agricultural practices in Mexico, which allowed farmers to irrigate their fields with poorly treated wastewater. She took a patronizing attitude towards me, enjoying the opportunity to show me, a student at MIT, how little I knew of the world. She laughed, "What if you got sick, and I had to call your father to tell him that you were in the hospital from eating bad food? What would I say? 'Mr. Wanderer, your daughter, who is here studying biosecurity, is in the hospital'?" She enjoyed the irony of my apparent innocence of what she saw as basic biosecurity precautions. While in the United States I had become accustomed to having confidence in the federal agriculture system that regulated and monitored food safety. In Mexico, however, Ana taught me not to trust the system and instead to rely on my own individual practices for protection—rigorous use of hand sanitizer on the metro, careful washing of fruits and vegetables, and purchasing bottled water rather than drinking tap water.

At the same time as Ana advised me about biosecurity in the home, we were alerted to other security failings. Our apartment building housed a number of residents, and not everybody was careful about closing the door to the street. One day, the women from the floor below us knocked on our door, distraught. Someone had broken into their apartment, stealing personal belongings and money. Our apartment became a central space for tenants organizing for a secure living space as people gathered to create a petition to the landlord insisting that he had an obligation to provide safe and secure lodging. While there was a brief debate about contacting municipal officials about the robbery, the group ultimately decided that contacting the police would be ineffective. Security was determined to be the responsibility of the landlord and the individual tenants who needed to be more responsible by being vigilant about locking the door to the building and refusing to hold the door open for strangers.

The tenants, speculating on how the robbery happened, concluded that it was the group of teenagers who hung out outside the convenience store across the street. They suspected these teenagers not only of robbing the apartment but also of selling drugs, vandalizing cars, and generally making the neighborhood more hazardous. While the building's front door and hallway were equipped with video cameras, I learned that these were more symbolic than anything else, as they were unconnected to any recording devices. The idea was that the mere presence of these devices would deter thieves, and since their function was intimidation rather than data collection it was not necessary for them to record. At any rate, they were ineffective in this case. These symbolic devices reminded me of the half-completed, anticipatory infrastructure of the BSL3 lab. Like the cameras, it was not currently functional but its presence was meant to represent the promise of security.

My interactions with Ana had attuned me to some popular perceptions of biosecurity, while the AMEXBIO meeting highlighted the concerns of the government, scientists, and other laboratory workers. As the president and founder of the organization, Sevilla gave the opening address. He delivered a decidedly modest message for the audience, reminding everyone that bioseguridad in Mexico was in its infancy and that they had significant work to do. In these early days for bioseguridad, AMEXBIO was establishing training programs for scientists and a code of ethics. Aside from these professional and ethical concerns, Sevilla addressed the outlook of the group, calling for scientists to maintain their sense of optimism, even though they lacked resources available in other places, and to creatively imagine how to produce bioseguridad with minimal resources. Creativity and optimism were asked to stand in for financial investment, as Sevilla contended that Mexican scientists would have to find their own way to produce biosecurity rather than attempting to replicate what had been done elsewhere.

Noting that the keynote speaker came from the Health Canada lab in Winnipeg (one of the best-funded and most technologically advanced laboratories in the world, as well as one of the key sites for processing H1N1 samples), Sevilla warned the audience against invidious comparisons between Mexico and Canada, noting that AMEXBIO did not intend to hold Canada up as a model for Mexican or other Latin American labs. The underlying message in Sevilla's speech was that biosecurity in Mexico and Canada would inevitably look different. The Canadian government had invested $400 million in constructing the biocontainment lab in Winnipeg. In the absence of that kind of investment, how would scientists safely conduct research to protect the health of the nation? How could scientists translate biosecurity practices from their most expensive iteration in Canada to the daily work of microbiologists in regional and local laboratories in Mexico? The federal government provided Mexican scientists with minimal guidance on how to construct biosecurity. While in the United States and Canada federal regulations governed lab practices and organizations like the CDC produced guides establishing standards for laboratory work, Mexico had no equivalent regulations.

SCIENTISTS TALK CULTURE: RISK AND PERSONAL RESPONSIBILITY IN THE LAB

Difference in the laboratory was also articulated through the idea of culture, specifically something practitioners call "safety culture." I gave a presentation on my research at the AMEXBIO meeting, where, for the first time during my fieldwork, no one found it unusual that an anthropologist might be studying scientists.

Instead, many of the attendees pointed out to me that they were deeply concerned with culture, and well aware of its significance for science. In particular, they were interested in the problem of implementing safety culture and hoped that I might turn my research to this essential practical matter.

At the meeting, Patricia Delarosa, a scientist from an American research institute, gave a talk emphasizing the power of culture to create security. She suggested that rather than investing in technology or lab construction at the same rate as Canada or the United States, Mexico could produce bioseguridad through the development of a "culture of biosafety." Delarosa's talk, as well as the suggestions I received about the potential applications of anthropological research, reflected the widespread adoption of a particular notion of culture within the biosecurity community. Culture, in this case, was a set of rules or practices. It was understood to vary from place to place but also to be something that could be taught and enforced.

Delarosa elaborated, noting that some laboratories that she had observed had developed a safety culture in the form of the rigorous use of set procedures that allowed them to manipulate microbes safely. She contrasted this safety culture with lab practice in the United States, where complicated and expensive technological apparatuses were deployed in addition to rules and behavior to produce safety. She characterized the differences between these labs as a cultural one, noting that "there is a culture to safety in laboratories, and we need to recognize that culture." In these terms, culture was a resource that could be used in places where financial and technical resources were lacking. Safety culture was also a way of individualizing responsibility—as Delarosa described it, establishing a culture of safety meant making the individual lab workers responsible for their own safety, the safety of others, and the safety of the environment. The risk assessment workshop at INER was an example of this articulation of safety culture. Those attending the workshop were reminded that they were responsible for the risk assessment of their own workspace. In a country where formalized biosecurity regulations did not exist, reliance on individualized responsibility was the order of the day.

Delarosa's use of the term "safety culture" was not idiosyncratic. Susan Silbey has charted the growing popularity of the term in engineering and management fields, arguing that the dramatic increase in the use of the term after 2000 is related to the dismantling of the regulatory state and represents an attempt to rethink responsibility and risk. Talk of safety culture is a way to place responsibility on individuals and is connected with the dismantling of a regime of collective responsibility. The focus on safety culture was the outcome of a redefinition of what it meant to be a productive citizen, and Silbey argues that "talk of safety culture flourishes at the very moment when advocates extend the logic of individual choice, self-governance, and rational action from the market to all social domains."[51] Safety culture emerges as regulations and collective programs to manage risk and danger are dismantled in favor of "institutional flexibility" and risk-taking. Rather than collective responsibility and government safety nets, individuals and businesses should embrace market mechanisms to ensure productivity, efficiently manage risk, and distribute responsibility. Outside of the laboratory, the individualization of risk meant, for example, that in Mexico people were responsible for ensuring the safety of the produce they consumed or the security of their own living spaces.

Delarosa concluded by pointing out the importance of local biologies as well as local culture. She noted that "Mexico has endemic disease that doesn't exist in the US. There might be organisms that are more virulent here, and environmental stability and the availability of vaccines all vary from state to state." In assessing risk, scientists needed to account for the current and historic presence of an organism, the immunological status of the human population, and its rate of exposure to the microbe in question. Delarosa ultimately argued that the risk of working with particular microorganisms was something that needed to be established at the level of the nation-state. She concluded by pointing out that assessing risk required thinking about not only the microbe being studied but also the environment in which it was being studied.

Recent epidemics of infectious diseases like H1N1 and SARS have been interpreted as demonstrating the globalized nature of biology. Programs and regulations to address public health, like the IHR 2005, indicate a turn from state-by-state responses to disease towards efforts to produce universal, globalized responses. However, scientists encounter difficulty in translating research principles and practices to new places, calling into question whether biosecurity can go global. In the daily practice of lab work, biology does not appear to be global. Talk about safety culture and practices to manage bioseguridad upend conventional representations of the body of the scientist as universal and the space of the lab as unaffected by the place around it.

Instead, contextualization and particularity are the rule. The idea that scientific practices and techniques are not universals but instead need to be managed in accordance with Mexican particularity was repeatedly invoked in training sessions, scientific presentations, and daily lab practice. Scientists managing risk in the laboratory argue that the environment in which they worked is technologically, socially, and biologically distinct from other places and thus requires unique biosecurity practices that cannot be translated into a global system. Acclimatizing practices to Mexico and making security means paying attention to the context in which research is done, making it tractable, imaginable, definable, and controllable. Although the movement of life-forms around the globe that accompanies increasing trade and travel may appear to be producing biological homogeneity, through work to produce bioseguridad scientists assert the local heterogeneity of both biological life and scientific practice.

In particular, scientists focus on local microbial ecologies, characteristics of the human population's immune systems, and the aspects of the regulatory, economic, and political environment that affected lab practice. Contextualization and understanding of how the materiality of life was produced through relationships (for example, with nonhuman life-forms like bacteria and viruses) and interactions with the environment are thus essential to producing security. Practices of bioseguridad are a way of thinking through what is unaccounted for in stories of the global biological, that is, what is missing in stories that focus on circulation and mixing on a global scale. They reveal the national specificity of scientific practices, even those that are part of global regulatory and health systems. Differences in the Mexican environment, expertise, economy, and regulatory system make it difficult to transplant practices from the United States.

The experiences of scientists demonstrate the friction that is created in implementing globalized regulations. As Nancy Leys Stepan argues, scientific ideas are transformed as they are employed in different contexts and regions.[52] STS scholars in Latin America have shown how local settings shape the possibilities for autochthonous science, and how models from elsewhere are transformed as they are imported into Latin America.[53] The difficulties that scientists encountered in translating biosecurity principles reveal previously unobserved or unconsidered differences between places and undercut the supposed universality of laboratories. Historian of science Robert Kohler argues that in labs "placelessness becomes the symbolic guarantee that science done there is everyone's, not just someone's in particular." The power and credibility of laboratories has long been understood to be in their interchangeability, and labs are meant to be isolated from their environment in order to produce universal science. However, the challenges in translating these practices to Mexico reveal how they always engage with and are structured by the environment around the lab. The changes that must be made to implement lab practices in a new place provincialize the experience of Euro-American scientists and show that lab practices and lab spaces everywhere are context- and place-dependent.

4

Invisible Biologies,
Embodied Environments

MAKING THE INVISIBLE PERCEPTIBLE

The center of the Mexico City borough of Coyoacán is a lively square surrounded by historic buildings and streets paved with cobblestones (see figure 8). The square is a popular destination for families, especially on weekends when people line up at the Tepoznieves ice cream stand, street musicians play for spare change outside the cathedral, and vendors roam the streets selling toys, balloons, and even puppies. I occasionally accompanied a friend to the square while she walked her dog. We threw discarded soda bottles for the dog to fetch, gossiping while idly observing people relaxing and socializing in the square.

Most afternoons, however, I headed past the crowded center to go for a run in El Vivero Coyoacán, a nearby park. Running in El Vivero gave me cause to reflect on the interactions between bodies and the environment. El Vivero is an important plant nursery where gardeners cultivate the plant life of Mexico City, producing approximately one million seedlings each year. The park's long history dates back to 1901, when Miguel Ángel de Quevedo donated a hectare of land to the state to create a nursery. Quevedo, dubbed the "Apostle of the Tree" for his energetic advocacy for conservation, was deeply involved in Mexico's forestry initiatives from 1900 until his death in 1945, playing important roles in the administrations of both Porfirio Díaz and Lázaro Cárdenas.[1] His vision for El Vivero remains important in the present day, as seedlings from the nursery shape the urban environment through public projects that transplant them to locations all over the city, as well as through sales to home gardeners in the park's busy plant market.

FIGURE 8. Coyoacán Center. Source: Author photograph.

In addition to providing a resource for urban plant life, the park is an important space for the improvement of human bodies, a place where residents of Coyoacán work on their physical fitness. The two-kilometer gravel path encircling the park makes it a popular destination for runners like myself. It is also home to exercise classes, yoga sessions, and even massages, which are offered by therapists who set up portable chairs along the walkways. Food vendors are prohibited inside the park, but they cluster just outside the entrances selling juice and snacks, often touting the healthfulness of offerings like fresh fruit or bars made of amaranth, a quinoa-like grain popular throughout Mexico. As people participate in various activities, they engage in what Judith Farquhar has termed "peopling the city," claiming space and assertively occupying public places.[2] Their presence produces a particular kind of civic space; by taking possession of the park to work on their own health and bodies, they construct it as a communal place in which they have a right to be.

The production of civic space is only one part of the equation, however. At the same time as people are producing the city, their bodies are being shaped by their exposure to the environment. While El Vivero was a pleasant place for me to run, I found myself struggling to maintain my pace or catch my breath. I wondered if it was the change in altitude that left me feeling perpetually short of oxygen—Mexico City is 7,350 feet high, while Boston, where I had been living, is essentially at sea level. However, when I complained to a friend, he dismissed this possibility immediately, confidently asserting, "No, the problem is the air pollution here." Either way, whether my breathing troubles were caused by the thinness of the air or the contaminants in it, my experiences in El Vivero increased my awareness of the quality of the air and caused me to reflect on the effect of the environment on human bodies and how, through practices of urban citizenship, people both make the environment and are made by it.

In this chapter, I return to the lab to examine these interconnections. While spending time in El Vivero attuned me to the effects of the air around me and the urban environment more generally, working at the Instituto Nacional de Enfermedades Respiratorias (INER) reinforced the importance of air quality and its role in shaping the body. At the hospital, patient respiratory health was a central clinical concern, and air, both as a substance essential for life and as a potential carrier of contaminants or pathogens, was a major scientific focus. Through this research, biologists made perceptible to themselves aspects of Mexico City and of Mexico more generally that otherwise would have remained invisible or imperceptible. They drew attention to the dynamism of both environments and bodies, paying attention to their interrelation and mutual constitution. This porosity and permeability is not simply an artifact of laboratory work; Elizabeth Roberts has detailed how daily life in Mexico City is unequally shaped by experiences of toxicity, whether air pollution or other forms of contamination.[3] In the laboratory, however, this permeability is somewhat abstract and generalized, no longer associated with particular neighborhoods but rather with the population of the city and the country more generally.

Scientists interact with air in the laboratory, both by controlling its movement through their workspace and by making visible air pollution's effects on the human immune system. In the process, they establish one way that history and environment produce human populations. In addition to tracking research on air, I examine how scientists studying infectious diseases, specifically HIV, have produced evidence of how human bodies themselves constitute an environment that affects microbial and viral ecologies. This research makes apparent that human bodies are not the only ones that are porous, permeable, and malleable. Nonhuman life-forms are similarly connected with and produced by the environments in which they live, making them intimately connected with particular places. Drawing on historical and cultural ideas of the uniqueness of the Mexican population as a result of its status as mestizo, these researchers reinterpret mestizaje in genetic and immunological terms. By arguing that the interactions between human immune systems and viral populations produce ecologies unique to Mexico, they represent microbial life-forms as products of biomestizaje.[4] In this case, protecting human

bodies from these viral populations requires "care of the pest." Producing biosecurity means studying and knowing the particularities of life-forms that threaten
Mexico and understanding how all bodies, not just human ones, are produced
through relations with others.

While the previous chapter examined how biosecurity practices are acclimatized to Mexico and the improvisatory character of research, this chapter turns
to the assertions my scientist interlocutors made for the distinctiveness of biology
(as substance), tuning into the way these claims anchor arguments about the relationship between bodies and the environment and history. Historian of science
Hannah Landecker has suggested that scientists have begun to "molecularize" not
only the body but also the environment.[5] Drawing on their knowledge of bodies as
relational, scientists at INER examined how this molecularized environment
shapes biology, work which suggests that improving human health requires attention to the environment. Human biosecurity is thus intimately connected with
environmental biosecurity. This research also has implications for sociality; as scientists interpret the population as joined by a shared biological materiality and
substance, they produce collective identities.[6] Further, arguments of the way bodies and environments shape microbial and viral populations also serve as a critique of the politics and geography of scientific research, drawing attention to
neglect of populations outside of Europe or the United States.

THE LUNGS OF MEXICO CITY

Air was made tangible in the laboratory on multiple levels, both through practices
to control its movement and through research on immune systems that made the
bodily effects of the country's air pollution visible. As well as being important
for health, air is a socially significant substance. Anthropologists and STS scholars
have devoted considerable attention to other ubiquitous physical substances, notably water. They have examined the role of water in culture, including different
modes of valuing water, the governance of water use, and knowledge systems
through which people understand water.[7] However, while air quality and the effects
of airborne pollution are obviously important, as Timothy Choy has pointed out,
air has been neglected and taken for granted in social theory.[8] Perhaps because of
its apparent lack of substance, air has not seemed to matter or make a difference.
For scientists at INER, air has considerable significance, as something essential
for life that can also carry dangerous pathogens and that can produce unexpected
and usually unobserved connections between places. The Mexican Secretary of
Health reinforced the importance of air for biosecurity in a 2011 article for
AMEXBIO's annual journal, in which he argued for thinking about polluted air
in addition to infectious disease as a biosecurity issue that should be subject to
government intervention.[9]

Tlalpan, the neighborhood where INER is located, is distant enough from the center of the city to maintain some of its historical character as an independent village. It is home to green, open spaces, a rarity in the sprawling Distrito Federal (DF). Tlalpan is thought of as the lungs for the DF and its green spaces as essential to producing the air that allows the city and its inhabitants to breathe.[10] Plants absorb carbon dioxide during photosynthesis and release oxygen into the atmosphere, much as lungs remove carbon dioxide from the bloodstream and oxygenate blood.[11] The green spaces of Tlalpan are under threat as the neighborhood continues to urbanize; residents argue vehemently for the protection of these areas, claiming that their loss would cause serious air pollution that would not only reverberate throughout the borough, but also have consequences for the air of all of Mexico City. In June of 2011, the Bosque de Tlalpan was declared a natural protected area in order to "conserve a strategic space for the environmental equilibrium of Mexico City."[12] According to *La Jornada*, the goal of preserving this space was to "maintain its biological diversity, landscape, and ecological processes, such as recharging the aquifer, protecting the soil, capturing particulate pollution in the air, regulating the climate, and protecting against floods."[13] The process of establishing the park thus made a connection between biosecurity, protecting human health, and biodiversity more generally.

The area's green spaces were one of the reasons why INER was constructed in Tlalpan in the first place. Built in 1936 as a sanatorium for patients with tuberculosis, the wide lawns and open walkways linking the buildings reflected scientific ideas of the day about health and place. The buildings were designed to improve the health of patients by maximally exposing them to the neighborhood's healthy atmosphere and environment. The committee charged with planning the sanatorium selected the site primarily for the purity and dryness of the air, the atmospheric calm, strong light, clear sky, moderate temperatures, and the protection that the surrounding woods and mountains provided from the wind. Ismael Cosío Villegas, the first director of the sanatorium, lauded the choice of site, saying, "The project will come to affirm the physiognomy of the place."[14] A successful sanatorium would prove that Tlalpan was a healthy spot. Concern with the effect of the environment was often characteristic of approaches to treating tuberculosis, which had long been understood as what environmental historian Gregg Mitman calls a "disease of place."[15]

While doctors and architects in the thirties sought to expose tubercular patients to the atmosphere, contemporary physicians were not interested. Diseases, the environment, and understandings of their relationship had changed. The hospital was no longer exclusively or even primarily a tuberculosis sanatorium, and given the high levels of pollution in Mexico City, subjecting patients to the atmosphere was no longer a priority for physicians. Instead, the doctors who studied and treated respiratory ailments at INER saw the air as full of contaminants and microbes.

Research on infectious diseases required careful management of spaces and air-flows to keep scientists from getting infected or samples from being contaminated with the ubiquitous microbial flora that filled the air. The changes in medical beliefs and practices meant that scientists at INER bemoaned the Instituto Nacional de Antropología e Historia's (INAH) designation of these buildings as protected historic sites, which made it difficult to tear them down or remodel them. Chema, the scientist overseeing lab design, complained to me, "The place where our patients are treated is a very old building . . . It's not a nice place to attend our patients . . . These are old buildings, they are protected by the government . . . You can't change a thing from the outside." Scientists like Chema were frustrated at being confined to an architecture of the past. While the environment and health concerns had changed, they were stuck working in a built environment that did not reflect contemporary practices, which did not seek to expose patients to the air.

CHOREOGRAPHING THE AIR

I observed as scientists made the best of a variety of workspaces and thought about how to control air in all kinds of conditions. The BSL3 lab described in the previous chapter was one important site for thinking about air because it was designed for research on microbes that could be transmitted via inhalation and could cause serious or potentially lethal disease. Thus, the control of air was an essential component of work in the BSL3, and training activities often focused on managing airflow. As I observed scientists at work and participated in training activities, I, like other lab workers, became attuned to the invisible movements of air. The significance of these movements was heightened in the BSL3, where air could be carrying infectious pathogens. Ordinary lab activities, like pipetting a sample, could produce dangerous, unseen aerosols. Aware of this danger, scientists and technicians paid more attention to air, engaging with patterns of airflow and adjusting their movements and work patterns to minimize disruption to the air around them. One scientist told me that managing airflow and controlling microbes in the lab was "a matter of choreography—a dance inside of a BSL3." Working safely in the lab required planning, control, and perhaps even artistry.

Training programs preparing scientists to work in these labs demonstrated how difficult learning this choreography could be. One afternoon Sevilla and I traveled to La Raza, a hospital located a forty-five-minute drive from INER on the northern side of the city, so he could give a seminar on biosecurity. La Raza is a large general hospital run by the Instituto Mexicano del Seguro Social (the Mexican Social Security Institute, part of the Mexican Department of Health [Secretaría de Salud]). The hospital is adjacent to the Monumento a La Raza, a memorial comprised of a pyramid and a group of statues commemorating the founding of Mexico and the siege and defense of Tenochtitlan, the capital of the Aztec empire. Despite the geographic separation between INER and La Raza, people and samples frequently traveled between the two institutions. For example, the morning of the training session, Sevilla received a sample from a newborn patient at La Raza with a suspected cytomegalovirus infection. The physicians at La Raza wanted him to analyze the sample for resistance to antiviral medication so that they could determine the best course of treatment. Sevilla had special expertise in this kind of analysis and frequently received requests like this one. A few hours after receiving the sample, we found ourselves heading to La Raza, making the reverse journey along the Anillo Periférico highway, the beltway encircling the city.

Waiting for us at La Raza was a small group of graduate students who had gathered to learn how to work safely with airborne pathogens. Sevilla began the session by showing a video of a technician releasing smoke into a biosafety cabinet, a specialized piece of equipment where research with infectious agents ideally takes place. The smoke made the airflow in the cabinet visible, and the technician demonstrated how rapid movements would disrupt the smooth flow of air towards the back of the cabinet and away from the researcher. Work in a biosafety cabinet requires a measured, deliberate pace. Responding to an accident like a spill, for instance, requires remaining calm and controlling one's instincts to move quickly, since rapid movements will generate aerosols from the spilled substance. As scientists learn how air moves and how it can transport infectious agents, they seek to reshape their embodied practices.

However, as the training session demonstrated, it is not easy to incorporate this knowledge into practice. After the movie and a lecture by Sevilla, the class moved to a laboratory to engage in hands-on practice in a biosafety cabinet. Here, what had seemed a simple matter when viewed in a movie immediately became more complicated. Every move required calculation and was a balancing act in terms of working safely, efficiently, and with minimal wasted resources. Two students volunteered to demonstrate safe procedures and use of the cabinet. Although Sevilla had explained that for safety purposes and to avoid contamination students should wear two pairs of gloves, when one of the women who was demonstrating the cabinet asked if she should double-glove, the class leader hesitated. He noted that they did not have many gloves to spare. Assessing the situation, Sevilla responded that for the purposes of the demonstration, she could wear a single pair of gloves. As she worked in the biosafety cabinet, Sevilla reminded her that every time she used a pipette to transfer materials, she created aerosols. To avoid unnecessary risk or exposure, she should carefully plan her experiments to minimize pipetting. Sevilla frequently corrected her, gently reminding her which areas of the bench were clean and which were contaminated. She performed the practice procedures using a bright blue solution which made it easy to see and respond to spills and contamination. However, most lab work is conducted with more subtly colored liquids, which makes spills and droplets more difficult to recognize. As the students got their first experiences of working in a biosafety cabinet, the difficulties in learning this kind of work and in remembering the ways in which aerosolized and infectious particles spread became apparent. They made frequent mistakes, forgetting to stock all the materials necessary for the experiment in the biosafety cabinet at the start of work, running out of cleaning supplies, and accidentally removing contaminated matter from the secure environment of the cabinet. The limited resources available also made training more difficult—using only one set of gloves, students were unable to practice optimal containment techniques. It became apparent that it takes a long time to become accustomed to working in a biosafety cabinet and for the kinds of lab practices and slow, careful movements that the work demands to become deeply ingrained.

In the context of limited resources, work was more difficult, and exposure to risk was greater. Prior to coming to Mexico, I had conducted ethnographic research in a lab in Chicago, where I had been trained in biocontainment practices and had conducted experimental manipulations with microbes and small animals. The lab in Chicago was very well funded, a consequence of the increase in money for bio-defense research from the NIH after the anthrax attacks in the United States in the fall of 2001. One scientist in Chicago told me, "Here, everything's sort of disposable. I don't know if it's just because there's money. I don't know if every project has money like this one." Their safety practices and ability to work in the lab were a reflection of the significant government funding available for biodefense work. She went on to say, "It's not that we're using it [the money] irresponsibly, it's just that it's easier to do work when you don't have to worry about reusing things and watching. I mean, we watch the money, but we're allowed to get the things that we need or could use to make work easier." While in the United States fears of bioterror produced substantial funding for research, which in turn made laboratory activities easier, the trainees at La Raza did not have access to the same resources. They needed to exercise more care and learn alternate ways of protecting themselves against exposure.

Even the biosafety cabinet, one of the key pieces of equipment for working with aerosols and controlling airflow, was a luxury. At INER, across the institute from the BSL3 lab, was a laboratory for research on infectious fungi (see figure 9). I spent a few weeks in the lab, where the lead scientist, Francisco, taught me alternative ways of controlling the air. While the BSL3 was housed in a new building, the infectious fungi lab was located in a much older facility. The lab was small and brightly decorated, in contrast with the generic and clinical appearance of the newer BSL3 and associated lab space. It featured blue and white talavera tile and walls decorated with fungi-related paraphernalia: a calendar with images of Mexico's edible mushrooms, a poster showing the growth of common pathogenic fungi in various media, and small sculptures of mushrooms. The décor was completed with a few pictures of popular Mexican tourist attractions like beaches. The shelves

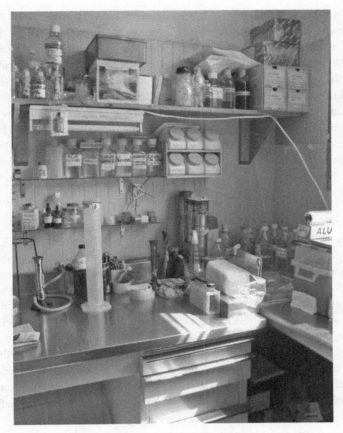

FIGURE 9. In the infectious fungi lab. Source: Author photograph.

were stocked with the usual laboratory materials—clear jars with distilled water, glycerol, lactophenal cotton blue (a solution used to stain fungi), sodium citrate, methanol, and various other solutions. Some of the more precious bottles were marked with Francisco's name and a warning— "no robar," or do not steal. The laboratory's one window was sealed shut in an effort to prevent the contamination of the lab or samples with fungi from the environment.

Francisco's research was not as well funded as that conducted in the BSL3 lab, and he had learned to work without an expensive biosafety cabinet. As he trained Guillermo, a student at a nearby university, and me on how to do diagnostic tests on patients suspected of having fungal infections, Francisco explained that to work safely with fungi you *should* have a biosafety cabinet. However, since his lab lacked one, he showed us how to use a mask and to improvise a workspace using two

Bunsen burners. With the Bunsen burners at either side of the bench and the equipment for the experiment in the middle, the hot air from the burners created an updraft, moving pathogens away from Francisco and from the materials he was using. Working between two burners was hot and sweaty, and the heat made it impossible to forget about the air around us. Regardless of whether research was taking place in a well- or poorly funded lab, scientists working with infectious materials became much more attuned to and aware of the air around them. The potential for inhaling dangerous pathogens transformed the ways they performed laboratory work and made the movement of air an issue of immediate concern. Scientists' understanding of how air moves and the materials it can contain shapes their embodied practices.

ENVIRONMENT AND PLACE

Scientists at INER were not only concerned with pathogens in the air. They were also deeply engaged with Mexico's problems with pollution. While lab practice made air tangible at a micro level, scientists at INER were also engaged in work that made air quality and its effects on human bodies at a larger scale visible. In this research, they produced evidence of the way air made connections among people and how bodies (both human and nonhuman) were produced through exposure over time to the environment. While air quality in Mexico City has improved since 1992, when the UN named it the most polluted city on the planet, poor air quality continues to be a significant problem. In 2012 the World Health Organization reported that each year in Mexico City there were four thousand deaths linked to air pollution.[16] Ailments connected to pollution include lung cancer, cardiopulmonary illness, asthma, and respiratory infections.

While the smog of Mexico City can be seen from airplanes and is noticeable when it obscures the nearby mountains, it is generally invisible on the street level as it enters the lungs. However, research at INER makes the effects of smog apparent. After working for a few weeks with Francisco, I moved down the hallway to the Department of Microbiology, where Gloria, a graduate student in her twenties, was looking at macrophages under a microscope. Dressed in jeans, sneakers, and a white lab coat with a name badge, she focused intently on the macrophages, writing in her lab notebook as she explained their function to me. Macrophages are part of the immune system—in her words, the cells that "eat everything." They engulf and digest foreign material, cellular debris, and pathogens. As I took a turn looking through the microscope, Gloria pointed out how dark the macrophages in this sample were. The sample had been taken from the lungs of a Mexico City resident, and the dark color of the macrophages was a result of the particles that the individual had been ingesting, the pollution and debris that were carried along with the Mexico City air.

Gloria observed to me that the notoriously bad air quality of Mexico City made it a good place to study the effects of pollution on the lungs and immune system. This sample was part of a project she was working on to compare the immune systems of people who lived in different areas and to analyze how changes in the immune system correlated with pollution levels. They were currently recruiting volunteers from both Mexico City and northern Mexico, which Gloria noted was even more polluted than Mexico City as a result of the intensive industrial development along the US-Mexico border.[17] The challenge in Mexico, she pointed out, was finding unpolluted areas from which to recruit volunteers. Gloria noted that most of their samples came from students, whom they regarded as the best volunteers. They understood the significance of the study, the value of their samples, and were able to give meaningful informed consent. The samples were extracted from subjects through a technique called bronchoalveolar lavage, in which saline solution is squirted into the volunteer's lungs and then extracted via a tube inserted into the nose. While Gloria and her colleagues assured me that the procedure was not painful, they did describe it as bothersome and uncomfortable. Well-informed students who were aware of what they were getting into were therefore seen as the most suitable volunteers.

Most of the participants in the study had worked in labs themselves and could understand the kind of research being conducted. They were often curious afterwards about the samples they had provided, asking, "How were my cells? What were they like?" The study and the analysis of their cells provided them with a new perspective on their bodies and health, making visible previously invisible and unfelt aspects of their biology. One researcher noted that in addition to the volunteers, the lab relied on contributions from everyone who worked there, as scientists often turned to their colleagues for blood samples. Drawing blood was a much less onerous process than bronchoalveolar lavage, and people were generally happy to do it. As a result, most of the scientists working in the lab had detailed insights into the characteristics of their own immune systems. Gloria noted that she produced a lot of interferon gamma, a protein involved in immune system regulation. If someone in the lab needed that, she would volunteer to provide a sample. The practice of regularly providing samples for the lab's experimental research meant that scientists made their own and their colleagues' immune systems visible in new ways.

At INER, air was conceptualized not as intangible or incorporeal but as substantial. We were aware that air carries material and even life-forms from one place to another. It is something that is both affected by human activities, from the motion of hands at a lab bench to the release of pollutants, and a medium that connects the inhabitants of an area, transmitting unseen materials from the lungs and breath of one person to another and materially making bodies. The impossibility of containing air, combined with its ability to carry matter, produces effects that undo the scales and connections we ordinarily assign to social interactions. For example, air connects the trees of Tlalpan to the rest of the city, allowing the greenery of one area to act as lungs for the city as a whole. International political economic issues like trade agreements that result in the construction of factories to produce goods for export become visible at a microscopic level in the lungs of Mexico. Through the study of air, scientists attend to the relationship between body and environment, producing evidence of the ways bodies are produced through interaction with the environment, and demonstrating how communities come to share bodily substance through shared exposure to the landscape. The importance of air in shaping bodies complicates the idea of place. While doctors looking for a "healthful place" for a sanatorium once paid the most attention to the environment close at hand, contemporary understandings of the movements of air have caused scientists and doctors to extend more broadly their conception of what constitutes the place that is shaping their patients' bodies. The darkened lung macrophages demonstrated the effects of large-scale environmental and political issues on the most intimate and microscopic levels, making visible in the laboratory the way that air connects human health with the broader ecology and making clear that pollution is a significant biosecurity issue. This emerging visibility could make it possible for air and the environment to become the subject of political attention and regulation.

MEXICAN POPULATIONS, HUMAN AND VIRAL

Air was not the only material through which scientists produced evidence of national biological connections. Outside the BSL3 at INER's Centro de Investigación de Enfermedades Infecciosas (the Center for Research on Infectious Disease, or CIENI) was a series of stainless steel, liquid nitrogen–filled tanks. In the tanks were blood samples, plasma aliquots, and peripheral blood mononuclear cells from HIV patients from twelve Mexican states. These tanks represented an archive of the recent history of Mexican populations, both human and viral. This was the raw material for the center's primary research project on the epidemiology and evolution of HIV in Mexico. Santiago Avila, the microbiologist in charge of this project, described the research to me as a study of how the "immune response is leaving footprints on the HIV genome at the population level that have to do with genomics of the different populations in the world." The samples were crucial for the researchers' efforts to establish both which viral subtypes were circulating in Mexico and the evolutionary history of the virus in Mexico.

I met with Avila in his office, where he both interpreted the work of the center and explained how he came to be part of it. A serious and intense young scientist, Avila remembered being drawn to biology even as a young child. He was an outlier in a family of artists and musicians, the only one to pursue training in science. As an undergraduate he studied pharmaceutical biochemistry (a popular choice in Mexico, where the pharmaceutical industry is well developed), and then traveled to England for a master's degree in microbiology. His first position upon returning to Mexico was researching vaccine-preventable diseases at the National Institute of Public Health in Cuernavaca. He eventually moved to Mexico City to begin a PhD program, and it was as part of his PhD research that he began studying HIV epidemiology and evolution in the Mexican population. At INER he played multiple roles, designing research projects, preparing papers and grant proposals, supervising students, and managing the financial and material requirements of the lab. His position within the lab allowed him to speak with authority on the intellectual and practical components of research, as well as its place within the global research economy.

Avila explained to me that the blood plasma samples came from HIV-positive patients at clinics around the country. From these samples they extracted and purified HIV RNA and sequenced its genome in order to document in great detail the epidemiology and genetic characteristics of HIV in Mexico. HIV is a highly diverse virus with at least ten different subtypes. Among these subtypes A, B, and C are the most common; almost 50 percent of HIV infections worldwide are subtype C. The distribution of subtypes across infected populations is not random, but instead varies geographically. Subtype C is prevalent in southern Africa and India, while subtype A is more common in central and eastern Africa and among the former Soviet satellite nations in eastern Europe. Subtype B predominates in western and central Europe, the Americas, and Australia.[18]

While HIV in clinical populations is highly diverse, in the lab it is more homogenous. The majority of research is conducted on subtype B viruses (the strain most common in western Europe and the United States), specifically on reference strains isolated by laboratories in the United States and France. As Johanna Crane has shown, the choice of reference strains and research standards for HIV is the product of the molecular politics of infectious disease research. In the context of a highly diverse global viral population, the selection of one strain of HIV as a normal, representative, reference strain privileges certain populations and excludes others.[19] By collaborating with health centers across the country and establishing what HIV looked like in Mexico, researchers at INER sought to intervene in the narrow focus of HIV research that had often neglected Latin America.

Avila told me that the research CIENI was conducting allowed the team to establish how HIV was evolving at a national level with a very high degree of sensitivity. This work was particularly important, he argued, because previous studies had looked only at individual states or at a few high-risk patient groups. The center's research, on the other hand, looked at HIV at a national scale and characterized the genomes of the viruses circulating in the entire Mexican population, giving them a better picture of the epidemic as a whole. While most infections in Mexico and the rest of the Americas are subtype B, CIENI researchers found that there were still very important genetic variations within the subtype that were not captured by reference strains. Understanding the viral life-forms infecting Mexican patients was important both for guiding choices of research materials and for establishing effective treatment plans.

In addition to studying the epidemiology of HIV, researchers at CIENI asked how these viral life-forms came to have their particular genetic characteristics. Why was HIV different in Mexico? HIV evolves very rapidly due to its fast replication capability, its high mutation rate, and the high probability of recombination. This rapid rate of evolution makes it possible for the virus to adapt to multiple selection pressures, like those applied by the human immune system or antiretroviral therapy. Scientists at CIENI theorized that one reason HIV in Mexico varied from other places was because the human population of Mexico was genetically unique. These genetic characteristics then shaped the evolution and genome of HIV. In addition to extracting HIV RNA from the blood samples, they obtained the patient's genomic DNA, which they used to characterize the human leukocyte antigens (HLA) of each patient. HLA molecules are components of the immune system, affecting how it responds to pathogens in a variety of ways. They play an important role in the function of cytotoxic T cells, a type of white blood cell which destroys infected or damaged cells. In a presentation on his research, Avila noted that HLA is highly variable and that these variations are "reflected at a national or population level." That is, the Mexican population was characterized by a specific pattern of HLA alleles.

Avila emphasized that HLA characteristics and related cytotoxic T cells produce an environment with strong selective pressures that lead to viral evolution. In this case, rather than environmental factors producing human biology, human biology itself is an environment that shaped nonhuman life-forms. Comparing each patient's HLA alleles with the genome of the virus that infected them, they found links between particular HLA alleles and the presence or absence of amino acids in the viral genome. Avila interpreted a graphic that represented these linkages for me, explaining:

Avila: Well, that's a very nice model that was developed by Microsoft in
        Washington. One of the people we collaborated with, Jonathan Carlson,
        developed this model. Here we're just seeing associations between the
        immune response and the viral genome. What you see here is a circle;
        each position in the circle represents a position in the viral genome. In
        this case, it's the protease and the RT gene [protease is an enzyme
        involved in the breakdown of proteins into amino acids and the RT gene
        is the gene coding for reverse transcriptase, the enzyme that produces
        complementary DNA from RNA]. And outside the circle you see some

numbers. Those numbers correspond to human genes; they're called HLA alleles. HLA alleles define some very important immune responses to control the virus. There are three HLA class one alleles, class A, B, and C, and there are many different variants of those genes that are expressed in different frequencies in different populations. The associations we're looking at between HLA genes and polymorphisms in the viral genome, what you see outside are the names of those HLA alleles. And what you see within the circle are associations between HLA alleles and the evolution of different positions in the viral genome.

Emily: So if you have a certain HLA allele, you're more likely to have this mutation.

Avila: Exactly, mutations in the viral genome. For example, these HLA alleles are associated with changes in this particular position in the viral genome. But the virus, the different positions in the virus also coevolve. And that's looked at in this mathematical model. So you see that changes in this position are associated with changes in *this* position and maybe in this other position, and *this* other position. So that's what those lines mean. That's how the virus is adapting. Because sometimes one mutation is not enough, or maybe one mutation causes the virus to not replicate effectively, so another mutation will have to come to compensate for those cuts in viral replication. That's why many different mutations appear.

Another CIENI biologist explained the group's research by showing a map of the global distribution of HLAs. He emphasized that HLA alleles vary with geography and that the goal of their research at INER was to describe the genetic characteristics of HIV in what he called "the immunogenetic context of the Mexican population." In order to do this, they compared HIV and HLA alleles from Mexican patients with a cohort composed of Canadians, Americans, and Australians. They explained that the Mexican patient population is different from the others because it is a mestizo population, that is, "the result of the admixture of Spanish, Indian, and black genes."[20] As a result of this history of mixture, the Mexican population has unique patterns of HLA alleles, and the HIV virus has evolved in response to the particularities of the human population's immune systems. In addition to producing a unique viral population, the prevalence of protective HLA alleles can also produce clinical differences in the patient population, influencing the viral set point (a patient's viral load a few weeks or months after infection) and disease progression.

Scientists at INER read genetic and immunological difference and shared biology at the scale of the nation. This is not to say that researchers at INER argued that the Mexican population is homogenous: Avila explained to me that in biological terms "the Mexican population is very diverse. So we talk about Mexican mestizos, but the Mexican mestizos are very diverse—from a lot of different Indian populations, and black populations, and European populations. So you see a whole mixture of genes. But in the end, this is what you see, this is what you have in Mexico." Despite the acknowledgments of diversity, scientists at INER assumed that the geopolitical boundary of the nation demarcated a genetically cohesive and interesting population, the mestizo.

As Jenny Reardon argued in her work on the Human Genome Diversity Project, to produce scientific understandings of "human genetic diversity," scientists had to develop or deploy social understandings of the world that would enable their research. In these projects, scientists assumed that the natural order could be usefully represented by preexisting social categories.[21] Similarly, Michael Montoya, writing about genetic explanations for diabetes in Mexicano populations, described these explanations as an inversion of the biosocial (in which biology informs notions of self and identity). In this case, the social is informing the biological: population constructs, imagery, and social history have shaped the selection of biological units of analysis for diabetes research.[22] INER's claims about the genomics of the Mexican mestizo were in line with the findings of the Mexican Genome Project discussed in the introduction, which likewise argued for the distinctiveness of Mexican genetics.[23]

While these claims segment the population at the level of the nation, one could easily imagine research that divided the population into alternative groupings, constructing difference at a new scale: by city, by region, or (as commonly happens) by ethnic group. Scale is not neutral—it must be produced. Scale is politically powerful—framing problems within particular scales (whether global, national, local, or microbial) configures causes, consequences, and interventions differently.[24] Despite pointing out the heterogeneity of the Mexican population, in their analysis scientists at CIENI lumped all patients into a single cohort (the Mexican), interpreting the nation as a biological group. They posited a coherent, uniform national biology around which boundaries could be constructed. This uniformity applied not only to human, but also to viral life-forms. I asked Avila whether they observed any differences within the cohort of Mexican patients, and he responded that "no, virologically speaking, the viruses circulating in Mexico are very similar to each other. That's one of our findings. And almost all of the viruses are from the same subtype. The homogeneity of the viruses is remarkable, I would say, compared to what they've seen in the United States where there are a lot of non-B subtypes circulating in the population." This research produced distinctions between different nations, giving Mexico a particular identity and demarcating it from other places (notably the United States) in terms of human and viral populations. These distinctions made it possible to talk about the virus as a population. Extending Avila's comment about the homogeneity of the virus, we might call it a mestizo virus. Thinking in terms of biomestizaje means it is possible to interpret the process of mestizaje as applying to nonhuman life-forms like viruses, as their biological material is shaped by mixture and life within Mexico.

Researchers at CIENI did not attribute all of the differences that they observed between Mexican and other viral populations to the genetic characteristics of the Mexican population, although in their analysis that was an important factor. HIV adapts not only in response to the human immune system, but also to antiretroviral therapy (ART), developing resistance to the drugs used to treat it. Public efforts to provide universal access to ART began in 2001 and were fully implemented in 2003.[25] By the end of 2009, out of the 220,000 adults with HIV in Mexico, 27 percent were receiving ART.[26] As researchers at CIENI studied the epidemiology of HIV in Mexico and sequenced viruses in samples from around the country, they found a prevalence of 7.4 percent transmitted drug resistance mutations, slightly lower than most industrialized countries. Avila speculated that it was because "in Third World countries, antiretroviral therapies started later. That's one reason. Another is that, well, the use of antiretroviral drugs is different in different areas of the world. And we're just starting to see this large-scale use of antiretroviral therapy, this broad access to antiretroviral therapy, in Third World countries, and those are the characteristics of Third World countries." Countries like the United States, in which patients began antiretroviral therapy earlier in the history of AIDS treatment, started with what are now regarded as suboptimal, low-potency regimes that ultimately may have increased the number of drug-resistant mutations in their viral populations. The lower levels of resistant mutations and the different mutation patterns in Mexico may have been a product of different trajectories of access to antiretroviral therapy, which was broadly introduced later than in the United States and began with high-potency regimes. HIV in Mexico has thus been shaped by political choices and patterns of access to healthcare. These national variations meant that it was essential to study HIV in clinical populations around the globe. Avila explained to me, "These studies are necessary in many populations. This is one case where doing the same study in different populations is worth it. You need to do that, because it's so different what you can find in HIV adaptation in different populations." Differences in human bodies produce variations in viral populations, which may indicate that different approaches to treatment are necessary.

Ángeles Cruz Martínez, reporting on CIENI's work in *La Jornada*, turned this story of viral transformations into a reflection on national risk and the need for technological and scientific development. Even in the context of supposed global risk and porous borders, Cruz writes that "in this country, AIDS has genomic characteristics that make it stronger for different factors than that of other nations." As a result, HIV in Mexico needs dedicated scientific attention. It may be impossible to develop a universal vaccine; scientific research is key to the nation's health and security since "a potential vaccine will probably have to be adapted to each specific population."[27] Scientists studied and understood the people of Mexico as a population made similar through shared histories and exposure to land, food, and biomedical practices. This concept of population was extended to viral life-forms, which were likewise seen as malleable groups whose biology had been made in relation to human bodies.

The differences in viral and human life also provided scientists with a unique resource, one which set their research apart. CIENI's fifth annual meeting, in March of 2010, was a moment in which the center's staff reflected on the significance of their work in a national and global context, contemplated future directions, and received comments and criticism from outside observers. Held in the INER auditorium, the meeting was one of the few times when all the staff of the research center gathered to discuss their work. In addition to researchers from CIENI, the attendees included guests from other institutions inside and outside of Mexico. Including the guests, there were approximately fifty to sixty attendees. Attendance fluctuated over the course of the two days as people left to work in the clinic or to attend to experiments. Even during this moment of reflection, clinical and research work continued. The director of CIENI opened the meeting, taking the stage between two giant floral arrangements. The auditorium had been professionally staged for the meeting, with an audiovisual team providing simultaneous translation from Spanish to English and English to Spanish and projecting video of the speakers from multiple angles. The high production values were a significant upgrade from more routine lab meetings, demonstrating the importance of this event to CIENI.

In his opening statement, the director reflected on the challenges of treating HIV in Mexico, where many patients do not know their serologic status until relatively late. They arrive at INER very ill, suffering from opportunistic infections and in need of intensive care. Because HIV infections are generally diagnosed much later in Mexico than in the United States, patients often present with symptoms and illnesses that have not been seen in the United States for thirty years. He noted that despite the efforts to improve research and treatment, "we're still in the '80s compared to the US. Opportunistic infections are a reality. It's sad." Responses from outside visitors (who primarily hailed from the United States) to case reports reinforced his analysis of the differences in treatment and disease progression between the United States and Mexico.

In the meeting, multiple modes of constructing and understanding the Mexican population were on display. When Edna, a clinician at CIENI, gave a presentation on ophthalmological manifestations of HIV and described the various opportunistic infections experienced by AIDS patients at CIENI, a physician visiting from Massachusetts General Hospital (MGH) responded with animation to her presentation, saying, "Last year at MGH we published a case series in *Clinical Infectious Diseases* [a scientific journal] of patients with ocular syphilis. We only had thirteen patients over the course of twenty years. You have over double the number of patients in your study. It's a fantastic cohort and opportunity to study these diseases, and we just don't have these opportunities anymore, especially to study these in the context of advanced retroviral treatment. It's a fantastic opportunity." This foreign scientist perceived Mexican patients as living in a past that patients in the United States had moved on from, articulating the difference in patient health and experience in terms of a time lag, one that meant that Mexico was not temporally equivalent to the United States. Johannes Fabian described ethnographic narratives that placed their subjects outside of the time of the writer as an example of the "oppressive uses of Time."[28] The temporal discourse here placed Mexican patients outside of the modernity experienced by other North Americans, and enabled these cases of untreated ocular syphilis to be imagined as a resource to this scientist from the United States. This kind of rhetoric constructing the population as one untouched by modernity and therefore a purer form of biology echoed historical practices of biomedical and social science research that treated Latin America as a source of more "primitive" nature.[29]

While scientists at CIENI did not view their patients' suboptimal treatment and poor health outcomes as a resource, they did see difference itself as valuable. Many of the scientists at INER had studied outside of Mexico and participated in international collaborations. And in Mexico, as elsewhere, publication in internationally recognized journals was the standard for measuring scientific productivity. In this context, national differences in biology were important resources. Avila, describing the cohort of Mexican patients they had assembled, told me, "That's our asset. That's why there has been so much interest from other research groups in other parts of the world. There are things that can really be studied here that you cannot study in other parts of the world." They argued that the cohort of Mexican patients exhibited valuable biological differences, differences that could be seen in genes and immune systems and that were based in the Mexican history, politics, and social systems. Human bodies are not the only ones that are constituted as malleable and shaped in exposure to environment; viral life-forms are likewise produced in relation and interaction with their environment. This research constitutes Mexicans as a biologically distinct population, which provides a useful point of comparison with other groups that allows researchers to test hypotheses about the ways in which HIV has evolved in interaction with the human immune system.

VIRAL RECORDS OF SOCIAL LIFE

As part of their epidemiological research, scientists at CIENI used phylogenetic analysis to reconstruct a history of the HIV virus in Mexico.[30] They read social histories into viral gene sequences, studying them to understand where founder strains came from, how they spread through populations, and their evolutionary relationships with HIV viruses in other places.[31] Viral life-forms were used to interpret the human interactions and relationships that transmitted the disease, in ways that could be used to shape public health practices. Avila told me, "It's incredible what an infection can tell you about human character. And population diversity and things like that." He pointed to the research showing that the viruses circulating in Mexico were much more homogenous than the diverse viral population in the United States, using the differences in viral populations to challenge assumptions about the movement of life-forms between the two countries. He argued that, contrary to frequent claims in public health that "disease knows no borders," the circulation of viral life-forms does follow national borders. He noted, "Recombinant forms that have been introduced by migration? Well, those phenomena are not being seen in Mexico, even with the very high migration that is seen from Mexico to the States and back." Avila posited that Mexicans get the virus from other Mexicans, "that Mexican communities are closed, they're not so open." In other words, the history of treatment patterns and human genetics had been written into viral genomes, which were now being used to understand and interpret human behavior.

Knowledge about disease transmission patterns was then used to shape public policy and choices about how to intervene in disease transmission. For example, a team of scientists conducted phylogenetic analysis of HIV on the San Diego–Tijuana border. Confirming what Avila observed in his national analysis, the scientists concluded that there were important genetic differences in viral life-forms in the two cities, arguing that despite the extremely high rate of traffic across the border, which is perhaps the busiest land border crossing in the world, the epidemics in Tijuana and San Diego are distinct. The researchers used phylogenetic analysis to claim that cases of the disease being transmitted across the border were relatively rare, and occurred primarily during transactional sex involving female sex workers in Tijuana and male clients coming from San Diego. The scientists argued that analyzing the viral genome provided clues to how it traveled through social networks, data that could be used for prevention and detection efforts.[32] This research, like the work at CIENI, demonstrated the complexity with which the social merges into the biological, as human practices shape and leave traces on viral life-forms, which then inform social choices about interventions in public health.

SHARED ENVIRONMENTS, SHARED BIOLOGIES, SHARED RISKS

Since the late nineteenth century, Euro-American notions of disease tended to treat the environment as external and largely irrelevant to the human body. Emerging notions of the modern body constructed it as impermeable, self-contained, and autonomous, and the landscape was no longer considered an important producer of health and disease.[33] As Warwick Anderson and Ian Mackay put it, disease became ontological.[34] That is, it became an independent entity, separate from its manifestation in individual bodies, and doctors became more focused on disease-causing pathogens, rather than the environment more broadly. While Euro-American scientists have historically regarded genetic identity as fixed and the biological characteristics of bodies and populations as generally permanent and unalterable, these assumptions are far from universal. Andean and Amazonian understandings of the body have often treated it as porous, permeable, and malleable. For example, Beth Conklin has shown how social groups in Amazonian cultures are often constituted around the idea of shared bodily substances produced through social interactions. The materiality of the body is built up over time, and relationships and identity are produced through cumulative social processes and the sharing of substances, including bodily exchanges and the shared consumption of food or drink.[35] This malleability means that relationships and elements of identity, including race, may change over time.[36] Scientific research in Latin America likewise has often highlighted malleability, both in the neo-Lamarckian eugenics projects discussed in the introduction and up to the present day.[37]

The different ways that bodies and environments were and are interpreted in Latin America are consequential for biosecurity science. If biological characteristics are malleable and produced through interaction with the environment and landscape, changes in the environment can change populations, producing or eliminating difference.[38] As this chapter has shown, the human populations and bodies that security projects have sought to protect are not interpreted as stable and unchanging; rather, in producing biosecurity, scientists have been attentive to and made manifest the ways bodies are dynamically shaped by the environment. In this research, the environment is broadly construed, as scientists demonstrate how political decisions on issues ranging from trade and manufacturing to the distribution of healthcare shape the material substance of the population. Scientists at INER represent Mexicans as connected by virtue of their shared history, exposure to the environment, and viral ecologies, and they use the lab to produce evidence of the connections between environment, history, and the body. This research constitutes populations and biological difference as national phenomenon. In the process, researchers at INER produce biomestizaje, locating key attributes of Mexican identity at the cellular and molecular level, in the immune system, in genetic characteristics, in bodies shaped by access to or lack of pharmaceuticals. This identity makes Mexicans differently vulnerable to disease and produces new forms of microbial life, which in turn require special biosecurity measures and protections. By attending to biology as malleable and dynamic, these biosecurity practices draw history and politics into the laboratory. Scientists in Mexico have produced research that contributes to greater neo-Lamarckian trends in the discipline of biology as a whole, characterized by trends in postgenomics and molecular epigenetics which emphasize the genetic code as dynamic, fluid, and shaped by the social.[39]

Addressing changing perspectives on biosecurity, the Mexican minister of health, José Ángel Córdova Villalobos, noted, "There is a growing awareness that nobody is free of biological risk and that these risks must be taken seriously to create a culture of prevention and protection, and to eliminate risky attitudes or actions."[40] Talk like Córdova's highlights one of the effects of biosecurity discourse, which has been to present new ways of stratifying risk, locating it at the level of the nation.[41] This contrasts with Mexico's ongoing security problems associated with drug trafficking, in which risk is stratified by class and geography. It also contrasts with standard public health analyses of disease, in which risk may be stratified by class, age, sex, or other characteristics. In terms of biosecurity, all Mexicans are configured as equally at risk. This research has produced a national population through shared biological materiality and a national community through shared senses of danger or threat, enabling the government to intervene in civil liberties (as happened during the H1N1 epidemic). As biologists produce knowledge about life and health in Mexico, they produce a picture of a nation that is connected by history and shared environmental exposures, and define life and potential threats to it on a molecular level. Their work suggests that "living better" or improving human health in Mexico requires attention to the environment and how bodies are produced by the physical and social environment that surrounds them and how human bodies themselves constitute an environment that shapes microbial and viral ecologies.

The Bureaucracy of Genetic Modification

CORPORATE ECOLOGY

The Instituto Nacional de Ecología (the National Institute of Ecology, or INE)[1] is housed in a gleaming skyscraper in southern Mexico City, surrounded by outposts of multinational businesses. These include a nearby McDonald's, Pizza Hut, Six Flags amusement park, and the Perisur Mall, an upscale shopping center where wealthy Mexico City residents shop for designer clothing and go to the movies. Although the immediate impression given by the area is of a modern commercial center, there are hints at the longer history of human and non-human habitation. INE is adjacent to Cuicuilco, one of the country's oldest archeological sites, where the remains of a circular stone pyramid emerge from a grassy field. A small garden sprouts a few blocks away, next to Avenida Insurgentes, the busy multilane thoroughfare that bisects Mexico City (see figure 10). The garden is touted as a restoration of flora and fauna native to the area and a reintroduction of the desert scrub ecosystem that had characterized this southern Mexico City neighborhood prior to its urbanization. Designed in 2008 by landscape architect Pedro Camarena, it was intended to restore the historical flora to the urban ecology of this increasingly paved and vegetationless area.[2] The result was a small patch of grass, trees, and bare rocks, identifiable as a garden only by the sign labeling it the Jardines Nativos del Pedregal (Native Rocky Gardens) and prominently indicating that American Express had sponsored the restoration. The small garden and the effort to grow native vegetation are a small reminder of the neighborhood's mostly vanished ecological past. And, in its conjoining of big business and efforts to restore and protect indigenous plant life, it is an apt symbol for the work being conducted in the adjacent INE building, where scientists

FIGURE 10. Jardines Nativos del Pedregal. Source: Author photograph.

and administrators regulate and manage efforts by major businesses to transform the plant life and agricultural systems of the country.

Anthropogenic landscapes and organisms in Mexico are variously loved and despised. The changes in the land that have accompanied human activities are sometimes celebrated as essential to Mexican food security and identity and some-times rejected as degradations of valuable ecosystems and natural capital. For example, maize, which was produced through human domestication of the wild grass teocintle, is celebrated as materially and symbolically central to Mexican life and culture, a specifically Mexican life-form produced out of a long history of interactions between people and plants.[3] However, transgenic maize, made through human interventions in the laboratory, is often regarded as a problematic interloper into the nation's agricultural system.[4]

GMOs in general have been extremely controversial in Mexico, where there have been extensive debates over the risk of biotechnology for Mexican genetic diversity, agriculture, and food security.[5] In response to these lab-mediated transformations, Oaxacan campesinos and the ecologists collaborating with them to protect the diversity of the Mexican plant population turned their attention to the molecular. Maize plants were identified as good, "native" Mexican crops based on tests indicating the absence of transgenic elements.[6] This tactic relied on molecular analysis and located identity at the level of the genome. Opponents of GMOs in the United States often invoke images of contamination and the destruction of pure "nature" in their protests. This imagery of a pure, uncontaminated "natural" world that might be violated is, as Hugh Gusterson points out, a way of obscuring the way human agency has shaped the landscape.[7] Understandings of the threat of GMOs are generally different in Mexico, where people are quite explicit in their understanding that human and plant lives are interconnected. People have argued for the protection of particular crops not because they represented pristine nature, but rather based on how their materiality and genomes have been shaped by their entanglement with humans, that is, their status as products of biomestizaje. Transgenic crops, which have different histories from native landraces and are produced out of different social and economic systems, are seen as threatening both maize crops themselves and the communities who rely on them. Responding to widespread fears of destruction of a crop that was both an essential food item and a symbol of the nation, the federal government banned transgenic maize in 1998. This ban was subsequently lifted, and the first permits for the experimental use of transgenic maize were issued in 2009.[8] This chapter examines the new scientific bureaucracy of permitting, evaluation, and control that Mexico implemented when lifting the ban.

While the previous chapter detailed how bodies are produced in relation to landscape and environment, this chapter addresses the role of plants in understandings of landscape and territory and how government scientists produce knowledge about those plants and the consequences of those knowledge practices through ethnographic fieldwork in the Departamento de Bioseguridad at INE. Territory is produced both materially and symbolically.[9] Plants, as food, as key elements of ecosystems, and as essential parts of national identity, play important roles in producing territories. Plants have often been used to make borders and boundaries between two territories visible as well as to establish human claims to and control over land, marking it as cultivated or owned. Plant populations have been managed to make landscapes more legible and more easily regulated.[10] This chapter explores how plants may still mark territory even in cases when the identity of the plant is nonobvious, not immediately knowable, and, in fact, requires careful expert work to be made legible. In this case, plants have become subjects of a debate over who has the authority to establish their identity. Examining the spread of plants and transgenic material in Mexico also draws attention to non-human agency and the way plants and genes, even in the context of ostensibly human-controlled and -dominated agricultural systems, spread and multiply in ways that exceed human intentions.

Plant populations and human lives are entangled; the particular plant populations of an area both index human practices and make human lives possible.[11] Debates over what kind of maize should grow in Mexico are debates over what human economic, social, and agricultural systems should be supported. Native landraces are taken to correspond with the systems of small-scale agriculture that had produced them, while transgenic corn is associated with transnational capital, industrial agriculture, and neoliberalism. Controlling, surveilling, and regulating plant life is an important way of constructing national boundaries, and work on transgenic organisms (whether against or in support of) makes clear that making life better and, more generally, managing and protecting the nation is a more-than-human project. The Mexican government, notably through the Instituto Nacional de Ecología and a few other federal organizations, attempts to control the circulation of plants in agriculture and the broader ecosystem. Regulating plants is one way of drawing a material and ideological line between Mexico and the United States, which have quite different relationships with maize and with GMOs. This boundary, however, is porous and frequently transgressed, particularly by people who do not interpret genetically modified life-forms in the same way that the government does.

BIOBUREAUCRACY

At INE, Federico and Carlos are two of the scientists involved in the process of characterizing and making legible the plant life of Mexico. Both in their twenties, they had been independent contractors in the Departamento de Bioseguridad at INE for about four years since receiving undergraduate degrees in biology from the Universidad Nacional Autónoma de México (UNAM).[12] Scientists in the Departamento de Bioseguridad play an important role in regulating the use of genetically modified organisms, reviewing any application for experimental or commercial use of GMOs. Their role in the regulatory process makes INE and its bureaucracy obligatory passage points for the legal entry of GMOs into the Mexican nation and ecosystem. Any person or corporation (and in practice, applications are nearly always made by corporations) who would like to use GMOs for experimental or commercial purposes must apply to the federal government for permission. Once an application for a permit had been submitted, the INE Departamento de Bioseguridad assesses the risk of the proposed activity and advises whether or not to grant a permit.

Biosecurity at the Instituto Nacional de Enfermedades Respiratorias (as discussed in chapters 3 and 4) is about the relationship between the environment, microbial life, and the human population. However, biosecurity has a different meaning at INE, where concerns about human health have emerged only secondarily. The primary focus of the Departamento de Bioseguridad is the effect of GMOs on Mexican ecosystems. And while work at INER involves the collection of biological material from around the nation and laboratory research to make visible unseen biologies, the Departamento de Bioseguridad at INE is primarily a deskbound operation. I had come to INE intending to study how ecologists monitor the environment, the effects of GMOs, and the effectiveness of biosecurity measures. I wanted to learn how scientists make use of the sciences of ecology and molecular genetics to establish the identity of local, native biologies and potential changes caused by GMOs. However, while I did spend time in INE's laboratory, observing scientists as they processed samples and tested them for the presence of transgenic material, making biosecurity in this case was not primarily a field or laboratory science. Rather than the scientific or technological processes of ecological assessment and genetic analysis that I had expected to observe, the central technologies involved in understanding GMOs at INE were technologies of bureaucracy.

Understanding the management of plants required digging into bureaucratic documents. The format and design of bureaucratic documents has long been analytically invisible, neglected by anthropologists because they were regarded as providing direct and transparent access to the material they were documenting.[13] Through ethnographic research at the National Institute of Ecology (INE) in Mexico City, in this chapter I look at the regulation of plant circulation in agriculture and the broader ecosystem, examining the ways biology and bureaucracy intersect in the development of what could be called a *biobureaucracy*.[14] This biobureaucracy and the process of granting permits make some aspects of plant and ecosystemic life legible to the state and others invisible. Ethical choices are built into bureaucratic classification and documentation practices, valuing some plant and animal life over others and creating areas of knowledge and ignorance (ones which scientists outside the department contest). The emphasis on documentation and accreditation is used to sanction state knowledge production and devalue other knowledges. In the process, the office becomes a key place and documents key technologies for determining what life-forms are visible to the state and its protections and which are not, and how the mobility, stability, and security of plants and ecosystems more broadly are determined. I examine how the movements of paper (or pdfs or docs) are made into authoritative statements about the patterns of plant life.

This work takes place in multiple spaces, but primarily the office and the lab, which produces legibility in different ways. In the office of the Departamento de Bioseguridad, scientists including Federico and Carlos convert GMOs into bureaucratic objects and the subjects of technocratic administration. The office is a key domain in which plants and other life-forms are ordered and classified, marked as Mexican or foreign, conventional or genetically modified. Plants get sorted into these categories through bureaucratic processes, and these representations of plant and other life-forms have material consequences, primarily in whether or not people are permitted to release transgenic organisms. Studies of bureaucracy raise the methodological question of how to study an extensive organization ethnographically, especially one in which the majority of work analyzing documents is individualized labor done on a computer.[15] My approach at

INE was to primarily follow two individuals, analyzing the bureaucracy as they experienced and engaged with it. I observed as Federico and Carlos spent their days interpreting data about the current status of Mexican ecosystems and the possible consequences of the use of GMOs, particularly how they might affect what were termed *nontarget organisms*, that is, the other species that comprise an area's ecosystem. In their research, they made plants legible through forms, databases, and computer programs. These instruments are important tools in shaping the representation of plant life, admitting some kinds of knowledge and authorship while excluding others, and producing strategic lacunae in institutional knowledge.[16]

Scientists outside the organization critiqued the biosafety and biosecurity procedures related to genetically modified organisms as inadequate because they were purely bureaucratic. At UNAM, I met with a specialist in plant evolution and development, who criticized the GMO monitoring and biosafety practices undertaken by the state as being unscientific. She argued that the scientists involved "forgot about their scientific nature" to advance an "economy of promise. Not even economy of something material. An economy of promise based on false scientific argumentation." The bureaucratic processes that govern these practices are too reductive, treating the complex systems into which GMOs are released as predictable, linear ones, and as a result do not properly evaluate the risks or consequences of using GMOs. Antonio Serratos, a scientist at the Universidad Autónoma de la Ciudad de México who specializes in plant molecular biology, complained about the permit application process in a newspaper article, arguing that the material called for was incomplete, containing little data on how effective transgenes were at controlling pests or what their effect might be on the genetic makeup of Mexican plant life. Critiquing the paucity of scientific data in these applications, he went on to say, "The research of transnational companies should be carried out at a molecular and ecological level, but what they are doing is a bureaucratic process."[17] As Serratos's complaint illustrates, the central technologies of understanding GMOs and interpreting their presence in the country are *not* those of the lab, but rather of the office and the bureaucracy. While he viewed this as a flaw, turning knowledge about GMOs into the outcome of a bureaucratic procedure facilitates the regulatory process. As this chapter will show, it strictly delimits the kinds of data that can be used and ensures that the state is the only authoritative source of knowledge.

While the office is central, the decisions made there are not divorced from lab research. Samples from around the country are sent to INE's lab, where scientists carry out monitoring processes, interpreting and classifying plant life by making visible the signifying properties of plants themselves through genetic analysis.[18] Plant identity is reduced to the molecular scale and to data that can be translated into documents and forms legible in the office.[19] While consumers and others have relationships with maize based on characteristics like taste and appearance, qualities that are connected to subjective, emotional, and personal experiences and history with plants, there is no space for these in the regulatory apparatus. With the emergence of biosecurity discourse, plants are increasingly understood in molecular and bureaucratic terms. This understanding serves as a gatekeeping mechanism, restricting who can make authoritative statements and turning government scientists (rather than farmers, academics, or others) into key figures shaping the nation's plant life. To understand these processes, I will briefly discuss how biodiversity has been treated as national patrimony, the history of GM crops and their use in Mexico, and then return to the office and lab at INE to show how GMOs are made legible.

HISTORIES AND MEMORIES OF MEXICAN PLANT LIFE

The Mexican government prides itself on the country's status as a megadiverse place, one of the twelve countries with the highest richness and variety of biological diversity, and the center of origin for a variety of crops.[20] INE in its official publications connects biological diversity with Mexico's cultural diversity: one supports the other, as Mexico's large indigenous population connects with the environment through its "diverse traditional uses and strong connections to the biodiversity around them."[21] People often link human and plant life in debates over plants as patrimony and as a unique national resource, and express concern over the preservation of *razas de maiz*, or races of maize.[22] Maize in particular has been a longstanding symbol of Mexicanness, transforming from a symbol primarily associated with indigenous populations to one associated with the idea of a unified mestizo nation in the mid-twentieth century.[23] While maize is central, Mexico's importance in cultivating and trading plants extends to a variety of other crops including beans, lima beans, squash, chili, potatoes, avocadoes, cacao, papayas, guava, sapodilla, annonas, cotton, sisal, chayote, sunflowers, and vanilla. Biologist and expert in the origin and evolution of maize Garrison Wilkes marvels at the human contribution to the evolutionary history and development of a wide variety of crops in Mexico, noting that they are "the product of 8,000 years of accumulated mutational events evolved by recombination and inbreeding in geographic isolation into more productive genetic systems selected under domestication by the indigenous people in the varied habitats of Mexico."[24] Domesticated plants and their varieties are deeply shaped by and shape human life.

Plants were identified as national patrimony (that is, belonging to all the nation, rather than to particular indigenous groups) during the period of pharmaceutical nationalism in the 1970s, and again during debates over contemporary bioprospecting. Cori Hayden has demonstrated how plant research in Mexico was part of ongoing nationalist projects that sought to turn traditional knowledge and indigenous materials into national resources. As she points out, the use of traditional knowledge about plants to produce modern pharmaceuticals has been a nation-building enterprise, from the first efforts to develop a Mexican pharmaceutical industry during Porfirio Díaz's presidency to contemporary efforts to produce internationally competitive Mexican pharmaceutical enterprises.[25] Use and exploitation of these plant resources produced structural changes in political, economic, and social life.[26]

Practices to protect plant population diversity existed before biosecurity discourse. Between 1920 and 1930, Russian biologist Nikolai Vavilov, working for the Institute of Plant Industry in Leningrad, catalogued extensive collections of corn from the New World and determined that Mexico was the world's center of corn diversity.[27] In early 1951, the National Research Council and the Rockefeller Foundation established a Committee on the Preservation of Indigenous Strains of Maize, sounding an early alarm about threats to maize diversity in Mexico. The committee reported, "There are countless strains of maize which are in danger of dying out because of the inroads of corn introduced from the outside. Reliable reports indicate that, if nothing is done to preserve these strains, some of which represent the product of thousands of years of domestication, a very large proportion of them will be extinct within from one to three decades. This would be a major disaster."[28] Maize was and is a staple of Mexican cuisine and the primary ingredient in the ubiquitous tortillas sold from kiosks throughout the country and served with every meal. The Rockefeller Foundation argued that the loss of Mexican corn diversity threatened both food supplies in Latin America and corn improvement programs in the United States; to protect the diversity of maize, they developed a program to save samples of seeds from all the landraces of corn in Latin America in four "germplasm banks."[29] The problems confronted by the Rockefeller Foundation and the solutions they found for them have commonalities with contemporary biosecurity.

The importance of tortillas and maize more generally were evident in the 2011 presidential campaign. Enrique Peña Nieto, the candidate of the Partido Revolucionario Institucional (PRI) and the frontrunner in the election, briefly became the butt of jokes when the Spanish newspaper El País asked him the price of a kilo of tortillas. Peña Nieto responded that he did not know how much a kilo of tortillas cost, nor should he, since, as he pointed out, "I'm not a housewife." His comments were widely publicized, and he eventually took to Twitter to try to reframe them, stating in a series of tweets, "I regret and am surprised by the reaction to a comment I made in the interview with El País. I said, 'I am not a housewife,' referring exclusively to my home, not as a disrespectful or offensive statement on women. In consequence, I am sorry that this expression has been misinterpreted in order to discredit my appreciation, respect, and admiration for women."[30] Even though Peña Nieto's remarks and his ignorance of the price of tortillas made him seem both disrespectful of women and out of touch with the concerns of ordinary

Mexicans, he ultimately won the election to succeed Calderón as president and took office in 2012.

People are particular about the taste of tortillas. I joined a friend and his family on an excursion to Tepoztlán, a small village in the mountains of the state of Morelos, where we bought handmade tortillas from a vendor on the side of the road. We ate them with just a sprinkling of salt while walking around town. When I enthused about how delicious they were, my friend's wife commented that while they were good, tortillas in Mexico used to be much better. To her taste, corn in Mexico was different now, and the tortillas were not the same as she remembered from her childhood. Her comments came back to me when I interviewed Jorge Larson, a biologist at CONABIO who was involved in maize biosecurity projects. I met with Larson at his office down the street from INE. The director of a project to plan how Mexico could best make use of its biodiversity, he was in charge of a number of employees. As we walked to his office he greeted people, responded to questions, and gave instructions for how to proceed with various projects. As the interview began, he appeared distracted, shuffling papers on his desk and checking his email while answering questions. However, once my questions turned to the status of maize and other plants in Mexico, he became engaged and attentive.

Larson was optimistic that a neoliberal, market-based solution would protect Mexico's diversity of maize crops. Educated consumers like my friend's wife were crucial to this plan. "In Mexico we still have one generation of nostalgia markets. One remembers. And there is a generation right now that still remembers. My grandfather used to drink that. I ate this with my grandmother. So, there's a market there," he said. People's recollection of and attachment to food traditions would ensure that farmers would continue to grow traditional crop varieties. However, he was concerned about whether these consumer memories and desires were being properly channeled, asking, "How does this eventually connect with biosafety and how is biosafety implemented by government or visualized by academia in Mexico? I don't think such a vision exists in terms of the integrity of biological and cultural landscapes." Consumers' desires for corn tortillas that tasted the way they remembered needed to be translated into terms that would be visible to government risk assessment processes in order to have an impact on the agricultural system and the ecosystem more broadly.

Larson argued that without first producing enough corn for everyone to eat, "you don't have the conditions for legitimate biosafety. Because first you have to build, you have to rebuild basic corn self-sufficiency, from the household, to the region, to the country. And then we can discuss GMOs. You see what I mean?" He used biosecurity to refer to both the human population's ability to survive at a most basic level and the survival of nonhuman populations and biodiversity. This is in line with long-standing concerns within the government about levels of food production and the country's lack of self-sufficiency in growing maize for food.

Arturo Warman, an anthropologist who was director of the Instituto Nacional Indigenista (INI, or the National Institute for Indigenous People) and then of the Secretaría de la Reforma Agraria (Department of Agrarian Reform) in the 1990s, supervised a report that exemplified the government's sense of maize production as a problem. Written in the 1980s, *El Cultivo de Maíz en México* reported that "insufficient production of maize has been a chronic phenomenon in Mexico's recent history." Maize is both symbolically and practically important, as the fundamental component of the majority of the population's diet. "In almost all of Mexico, the existence of maize is the hedge against hunger," and its production and consumption influence economics, domestic work, family structure, exchange, and the spatial organization of the country.[31]

MAKING TRANSGENIC CORN

In 1998, Mexico identified genetically modified strains of corn produced by agritech companies as a threat to the genetic diversity of Mexican corn and temporarily banned planting transgenic corn. Genetically modified organisms are organisms whose genetic material has been changed using genetic engineering techniques. Modifying genetic material became possible in the 1970s with the development of recombinant DNA (rDNA) technology. Biologists at Stanford developed a technique to disassemble DNA molecules, isolate individual genes and insert them into plasmids, and move these genes between bacterial strains.[32] By the 1980s, molecular biologists had sufficiently developed rDNA techniques to enable them to move genes not only between bacterial strains but between organisms in different kingdoms, making it possible to manipulate the genetic material of plants and animals.[33] The first genetically modified crop was introduced in 1988 when China developed a variety of tobacco resistant to tobacco mosaic virus. In the following decade a variety of new crops were introduced, most famously the FlavrSavr tomato, a tomato developed by the biotech startup Calgene that, thanks to a change in its DNA that inhibited the production of a particular protein, rotted more slowly and was easier to transport.[34] After the FlavrSavr came crops that were modified to be resistant to herbicides and various insect pests. According to the Food and Agriculture Organization of the United Nations, there are approximately one hundred million hectares of genetically modified crops being grown worldwide, primarily soybean, maize, canola, and cotton.[35]

GMOs have variously been interpreted as potentially lifesaving or as catastrophically destructive, as proponents argue that vitamin-enhanced plants will save lives, while opponents claim they will damage farmer sovereignty and the environment more generally. Corporations producing GM crops often cite the long history of human modification of plant life, positioning GMOs as merely an extension of or equivalent to the process of domestication. Opponents, on the other hand, view them as a radical break, not only in the novel scientific procedures deployed, but also in the new forms of intellectual property and commodification of life that result. Their critiques focus on the way these concentrate power, money, and intellectual property rights in the hands of multinational corporations.[36] Debates over GM crops can also be debates over sovereignty, as anti-GM activists have characterized them as foreign threats to national or local sovereignty. Activists in Costa Rica successfully advocated for the construction of "transgenic free zones" on the grounds that GMs were contaminating life-forms threatening the pure nature of the nation, violating its borders and the integrity of biological life within them.[37]

The 1998 ban on transgenic maize was the government's response to widespread fears of contamination or destruction of a crop that was both an essential food item and a symbol of the nation. The ban was lifted in 2009, when a new law was enacted requiring individuals or corporations to apply for a permit in order to legally experiment with or grow genetically modified organisms. Titled the Ley de Bioseguridad de Organismos Genéticamente Modificados (the Law on the Biosecurity of Genetically Modified Organisms), this law established the permitting process for GMOs. The growing use of GM corn is part of what Elizabeth Fitting terms the "neoliberal corn regime," which advances capital-intensive agriculture and the production of corn for export.[38] This regime focuses on exporting corn despite the fact that Mexico does not produce enough corn for its own use and has to import corn for domestic consumption from the United States. It is in this process that INE and the Biosecurity Department are most involved in the bureaucracy surrounding GMOs (and the moment in which the state intervenes most aggressively in the use of GMOs).

NATURE ON PAPER

The Departamento de Bioseguridad was housed in a small office crowded with five desks and computers. In addition to Federico and Carlos, the department's two administrative assistants, Alicia and Teresa, worked out of the cramped office, which was also equipped with a couple of filing cabinets and two bookshelves crammed with binders of files on various crops, herbicides, permit applications, scientific publications, and other paperwork. On the walls were maps marking the national territory, making visible the space the department sought to secure, as well as maps showing the use of GMOs around the globe, indicating the global presences of these organisms. A nearby whiteboard was covered with scribbled notes outlining plans for the future and reminders of ongoing tasks. In one corner of the office was a pile of tangled metal equipment—currently unused pollen collectors that were waiting to be deployed in a future ecosystem-monitoring project, hinting at the field and lab processes that supported the regulatory work of the office.

Federico and Carlos insisted that following the applications for permits was essential to understanding the use of GMOs in Mexico. They argued that rather than the assays being run in INE's lab across town or the fieldwork they occasionally conducted, the center of action was with the documents in their office. Reviewing documents was their primary responsibility, and it was through various documents that they assessed the risks of proposed activities and made judgments about potential ecological effects and necessary biosecurity measures. The importance of documents and documentation for making nature legible became apparent soon after I began my participant observation in the Departamento de Bioseguridad, when Federico, Carlos, and Yolanda, the director of the Biosecurity Department and Federico and Carlos's boss, all sent me documents to review—a copy of the Cartagena Protocol on Biosafety (an annex to the UN Convention on Biological Diversity that addresses the management of GMOs), recent permit applications, and risk assessments that they had written in response to permit applications. Yolanda sent all of us a copy from INE's equivalent in Spain so that we could "see that our [Mexican] reports are better constructed and justified." Comparing documents from other countries was a way to establish Mexico's relative competence at managing the use of GMOs.

Yolanda had a private office located down the hallway from the rest of the department. She is an energetic and fast-moving biologist, with undergraduate and doctoral degrees from UNAM, where she focused on plant ecology. While pursuing her doctoral degree, she found herself stymied by the lack of laboratory facilities. Unable to complete her research in molecular biology in Mexico, she won a scholarship that allowed her to finish her lab work in the United States, where she went on to do a postdoc that entailed fieldwork in Africa and coordinating laboratory research in the North America and Europe. When she returned to Mexico, she took a temporary position working with the INE. Finding the work engaging, she stayed on as director of the Departamento de Bioseguridad, where she focused on assessing the risk of genetically modified organisms, meeting with representatives of companies, scientists, farmers, and other government officials, as well as supervising the work of Federico and Carlos and the functioning of the department's laboratory.

Since the implementation of the Law on the Biosecurity of Genetically Modified Organisms, in order to legally experiment with or grow genetically modified organisms in Mexico, individuals or organizations must apply for and receive a permit. The vast majority of applications are submitted by major agritech companies. In 2011, Syngenta, Bayer, Pioneer, Monsanto, and Dow Agro-Sciences, all major multinational corporations, submitted applications. The only non-profit to submit an application that year was the Centro Internacional de Mejoramiento de Maíz y Trigo (the International Maize and Wheat Improvement Center). In 2011, the Mexican government granted new permits for the use of genetically modified cotton, maize, soy, and wheat. Of these, the most commonly grown GM crops were cotton and soy.[39]

The process of granting a permit incorporates many government agencies, hinting at the many constituencies concerned about GMOs. Permits are granted by SAGARPA, the Ministry of Agriculture, Livestock, Rural Development, Fisheries, and Food, which is also principally responsible for monitoring the use of GMOs after the permits are granted. While SAGARPA has the final authority over whether permits are authorized, a variety of other agencies also give opinions and recommendations. The Biosecurity Department at INE is among these agencies, as are CONABIO (the National Commission for Biodiversity) and COFEPRIS (the Federal Commission for Protection against Health Risks).

Each of these organizations is intended to represent the interests of a slightly different constituency—the Departamento de Bioseguridad at INE is concerned with protecting the ecology and biodiversity of Mexico and assessing the risks that releases of different GMOs pose to the ecosystem. That the state is not a monolithic entity is abundantly clear in the permitting process, which vividly illustrates Andrew Mathews's description of the Mexican state as "a shifting group of loosely connected institutions that are unstable and often in conflict with one another."[40] The institutions involved in permitting frequently disagree, although their debates and differences are made invisible once a permit, which contains no record of dissenting voices, is issued. These conflicting agencies are governing a country with diverse responses to GMOs, which present different biosecurity issues in different parts of the country. A law student studying GMO issues described to me the Mennonite communities in the north of Mexico. With a mixture of admiration and chagrin, she said, "They're very hard-working people. They make the desert grow, but they don't pay attention to laws." Members of these Mennonite communities often had relatives in Texas, and might acquire seeds from them, with no regard to whether they were genetically modified or not. Unlike in Oaxaca where, she said, "people ask, 'where is the GMO field so we can burn it?,'" in northern states like Chihuahua, they needed to explain to people that GMOs could not be planted without permits. This distinction in attitudes and use of GMOs in the north and the south was reiterated to me by many people, reinforcing the notion that the disparate assortment of conflicting institutions that constitute the state are engaged in governing an extremely heterogeneous territory, and demonstrate the ways that GMO practices are used to create and demarcate territorial and cultural differences.

The risks with which INE is most concerned are those related to biodiversity—namely, the possibility of gene flow between GMOs and their wild and domesticated relatives, the potential of GMOs to escape the area where they are being cultivated and become weeds, and possible impacts on unrelated organisms. The department reviews applications, recommends biosafety measures to protect biodiversity, and also does some of its own monitoring to ensure that these measures are effective in limiting the effect of GMOs on the broader ecosystem. The division of labor and areas of concern among agencies delimits what INE pays attention to. Effects on human health are outside their purview, as are effects on agriculture as a whole. The sole concern of INE is whether the use of this biotechnology will affect Mexico's wild plants and animals. Carlos and Federico both seemed to regard their efforts as a necessary if somewhat futile battle to create space for the coexistence of agriculture and other kinds of life-forms. This was something that the bureaucrats at SAGARPA, who were primarily concerned with controlling pests and increasing production, were not interested in. One scientist at the Department of Biosecurity described SAGARPA to me as very much in favor of GMOs, an organization with only one object in mind: "produce, produce, produce."

CASE-BY-CASE, STEP-BY-STEP

Yolanda viewed her role at INE as overseeing the implementation of the Cartagena Protocol, noting that "case-by-case and step-by-step is the religion of the Cartagena Protocol," and making this her mantra for the department. The Cartagena Protocol is an international agreement intended to protect biodiversity against possible risks posed by genetically modified organisms. It went into effect in 2003.[41] Case-by-case means the individual evaluation of GMOs, supported by the available scientific and technical data, taking into account the organism that is being modified, the characteristics of the modification, the history of use of the organism, the area where it is being released, and the benefits compared with alternate technologies. Step-by-step indicates that the department should conduct risk assessments of all GMOs intended to be released and report the results of experimental and pilot releases.

To do this case-by-case analysis, Federico and Carlos used an online program called Análisis de Riesgos para la Liberación de Organismos Genéticamente Modificados en el Medio Ambiente (Risk Analysis for the Release of Genetically Modified Organisms in the Environment, or AROMMA). According to Federico, "It's your guide so that you can make decisions. The decision tree. It's a manual, a document that helps you decide on the level of risk, which you put together with the information that the business or institute gives you. And the bibliographic information or information from earlier monitoring." It is a technologically simple, primarily text-based program that asks the analyst to respond to a series of questions, beginning, for example, with a straightforward question about how widespread the release will be. Will the GMO be used in a confined area, or released into the wider environment? While AROMMA was designed specifically for the Biosecurity Department's use, it is also available online to anyone who is interested, a gesture towards transparency and the idea of bureaucratic objectivity—that anyone inputting data into the program should come to the same conclusions. Federico and Carlos guided me through these documents and computer programs as a way to understand their work, training me to interpret the permit applications and the process through which they were accepted or rejected. As they trained me to use AROMMA, it became apparent that despite the hoped-for objectivity, using the program and interpreting the applications required professional expertise and judgment.

In the process of assessing a permit application, Federico and Carlos had to make determinations about what information or data was legitimate. These judgments reflected their framing of expertise and what counted as reliable knowledge. For example, Federico specified for me what constituted a legitimate source when he was forming his technical opinion. He would only consider data generated in official monitoring processes or published in scientific journals to be relevant. He noted, "I don't think that it's valid to put in a technical opinion with informal information," dismissing unpublished reports from campesinos, or even monitoring done by scientists not affiliated with the government. On the other hand, he did not view all scientific publications in the same light, telling me that he had to be very careful about which publications he cited. While he did not necessarily have to read the entire publication, if he was going to cite something to support a decision, he needed to read the title, the abstract, and, perhaps most crucially, where the authors came from. Not all authors were equally credible for the purposes of producing data that could be used in the permitting process. "Imagine if we cited something from Monsanto," he asked me, indicating that such a citation would be seen by anti-GMO activists as an indication that the entire risk assessment process was flawed and dictated by multinational corporations.

Carlos and I reviewed an application from Dow AgroSciences for permission to do an experimental planting of GM maize in two states, Coahuila and Durango, both in northern Mexico. In their permit application, Dow AgroSciences attempted to present authoritative knowledge about first, the organism they sought to plant, and second, the environment in which they would plant it. The application was for an experimental planting of maize HX1. As the application described, maize HX1 is characterized by the insertion of two genes derived from bacteria that confer resistance to insects and herbicides.[42] Carlos used the AROMMA program to make expert judgments about the risk of releasing this organism. As in a choose-your-own-adventure text or game, the risk analyst selected one or the other option based on the information provided within the application. Each response led to different questions and different analysis modules. AROMMA, with its prespecified questions and answers, elicited particular kinds of responses and channeled the analyst's assessment.

The permit application submitted by DowAgrosciences provided specific details about the plant (maize HX1), particularly what new proteins would be expressed, the effects of these proteins on susceptible insects, how the new genes were inserted, the number of copies of each gene that had been inserted, and how to detect the presence of the GMO in the field and the laboratory. The application also enumerated the potential health effects of this variety of GM maize for humans, assuring the reader that the allergenicity of the maize was very low.[43] The detailed reports on testing for human health indicated the multiple audiences for the permit application—while a reviewer from the Department of Health would be quite concerned about potential effects on humans, at INE human health was not a major concern. Federico and Carlos were instead concerned with adverse effects on biodiversity. While their goal was to identify risks and possible adverse effects, Yolanda pointed out that this was not straightforward. She asked, "What is adverse? And for whom? Who establishes what is adverse? Often it's politicians. Often it's not you, the scientist, who says what is adverse." In general, though, the department wanted to know how the proposed planting could affect the growth of invasive species, change populations of nontarget organisms, transform soil bacteria, or spread beyond the initial area of cultivation. They used AROMMA to move step-by-step through potential consequences or adverse effects.

For Federico and Carlos, the sections of the applications that referred to the environment in which the GMO would be used were the most important. Here, Dow AgroSciences provided general information on the climate, type of soil, hydrologic characteristics, and land use of the states in which it would cultivate the maize. It provided very extensive, but generic, information about the entire state even though the planting would only be in a limited area. Here, play with scale was important. Providing a large quantity of data at the scale of the state could obscure the absence of the specific data at the scale of the farm or field that would have been more relevant. Scaling the information provided was a way of complying with the demands of the application while not providing the most significant data. While biodiversity science is noteworthy for the quantity of information and classifications generated,[44] the attention to the biodiversity of the environment in which the maize would be planted was extremely cursory. The kind of information available was very important: it circumscribed what the federal government could consider as at risk or threatened by the transformations in the agricultural system.

Elements of ecosystems were legible to the government once they were included in inventories, registries, or databases of organisms that established the baseline for biodiversity in an area. Organisms needed to be made visible in the office in order to be protected; the things that do not get classified are not considered important. If these applications are performative, as Geoffrey Bowker argues that biodiversity databases are, and conservation and biosecurity efforts only protect those things that have been counted and classified, the lack of information puts the ecosystem in which the GMOs are being cultivated at risk.[45] Yolanda told me that "to say that we're going to protect biodiversity is to say nothing. You have to be more specific, to say what you're going to protect." However, this is particularly complicated in a country like Mexico, which has a high level of biodiversity. This biodiversity is not always well characterized—for example, few biologists study insect life in agricultural areas, and farmers view insects as merely pests. As a result, inventory on insect life is quite incomplete. In addition, as a center of origin for a variety of crops, there are also more wild relatives of organisms like maize, which would facilitate gene flow from GMOs into the ecosystem at large. Risk assessment is more complicated, and scientists at INE acknowledged that their information was limited.

The very brief description of the effect of GMOs on nontarget organisms included in the application from Dow AgroSciences did not provide any specific details about the kinds of organisms that live in Coahuila or Durango, only that there are no endangered species and that, as the application points out, "intensive agriculture has generally been an activity that has diminished biodiversity. Overall, with greater intensification of agricultural practices, the greater the reductions in biodiversity in these ecosystems." Carlos and Federico concurred that agriculture in general, regardless of whether GMOs are used or not, is bad for biodiversity. Even before the advent of GMOs, the Green Revolution had had a significant impact on the landscape. They noted that far more important than the use of GMOs in terms of biodiversity was the kind of agricultural system in place. Large farms that grow a single crop using heavy machinery and herbicides have a negative effect on biodiversity, while traditional milpa systems, in which a variety of crops are grown together and tended by hand, are less destructive. However, although applications for projects that would use GMOs in industrial monocrop systems would inevitably be detrimental for biodiversity, the particular agricultural practices being proposed were regarded as beyond critique.

In this example, as in others, businesses submitting applications were cannily attentive to the fact that biodiversity around agricultural areas was generally diminished. Turning to a definition which restricted "nature" to pristine areas, these applications drew attention to the ways in which human activities had shaped the environment around farms. They treated agriculture and human activity of all types as inevitably destructive of biodiversity and implied that nature, in order to be worth protecting, must be pristine and unaffected by human activity. This perspective fails to take into account the way the milpa and other agricultural systems in Mexico have substantially *contributed* to the genetic diversity of maize by producing a wide variety of landraces and the significantly different impacts agricultural systems can have on biodiversity. Deploying a Euro-American conception of the divide between nature and culture, the permit application essentially argued that human activity in Coahuila and Durango had already ruined "nature" in those states, meaning that there was no longer any need to worry about biosecurity. Carlos described the thinking of big businesses with an analogy: "You already have lung cancer, what does it matter if you breathe polluted air?" Despite the frequent dismissals of the value of ecosystems around farms, Carlos and Federico strove to make visible why the release of GMOs mattered and to articulate the importance of plants and animals living in environments that were obviously shaped by human activities. They sought to make biodiversity and GMOs legible in the paper world of bureaucracy and permitting. As they reviewed applications, they kept in mind potential effects GMOs might have on nontarget organisms, attending to the maintenance of biodiversity even in environments radically shaped by agriculture. For them, biodiversity counted even if it was not in a place that could by any stretch be considered untouched or pristine "nature."

MAKING RISK VISIBLE

A meeting with a group of Colombian scientists who had traveled to Mexico to learn how INE processed permits and monitored GMOs revealed the work that went into making risk visible. We met in the institute's reading room, a wood-paneled library filled with a variety of books and pamphlets. Sitting around a long green table, the five Colombian scientists introduced themselves and their primary research projects. They were all biologists, working at a variety of laboratories and institutions in Colombia. One of their major questions was how to translate the Cartagena Protocol and its mandate to monitor GMOs and protect biological diversity within national territories. They were concerned with how to translate the protocol into a workable bureaucracy. While the meeting began with a presentation by Yolanda about her experiences analyzing and monitoring the risks of GMOs, it quickly turned into an opportunity for the participants to trade war stories and to vent about the difficulties they encountered in their work. One Colombian scientist complained: "They want to monitor everything in Colombia. It's not possible." The expansive vision of a system monitoring the genetics of an entire country's ecosystem was a fantasy that the scientists could not accomplish. Scientists had to make choices about which elements of the ecosystem would be monitored as they made GMOs and ecosystems into objects of governance.

Yolanda agreed that it was difficult, contrasting the case in Mexico with places like England. "In a country with few resources and high biodiversity, it is difficult. It's not like England, where they have three butterflies." While in England there is very little biodiversity to protect, in Mexico there are significantly more potential interactions between GMOs and other organisms. Yolanda described how her department had solved this difficult problem—it was *not* by monitoring everything. Instead, she explained how the risk assessment process in Mexico had turned GMOs and the environment into bureaucratic objects, deliberately limiting the scope of the government's assessment of the potential effects and what needed to be monitored. Watching Yolanda explain to the Colombians how to do a risk analysis made clear how the bureaucratic process has made some risks visible while excluding others from consideration. The first step in a risk analysis is to describe each possible adverse effect—for example, if the DNA that has been modified produces a protein, whether this protein might be allergenic for certain populations. Yolanda pointed out that in INE's portion of the risk assessment, they were only interested in the ways that GMOs affected biodiversity. Other changes were not considered important or incorporated into the risk assessment.

She elaborated further. One of the tasks of conducting a risk assessment is establishing what unintended effects the new organism might have on other desirable organisms. "Desirable" becomes a key concept in restricting what needs to be considered. Yolanda complained that it is not easy to establish what organisms are desirable, highlighting the flexibility of the term. For example, she said, "Someone who is a conservationist or environmentalist might say *all of them*. All are desirable . . . Here in Mexico, the monarch butterfly is very important. It arrives in Mexico on the Day of the Dead, and it's like a symbol of the souls of the dead. Culturally they're important, but ecologically they're not. The animals that eat them could eat other things. They don't have an ecologically important role." Here she distinguished between desirability and symbolic significance to humans and significance within an ecosystem. The cultural significance of the monarch was outside the purview of INE; its desirability as an element of Mexican culture was not something they could consider. Federico described their risk assessment process in similar terms. "It's like the Cartagena Protocol says—case by case: What are you going to liberate? Where are you going to do it? What modifications did you make? What did you do? Then it's case by case. We take many things into account in that sense, but only in biological terms. We don't take into account the cultural." Even as they acknowledged the myriad ways in which culture and biodiversity are intertwined, they refused to encompass cultural questions within their process.

The division Yolanda articulated between ecologically significant and insignificant plants and animals was a curious one, in which the value of an organism to human groups was irrelevant, and the only thing that INE could take into account was an organism's place in the nonhuman world. Even given this strictly limited understanding of what constitutes a risk and what needs to be protected, it still takes substantial work to make these risks visible within INE's bureaucracy. Understanding an organism's actual or potential effect on biodiversity requires that the material substance of an ecosystem be transformed into documentation that will be accepted in the office. Across the city, in INE's laboratory space, scientists and technicians work to do that and to make plant life visible by monitoring local biology.

PRODUCING AUTHORITATIVE KNOWLEDGE

Monitoring GMOs proved to be complex. The effectiveness of Mexico's ban on transgenic maize had been called into question in 2002, when Ignacio Chapela and

David Quist, biologists from the University of California, Berkeley, reported that transgenic corn genes could be found in remote areas of Oaxaca far from the areas where GMOs were permitted. Chapela and Quist described this finding as both tragic and potentially dangerous, arguing that the genetic diversity of maize in Mexico was not only a national resource, but also essential to the security of the global food supply.[46] In the aftermath of this report, INE sought to test Chapela and Quist's claim. To produce its official accounts of Mexican ecosystems, the Departamento de Bioseguridad collected its own maize samples from Oaxaca, sending them out to two laboratories for testing. After long delays, the labs returned conflicting results about the presence of transgenic material.[47] Responding to these inconsistent results from local laboratories, INE constructed its own monitoring lab in Mexico City, funded by the UN and the federal government and accredited by the Entidad Mexicana de Acreditación (EMA, or the Mexican Accreditation Agency).[48] Accreditation became a key tool in asserting the power to produce authoritative knowledge and to reject other forms of knowledge. Without the official documentation and specific procedures required to receive accreditation, no findings on GMOs would be accepted as valid.

In addition, the Departamento de Bioseguridad developed the Red Nacional de Laboratorios de Detección de OGMs (the National Network of GMO Detection Laboratories) with the goal of establishing a group of labs that were competent to monitor the nation's biology and would provide consistent results from one laboratory to the next. Alongside the national network of labs, INE recruited NGOs, companies, researchers, and other individuals from across the country to join the Red Nacional de Monitoreo de OGMs (the National GMO Monitoring Network). These groups would assist with reporting and monitoring the environmental effects of GMOs. As with the Red Nacional de Laboratorios de Detección de OGMs, INE coordinates the efforts of this network in order to establish consistent monitoring procedures, particularly the collection of plant samples from the ecosystem and the use of PCR analysis to establish whether genes from GMOs have transferred from the approved release area to the ecosystem at large.

INE's need to prove to itself the veracity of Chapela and Quist's report was indicative of the challenges in converting plant life from a material substance into a discursive form that is legible and acceptable within the bureaucracy governing genetically modified organisms. In the following section, I describe how plants are transformed from living organisms into acceptable documents and who is allowed to make these representations. Analyzing this process, with its exclusions and erasures, shows how the functioning of the regulatory system relies on the production of ignorance and silence.[49] Rejecting reports produced by others is a way to assert that only the bureaucracy is able to produce universal knowledge and, as Mathews puts it, "imprison their audiences in a slot of local knowledge."[50] By strictly delimiting the kinds of labs that are capable of producing universal knowledge about agriculture and ecosystems in Mexico, the bureaucracy conceals alternate forms of knowledge, including those in peer-reviewed scientific journals.

The lab for the INE Departamento de Bioseguridad is on the campus of the Universidad Autónoma Metropolitana Unidad Iztapalapa (UAM Iztapalapa), in a southeastern borough of Mexico City. The streets around the campus are lined with single-story homes and tiny stores selling an array of groceries and clothing. The crowds of vendors hawk all kinds of food to passing students, and the unattached dogs roaming the streets all contribute to the neighborhood's generally chaotic and unkempt air. Iztapalapa urbanized relatively recently: in the 1970s it was still a predominantly rural area. However, since then it has become Mexico City's most populous borough, as well as the one with the highest crime rate.[51] The campus of UAM Iztapalapa is dominated by massive concrete buildings of a style that reflects its founding in the 1970s. The primary impression they give is of stolidity and prac-ticality. While many of the structures are worn and a bit run-down, the lab is located in one of the nicer buildings, a more recent construction with a glass atrium. Its appearance gives the impression of institutional investment and care.

The Departamento de Bioseguridad's lab was located past a seemingly indiffer-ent security guard, who waved me in without checking identification or confirm-ing that I was expected in the lab. When I entered the lab, I was greeted by Laura, the scientist who was in charge of day-to-day operations. Laura told me that she was somewhat surprised to find herself running a lab, her days dominated by paperwork. As a student, she had envisioned herself working outdoors, wearing boots and getting muddy doing fieldwork. While doing her PhD, she studied both ecology and molecular biology. As she was completing her degree, INE happened to be looking for someone to manage the new lab, a position that required exper-tise in both ecology and molecular biology. She chose to take the job rather than pursue a postdoc, and considered herself very lucky to have found work so quickly. She spent her first year essentially alone in the lab, purchasing equipment, estab-lishing and validating lab techniques, setting up quality control systems, and writing standard operating procedures—everything necessary to get the lab run-ning and accredited. Turning GMOs in the field into results that mattered in the office across town was complicated. Laura explained to me that the challenge in monitoring for GMOs is not with the technical procedures, but with the laws. She noted, "As a scientist, if you see the [PCR] gels, you can be satisfied. In the technical part, we have advanced very well." Legal validity, on the other hand, is more difficult to achieve. Her first year was dominated by paperwork and prepara-tion, all in order to make the results produced by the lab authoritative and univer-sal (see figure 11).

When she started, she didn't know of any other labs or people in Mexico doing this kind of detection work. At the beginning, while she was setting up the lab, she had no access to the DNA sequences used in genetically modified crops, which

FIGURE 11. Processing samples in the Departamento de Bioseguridad's laboratory. Source: Author photograph.

made her task of detecting them very difficult. Foreign collaboration was essential, primarily with US businesses that did detection work. For example, Genetic ID, an American company that touts itself as "the world's expert in GMO testing services,"[52] was an important ally, sending kits and material. The INE lab also collaborated with research centers in the European Union that had validated materials and methods available. Since then, Mexico has mandated that companies using GMOs provide reference material and methods of detection, which has made Laura's work simpler.

LABORATORY PROCESSES

Now that the lab was established, it received samples of crops from around the country, including many from the Sierra de Juárez region of Oaxaca, where Quist and Chapela had first reported GMO contamination. Samples might come from a monitoring program, or as a result of reports of the unauthorized use of GMOs. INE's monitoring focuses primarily on places of high biodiversity, or where there have been reports of GMOs being used. Monitoring was begun as a way to develop a baseline understanding of what was happening across the country. Ten states were chosen as places to monitor, a mix of centers of origin like Oaxaca and Puebla, places where a large quantity of maize was imported like Veracruz, and places close to the United States like Tamaulipas. While general environmental monitoring rarely returned positive results, tests directed at areas where people had reported GMO plantings were more often positive. For example, SAGARPA had received an anonymous denunciation that accused a group of Mennonites in Chihuahua of planting GM crops. SAGARPA's initial field tests supported the accusation, and INE's lab tests of the samples further confirmed that the crops were genetically modified. In addition, the lab had received reports of cases in which GMOs were unintentionally released; by way of example, Carolina showed me a picture of an accident in which a train transporting maize intended for consumption had spilled its cargo. Despite efforts to contain and clean up the seeds, some inevitably remained.

While most of the samples are maize, they also receive and test cotton, soy, rice, and alfalfa, looking for potential GMO contamination in all of them. The lab tests a variable number of samples each year, from two hundred to eight hundred, enough to keep two full-time lab technicians and two additional independent contractors busy, but still representing a minuscule proportion of the 20.6 million hectares of cultivated land in Mexico.[53] The institute has funding that supported the costs of monitoring and detection work, and in addition the lab occasionally tested samples for other institutes, usually in exchange for donations of supplies or equipment. Carolina, one of the full-time technicians, showed me around the lab and explained the testing process. Carolina had been there for about a year, which made her a veteran in the lab. She noted that the lab experienced a high degree of turnover. While Laura, the head of the lab, had been there since the beginning, she was unusual. The independent contractor positions were not permanent and provided little job security, so people tended to move on. The transitory nature of the workforce meant that the documentation and standardization of practices were all the more important as a way of producing institutional memory (see figure 12).

Carolina showed me around the lab and explained its procedures to me. There were a number of field tests that INE used to detect genetically modified organisms. First and most immediately, maize or other plants could be tested through an application of herbicide. If the plants died, they were not genetically modified. There were also test strips that could be used in the field to indicate the presence of GMOs. To use them, technicians ground the samples of maize in a cold buffer solution. They then dipped the strips in the buffer. If the protein they were looking for was present, a line would appear on the strip. Carolina laughed as she described them to me: "They're like a pregnancy test!" The strips were often used in the field for a quick answer, but they were not regarded as trustworthy, and the results always needed to be validated in the lab.

While the presence of GMOs might be revealed by simply spraying the suspected crops with herbicide, the work of the lab was to extract signs or

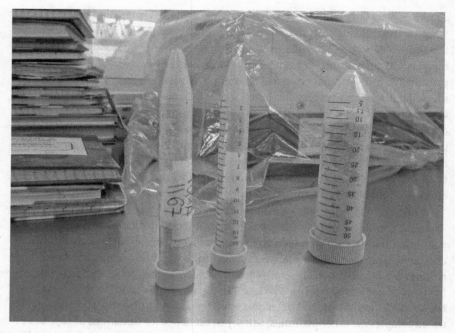

FIGURE 12. Samples being processed in the laboratory. Source: Author photograph.

representations from the material of plant life. Carolina explained that there were three stages to lab work: detection, identification, and quantification. The treatment of samples was made as regular and routine as possible. Once the lab received a sample, which might be in the form of seeds or leaves, the technicians documented its arrival in their database and gave it a number. They then inspected it to make sure that it was clean and pest-free, and that it had not degraded while being shipped. Part of this inspection was also a qualitative assessment of the physical characteristics of the maize or other crop. There are a huge variety of maize types, particularly in Mexico, and each has a different color, shape, and hardness. While handling and treating the samples, they worked carefully to keep them pristine, cleaning everything with water and Clorox to prevent contamination. When they processed the sample, it was identified only by number. Carolina observed that the technicians had emotional responses and feelings about different regions of the country. The states of Oaxaca and Puebla in particular were seen as producing maize that was the most typical and most representative of the country. Identifying the sample by number was a way to make the process more objective and avoid the possibility that the results or the technicians' work would be influenced by their emotional response or their perception of the area where it came from.

After examining and documenting the sample, they ground one hundred to five hundred grams into a fine powder, pushing it through a sieve to remove any large particles. They extracted and amplified the DNA from two grams of the remaining fine powder using polymerase chain reaction (PCR). They used PCR to look for the presence of particular DNA sequences which would indicate that the sample had been genetically modified. Most GM crops have at least one of two sequences, a promoter and a terminator, which do not exist in the genomes of unmodified plants. For example, they might look for the 35S promoter. Finding this sequence, which is derived from the cauliflower mosaic virus, in a sample of maize would indicate that it had been genetically modified. After detecting whether or not the sample was transgenic, they looked to see what the nature of the modification was. What proteins was it producing? Were they for the control of insects? Resistance to a virus? Some samples were multiply transformed, producing multiple new proteins. Endpoint PCR, the most commonly used technique, generated a gel with bands marking the presence of different DNA sequences associated with genetic modifications. This gel transformed the material of the plant into a graphic representation of its genetic material. In addition to doing endpoint PCR, which provides a qualitative sign of whether or not the sample is genetically modified, the lab does real-time PCR, a procedure that produces graphs quantifying the degree to which the sample consists of genetically modified organisms. They tested every sample twice, to confirm their results, and preserved each sample for four years in case they ever needed to be reanalyzed.

While dumping herbicides on a field to see which plants live or die or looking at a plant's genetic signature on a gel might appear to be compelling material evidence, these tests are not sufficient to make GMOs visible within the bureaucracy of ecological and agricultural regulation. For evidence of GMOs to count, it needs to be produced in fully accredited, validated ways. As part of the accreditation process, the lab has to fully document its activities. Life in the INE lab is structured around producing this documentation and validating its practices in order to ensure that the abstractions it produces from material traces of plant life are acceptable and authoritative. Only by writing standard operating procedures, documenting each step, and going through the other processes necessary to become an accredited lab would a group's findings on GMOs be visible to the state. Authoritative, universal knowledge is reserved for people with access to these limited resources.

When the Instituto Nacional de Ecología investigated Chapela and Quist's report on the presence of transgenes in maize in Oaxaca in the years before INE had established its own lab, it turned to commercial laboratories in the United States to produce evidence. After sampling 164 plants in 2003 and 706 plants in 2004, INE scientists sent the seeds to Genetic ID and GeneScan, companies that specialize in testing for GMOs. They justified their choice of these companies by noting they were "certified for compliance with international standards set by the International Organization for Standardization," a certification that gave their results more authority. Based on these results, they reported that there was no evidence of transgenes in the maize population.[54] These results were often interpreted as proof of the absence of transgenes and the efficacy of Mexican policies limiting their use.[55] Few labs could afford the expense of becoming accredited, and the insistence that only certified labs could produce authoritative data was a way of devaluing other forms of knowing—farmers' expertise, field tests, or even work done by academic scientists. The specialist in plant evolution at UNAM told me that Genetic ID had critiqued her research team for not "being scientific in doing biological monitoring, in contrast to their protected technology." Certification and proprietary technology all became tools for discrediting others' results. She argued that the standardization that Genetic ID deployed in fact made it less suited to do monitoring in Mexico, since its controls were set up according to gene expression patterns that characterized maize populations in the United States, which were much more homogenous than Mexican maize.

LIBRE DE TRANSGÉNICOS?
LABELS AND THEIR EFFICACY

The lab is an important resource for the country because of its role looking for and testing for the unintentional or accidental distribution of GMOs. However, the limitations of the lab make it seem that the state's surveillance and control over agriculture is perhaps primarily symbolic. The lab does not have the capacity to monitor the entire country, and relies on active denunciations in order to locate unauthorized GMOs. In communities where GMOs are embraced, farmers may be unlikely to report one another to INE or SAGARPA, and as a result remain invisible to the state. Furthermore, the state imports and distributes GMO grain across the country. A recent paper on the spread of GMOs points out that "millions of tons of non-segregated grain have been imported and distributed throughout Mexican rural areas by the public retail network Diconsa."[56] While this grain is intended to be used only as food, it can easily be planted. Carolina noted that not everyone distinguishes between maize for food and maize for seed. She said, "People might think, 'Oh, I could eat this bag of maize, or I could plant it and then have ten bags,' or whatever. But it's GMO, so they really shouldn't plant it." She added, "The government gives seeds as food, and then they can't really control how it is used, and people might plant it even though it's not approved for that." Labeling plants as grain or seeds was an effort to shape the way people used maize, but it had limited efficacy in actually controlling people's actions. Permits and labels are only partially effective in shaping social processes around the nation. Imported maize, while intended for consumption only, may not be treated that way by consumers and farmers.

Carolina noted that while labels are meant to help produce a particular reality (that these seeds will only be consumed, rather than planted, for example), they may sometimes impede the outcome they were intended to produce. For example, she argued that asserting a country is free of GMOs is problematic, drawing on the example of Ecuador. In its 2008 constitution, the country declared itself to be free of transgenic crops.[57] Carolina scoffed at this declaration. In an era of globalization, it is essentially impossible for a country to maintain this standard, and Ecuador imports products from the United States and Argentina, both notorious producers of GMOs. Carolina noted, "It's a fantasy to say 'They are not allowed here.'" Beyond the label being merely an indulgent fantasy, it has material effects on the development of scientific and technological networks and research. She claimed that because the country had labeled itself as free of transgenic organisms, it had not invested in the kinds of monitoring systems and infrastructure that Mexico had. Declaring a country to be free of transgenes produces a kind of official ignorance about the plant life of the country, allowing politicians and scientists to ignore their presence and to keep them invisible. While Mexico did not label itself as free of GMOs, it similarly pursued policies of official ignorance and invisibility. Transgenic crops did not have to be labeled, making their presence harder to detect (and practically impossible, without access to a lab).

PRODUCING AUTHORITY

People arguing both for and against the use of genetically modified organisms make broad claims about the consequences and necessity of their use. INE, in its role managing the use of GMOs, seeks to produce credible knowledge about the risks that will satisfy actors on all sides. These bureaucratic practices frame the knowledge produced about GMOs and their risks in order to circumscribe debates and control controversy. As the state makes decisions about what life-forms are essential to Mexican life, which should be protected and which eliminated, the work of gatekeeping that admits some kinds of data and excludes others is extremely important. In turning the regulation of GMOs into a bureaucratic exercise, the various, often conflicting institutions of the state have managed the production and flow of knowledge, establishing the state's labs as the only ones that are competent to perceive and measure the threat or risk posed by GMOs. In the process, the state asserts its authority over ecological health and security by controlling both knowledge and ignorance of the country's ecosystems.

Conclusion

Vivir Mejor and the Biodiverse Nation

A small, mud-colored salamander lives in the canals of Xochimilco, a neighborhood in southern Mexico City. The salamander, the axolotl, is a charismatic species with deep connections to Mexican history and identity. It has a striking appearance—broad, flat body, large head framed by feathery gills, wide-set eyes, and expressive mouth. Its name derives from a Nahuatl word that has been variously translated as water toy or game, aquatic monster, water twin, or water dog. Many of these translations reference the linguistic and mythic connections between the axolotl and the Aztec deity Xolotl, the canine twin of Quetzalcóatl, and the god of twins and monsters.[1] It is found in the wild only in the anthropogenic environment of Xochimilco. As described earlier, Mexico City is located on what was previously Lake Texcoco. Little remains of the lake today, as the water features that characterized the area in pre-Columbian times have mostly been drained. Xochimilco, where a maze of canals wind around small, artificial islands, is one of the few contemporary reminders of the watery history of the area. The canals and islands are the result of intensive engineering that transformed the land and water of the lake into an immensely productive agricultural site. Farmed since pre-Columbian times, the islands were essential resources for feeding the population of Tenochtitlán and subsequently Mexico City. The human engineering that transformed the landscape produced new habitats, notably the deep canals which became home to the axolotl. Making its home in an environment developed by human activities, the axolotl is an exemplar of the kind of nature that has animated all the projects analyzed in this book, one that is deeply entangled with human lives and activities.

The axolotl's unique life cycle means that it relies on the environment that agricultural activities produced in Xochimilco. Unlike other salamanders, including

144

FIGURE 13. Axolotl. Source: Stan Shebs, licensed under CC by 3.0 (https://creativecommons
.org/licenses/by-sa/3.0/deed.en).

the tiger salamanders from which they evolved, axolotls are neotenic. That is, they
do not undergo metamorphosis. Instead, they retain their juvenile characteristics
and the morphology of larvae as reproductive adults, remaining aquatic for their
entire life span. Stephen J. Gould speculated on the significance of the axolotls'
unusual development in *Ontogeny and Phylogeny*, hypothesizing that their delayed
somatic development (in which they reach sexual maturity before going through
the developmental stages typical of a salamander) offered them a selective advantage in the environmental conditions of Xochimilco. In Gould's formulation, they
have "repeatedly abandoned their facultative status for an irreversibly determined,
permanent larval life."[2] He noted that "if they transform, they are forced to trade a
favorable pond for harsh ground."[3] Unlike salamander larvae in vernal pools,
which dramatically alter their bodies to correspond with a radically changing
environment, the axolotls responded to the constancy of the canals of Xochimilco

by delaying (forever) their transformation into the adult form, becoming sexually mature while still in a larval stage (see figure 13).

While the axolotl is finely adapted to the historic environmental conditions of Xochimilco, the neighborhood has been undergoing rapid change as it urbanizes and as invasive species arrive in the canals.[4] Restoration ecologists, who study damaged or disturbed ecosystems and the efforts to repair them, have been attentive to how these changes have decimated the formerly abundant wild axolotl population. In 2006 axolotls were listed as critically endangered by the International Union for the Conservation of Nature and are now protected under the Convention on International Trade in Endangered Species (CITES) agreement. A 2014 census found a total of only five hundred to one thousand left in the wild, down from a population of six thousand per square kilometer in 1998.[5] The axolotls have relied on a human-produced landscape for their habitat; as human practices have changed that environment, they have become increasingly vulnerable. Conservationists in Mexico City argue that protecting the axolotl requires rethinking human practices.

"A SYNTHESIS OF CULTURE AND NATURE"

The present-day canals of Xochimilco are popular destinations for residents of Mexico City and tourists alike. People come for rides in trajineras, festively colored boats that can carry up to thirty people and are available for rental by the hour or the day. As the boats make their way slowly through the canals, they are stopped by vendors offering drinks, multicourse meals, or serenades by mariachi bands. The whole area has the atmosphere of a party, and few people seem to take notice of the extremely murky quality of the water the party is floating on. In 2011, I went to Xochimilco with Luis Zambrano. As director of the Laboratorio de Restauración Ecológica (Laboratory of Ecological Restoration), he studies aquatic ecosystems and organisms, with a focus on the axolotl. His work in conservation and restoration has made him well-known, and he has a high profile both within Mexico and internationally.

Shortly after we arrived in Xochimilco, Zambrano hailed a trajinera to take us to the site of one of his research and conservation projects, a refuge for the axolotl. Zambrano scoffed at the tourists, telling me that we would not be following them. We were going to what he called "the *nice* area. Not the tourist area." Eschewing the more populated canals, we headed towards the area where Zambrano was developing what he called an axolotl refuge, a space for the protection of the threatened axolotl population (see figure 14).[6] The refuge was one of the lake's artificial islands that had been restored to its historical function as a chinampa, or an area for labor-intensive agriculture. Like most of the chinampas in Xochimilco, it had been abandoned for decades. Chinampas had fallen out of favor as Xochimilco underwent

FIGURE 14. Axolotl refuge in Xochimilco. Source: Author photograph.

acute change, becoming increasingly urbanized while agricultural production was marginalized. The growing water needs of Mexico City and the accompanying diversion of water from Xochimilco resulted in declining water quality and food production and harmed the agrarian landscape.[7]

However, despite these changes, the Laboratory for Ecological Restoration had been able to transform this chinampa after acquiring the land with a grant from the federal government. It had once again become a thriving garden, demonstrating that the land continued to be remarkably fertile. Zambrano is collaborating with local farmers to work the land and had purchased the equipment, tools, and seed necessary to make it productive. They grew organic lettuce, broccoli, cabbage, and chamomile to sell in urban markets. To provide a refuge for the axolotl, they tended to and cultivated the canal, planting water hyacinth and other native plants, and constructed a filter to prevent nonnative fish from entering and to improve the canal's water quality. The improved water quality was also intended to improve the quality and healthfulness of the crops grown in the chinampa, which were irrigated with canal water.

Zambrano was optimistic about the refuge's promise to provide a haven for the axolotls and to protect the ecosystem in Xochimilco more broadly. The refuge began with one experimental canal and one control canal, subsequently expanding to four additional canals.[8] As we walked around the refuge, he told me that they had been working on it for the past three years, exclaiming, "And see the changes! From this experience, we know that in three years we can change the land. You need to have a good team. One person can't do anything alone." He went on to describe the refuge as a "synthesis of culture and nature." In this project, he was attempting to resurrect a historical form of agriculture in order to protect a species that had the status of a national symbol.

RESHAPING HUMAN AND NONHUMAN LIVES

The axolotl has thrived in the global circuits of biological research, traveling far beyond its origin point in Xochimilco to populate laboratories around the world. The proliferation of the axolotl is due to its popularity as a model organism, prized by developmental biologists for its neotenic retention of juvenile characteristics and its ability to regenerate a remarkable range of body structures at any point in its life cycle. It can regenerate entire limbs and tails, eye and heart tissues, and even the central nervous system. It can also be induced to change sexes. The unusual characteristics of the axolotl make it a valuable tool for scientists studying the molecular and genetic basis of organismal development and regeneration.[9] The University of Kentucky's Ambystoma Genetic Stock Center, one of the major producers of axolotls for use in research, has a breeding colony of axolotls and distributes fifteen to twenty thousand axolotls globally each year.[10] While the axolotl population in laboratories was growing, the wild population in Xochimilco was not. For Zambrano and other ecologists who were interested in the axolotl, it was not enough that this species survived in the aquariums and laboratories of the world. What was important was that the axolotl continued to thrive in Mexico, in Lake Xochimilco, and that Xochimilco retained its historical characteristics as a place where people engaged in small-scale agriculture and where axolotls and humans coexisted. While the axolotl endured in laboratory ecologies, spreading globally through its role in scientific research, Zambrano wanted to protect the axolotl in a particular place and to maintain the cultural forms associated with that place.

People are fascinated by the axolotl and the refuge project received significant attention from journalists within Mexico and from abroad.[11] The affective appeal of organisms, or their charisma, has been key to motivating conservation projects globally.[12] Zambrano intended to make use of the animals' charisma and significance for Mexicans to call for the protection of not only an animal or an ecosystem, but also the agricultural practices that historically characterized the area. This attention to the connection between ecology and culture contrasted with other conservation efforts in Xochimilco that typically paid little attention to the local community and often resulted in its dispossession in the name of protecting nature.[13] The refuge would both offer protection from encroaching urbanization, making it possible for the axolotl to survive in its native environment, and maintain the chinampa as a space for agricultural life and labor. The canals in which the axolotl lives could never be conceived of as pure spaces of nature; they are anthropogenic landscapes, tied to human practices, in which axolotl and human lives are produced together. In order to protect axolotls, Zambrano argued that Mexico had to maintain historic cultural practices through which human life and axolotls had coexisted for centuries.

The success of the chinampas depends on the development of a culture within Mexico City that values food attached to a specific locale. The concept of *terroir*, or "the taste of place," articulates the idea that the geophysical attributes of a place, like soil, topography, climate, ecosystem, combine with social and cultural practices of agriculture to produce particular tastes.[14] Zambrano and the farmers I spoke with at the chinampa described the produce as having a unique flavor. "The rosemary has a saltier flavor." "The earth is different. The epazote has its own taste." "Whatever herb we grow here, it has a different flavor." The process of constructing connections between a particular taste of food, a form of agriculture, and a particular place requires the development of a consumer market, one that is willing to seek out and support local foods and is invested in conservation. The growing prominence of fine-dining restaurants that emphasize the use of local produce suggests the possibility of generating an interest in the terroir of Xochimilco.[15] When I visited the refuge, the products produced there were not explicitly marketed as coming from Xochimilco. Zambrano and his colleagues hope gradually to get people to pay more for plants from Xochimilco because they are more delicious, and because supporting agriculture in Xochimilco means maintaining practices that produce places that are essential for nonhuman life forms like the axolotl.

Reports on Zambrano's projects described the conservation of the axolotl as crucial for the ecosystem of Mexico City, ascribing to the retiring and shy salamander tremendous ecological significance. Zambrano explained that "keeping the salamanders would imply that the urban environment had improved, and that Xochimilco had become a strong point for sustainability that would provide the city with water, climate, food, air, and vegetation."[16] Protecting Xochimilco would represent at least a symbolic commitment within Mexico City to protecting the environment. Zambrano argued that the health of the nation is tied to the preservation of life forms like the axolotl and that this preservation would come through a commitment to maintaining human ways of life that are tied to Mexican history. The management of nonhuman animal life entails management of human life, labor, production, and even taste. Saving the axolotl thus becomes a project that could reshape human lives in Mexico City. The refuge brings together nonhuman life forms and human practices to move past anthropocentric conceptions of a good life towards a more biocentric view, one which considers better living not only for people but also for Mexico's biodiverse life forms.[17] Nonhuman and human lives have long been entangled in Xochimilco, and this project, rather than seeking to address one in isolation from another, brings them together in the same frame.

VIVIR MEJOR AND THE BIODIVERSE NATION

In his study of Mexican nationalism, *The Cage of Melancholy*, Roger Bartra deploys the axolotl, which he identifies as "this very Mexican amphibian," as a metaphor for national identity.[18] Bartra translates the Nahuatl word *axolotl* as "game of water," drawing attention to the playful and fluid qualities of the animal. He suggests that there are "certain associations between social and biological phenomena, associations of ideas which traditionally have been at the root of national thought." In his telling, the biology of the axolotl, with its mysterious double nature as both larvae and salamander, the result of a perpetually delayed metamorphosis, becomes a representation of the Mexican national character. The biological properties of the axolotl for Bartra are a sign, "a message that comes to the Mexicans to instruct them on their condition, their origin, and their future." In this reading, the axolotls represent "the post-Mexican condition," a perpetual state of infancy or stalled development in regard to global trends.[19] The axolotl's mode of development, which diverges from typical salamander life cycles, becomes a metaphor for social life.

I connect the rejection of ordinary narratives of progress and development that characterize the axolotl's life with contemporary social movements of Buen Vivir or Vivir Bien that have emerged throughout Latin America in recent decades. Translated as "living well," the concept of Buen Vivir draws on values and experiences from indigenous communities to challenge capitalist practices and conventional Western notions of the good life. Buen Vivir rejects Western narratives and categories of developed and underdeveloped, and calls for alternatives to development that draw on indigenous lifeways and practices. The goal of Buen Vivir is to value harmony among individuals living in a community and between peoples and nature, and to move away from the anthropocentric logic of capital and development towards a more ecosystemic view of the world.[20] Buen Vivir has been written into the constitutions of Bolivia and Ecuador, where the idea of living well for all life-forms has been used to critique narratives that represent the global South as underdeveloped and in need of moving in the same direction as the developed world. The development patterns of the axolotl, in this light, might be reinterpreted not as stalled or infantile, but rather as a viable alternative.

Even as the refuge draws on contemporary Western scientific principles and is organized by a well-regarded, mainstream academic scientist, it exemplifies the challenges to Western scientific paradigms presented by Buen Vivir. The refuge rejects standard narratives of development in which nature needs to be rationalized and exploited, as well as the modern division between culture and nature itself. I read the axolotl refuge as an effort to draw on local indigenous and mestizo practices to find a new way forward, one that engages with concepts of terroir and taste of place, as well as historical forms of agriculture, to construct a new future in which both human and nonhuman life-forms are valued and thrive, and to imagine an economy based on solidarity, sustainability, wholeness, and diversity. The idea of remaking both human and nonhuman lives in the axolotl refuge resonates with these broader projects to challenge the divide that modernity and Western science have sought to produce between cultural and natural, human and nonhuman.[21] The creation of a refuge relied on the resurrection of a historical form of agriculture; the project demonstrated how protecting the biodiversity of the wetlands in which the axolotl lived was intertwined with maintaining the forms of human life that historically characterized the area. It is an important example of how scientists involved in biosecurity engage with human and nonhuman life forms as reciprocal actors who constitute one another.

Zambrano's work on the axolotl illuminates these kinds of efforts to produce better living in Mexico. Enlisting cultural practices to protect nonhuman life forms and environments, it exemplifies the way new scientific projects incorporate both the human and nonhuman and produce new forms of biopolitics as these populations are managed together.[22] Mexican biopolitics have become multispecies projects, encompassing animal, plant, and microbial worlds. As a result, disciplining and regulating the health of the nation entails thinking about many kinds of life-forms and their interactions. As this book has outlined, people have begun to perceive better living as a more-than-human project, one which moves past anthropocentric conceptions of a good life to incorporate a more biocentric view. This means thinking of better living not only for people but also for Mexico's biodiverse life-forms and thinking about both human and nonhuman life-forms as produced through the same historical and political processes. Scientists considering how to improve and protect human health, agriculture, and ecosystems make visible how all life-forms are malleable and how these biosocial processes are productive of distinctive populations. As scientists produce knowledge about the biotic substance of the nation, arguing that it is essential for the nation and needs to be considered in projects of better living, their work becomes an important locus for producing both science and the nation. This research has expanded notions about improving life outward, beyond the human.

The biosecurity science described in this book takes place in the context of the Anthropocene. The Anthropocene is the moment in which human activities have begun reshaping geological processes. There have been many debates over the term itself, as people have critiqued the use of the anthro- prefix for its implication that any and all kinds of human activity have produced these global changes, rather than more directly specifying which kinds of human activity have reshaped geology.[23] Despite these excellent critiques, the term remains useful, notably for pushing a wide array of people to confront a rupture with conventional Western divisions between nature and culture. If the very geological processes of the earth are shaped by human activities, dividing nature and culture into separate realms becomes increasingly untenable, and humans are no longer beings that act against an unchanging backdrop of nature. Biosecurity science usefully represents a way of thinking about life in a postnatural era, in which there is no longer any place that can be considered untouched nature, uncontaminated by human presence. Efforts to protect life and to make or let live various populations mean thinking about human and nonhuman populations together, whether caring for pests or safeguarding cherished species.

NOTES

INTRODUCTION

1. Gobierno de los Estados Unidos Mexicanos 2008.
2. Chilean writer Roberto Bolaño's widely acclaimed novel *2666* chronicles the femicides in Ciudad Juárez.
3. Camacho Servín 2012; Villalpando 2010. In comparison, New York City had four homicides per hundred thousand residents in 2013 (Sanburn 2014).
4. Kraus 2010.
5. Foucault 1978, 2008. As Nicole Shukin (2009) points out, the assumption that the species body at stake in biopolitics is always necessarily human has meant that animals have consistently been neglected in the analysis of biopolitics. Attending to biosecurity practices in Mexico makes apparent the way nonhuman as well as human life-forms are the subject of practices to improve and develop healthy populations.
6. See Foucault 1991; Lakoff and Collier 2008.
7. Goldstein 2010, 2016; Zeiderman 2013.
8. Bonfil Batalla 1996.
9. Latour 1993b.
10. Cruikshank 2005; Escobar 1997; González 2001; Todd 2016; Watts 2013.
11. Haraway 2003. Other anthropologists have further complicated and critiqued divisions between wild and domesticated and nature and culture. See, for example, Cruikshank 2005; Fuentes 2010; Raffles 2002; Viveiros de Castro 1998.
12. De la Cadena 2010, 2015.
13. Bartra 2007; Chorba 2007; Hernández 2001; Hill 2003; Paz 1994; Stephen 2002.
14. Córdova Villalobos 2011.
15. Córdova Villalobos 2011.

16. The term *biosecurity* first emerged in 1990 in New Zealand, referring to practices to protect livestock; see Masco 2014 for a history of use of the term. For its use in the United States, see Guillemin 2005; Lakoff and Collier 2008; National Research Council 2009; Vogel 2008.

17. Lane and Fauci 2001.

18. The first known incident was the contamination of salad bars with *Salmonella enterica* in Oregon by the Rajneeshee religious sect in September 1984. This incident caused illnesses in at least 750 people and 28 hospitalizations (King 2005: 433). For examples of the response to the 2001 anthrax attacks, see McPherson 2002; "U.S. Buying 100 Million Doses of Anthrax Antibiotic" 2001; Wallace 2001.

19. Lakoff 2008: 400.

20. Lakoff 2008: 400.

21. Armenta Núñez and Sánchez 1999; Diaz 1999; Guillén 1999a, 1999b.

22. Chen and Sharp 2014.

23. Helmreich 2009: 149.

24. For an elaboration of the concept of coproduction, see Jasanoff 2004.

25. Indigenista policies were prominent in Mexico, particularly in the period after the revolution. These were practices that celebrated some aspects of indigenous culture and identity and sought to incorporate them into the nation.

26. Collier and Quaratiello 2005; Hayden 2003; Soto Laveaga 2009; Stepan 1991; Vasconcelos 1925; Walsh 2003.

27. Stepan 1991.

28. Mendieta 2013.

29. Alonso 2004; Stepan 1991; Vasconcelos 1925.

30. López Beltrán 2011; Saade Granados 2011; Stepan 1991.

31. Vasconcelos (1925) 1997: 31.

32. Vasconcelos (1925) 1997: 32.

33. As Marisol de la Cadena (2008) has pointed out, in Latin America the categories of "'indigenous' and 'mestizo' belong to the same bio-political regime"; these identities are formed in relation to one another.

34. Roberts 2017; Stepan 1991; Strathern 1992; Weismantel 1995.

35. Roberts 2017.

36. Soto Laveaga 2013.

37. Aguilar-Rodríguez 2007, 2011; Stern 1999; Orisich 2018.

38. Orisich 2018.

39. Addressing nonhuman life-forms, this work joins a growing body of literature in anthropology engaging with multispecies ethnography (see Kirksey and Helmreich 2010 and Ogden, Hall, and Tanita 2013 for useful reviews of this literature).

40. Worster 2008; and see Cronon 1996 for an analysis of wilderness and nature in American history.

41. See Bordo 1987 and Merchant 1980 for analyses of the history of this division.

42. Wakild 2009, 2012; Simonian 1995.

43. Simonian 1995.

44. Wakild 2007: 103.

45. As elsewhere around the globe, the management of the environment contributed to the formation of subjects and regimes of rule. See, for example, Agrawal 2005; Fairhead and Leach 2003; Kosek 2006; Lowe 2006; Schiebinger 2004.

46. Banister and Widdifield 2014; Boyer 2012; Widdifield and Banister 2015.

47. Haenn 2005. The ejido system, which was part of the agrarian reforms implemented by Lázaro Cárdenas's administration in the 1930s, provided over three million campesinos with communal land tenure on more than seventy million hectares taken from prerevolutionary agricultural estates. It was a crucial element of the Mexican Revolution and a tool by which the government ensured the support of the peasantry from the time of its institution until its suspension by Carlos Salinas de Gortari in 1992 (Collier and Quaratiello 2005; Joseph and Nugent 1994; Mallon 1995; Stephen 2002).

48. While this is the dominant perspective, there are of course variations and alternative approaches. See, for example, Lynch 1988 for an analysis of how "subjugated" perspectives, like those regarding animals as capable of reciprocity, are present even in conventional US laboratory practice.

49. González 2001.

50. A landrace is a variety of a domesticated plant or animal species, one which has been adapted to the local environment through traditional agricultural practices. For more on the domestication of maize, see Bonfíl Batalla 1996; González 2001; Hartigan 2013.

51. Wilkes 2004.

52. Collier and Quaratiello 2005; Soto Laveaga 2009; Walsh 2003.

53. Blanchette 2015; Lezaun and Porter 2015; Lowe 2010.

54. See, for example, Kaufert and Lock 2001; Lock and Nguyen 2010.

55. Tsing 2005.

56. Lock 1993.

57. Katz et al. 2011.

58. Brown, Cueto, and Fee 2006.

59. Early estimates of the severity of this outbreak put the case fatality rate in Mexico at 0.4 percent. Seasonal influenza generally has a case fatality rate of less than 0.1 percent, so this was a significant increase (Taubenberger and Morens 2006). A case fatality rate of 0.4 percent would make the pandemic less severe than the 1918 influenza outbreak, the worst recorded influenza pandemic, which killed over 25 million people globally, but similar to a serious global pandemic that occurred in 1957 and caused widespread loss of life (Crosby 2003; Fraser et al. 2009).

60. Lacey and McNeil 2009; Lacey and Malkin 2009.

61. Chan 2009.

62. World Health Organization 2009.

63. Jacobs 2009; Lacey and Jacobs 2009.

64. McNeil 2009.

65. Nayan Shah (2001) describes how, in nineteenth-century San Francisco, public health authorities constructed Chinese immigrants as embodying disease.

66. See, for example, Ostherr 2005.

67. Instituto Nacional de Medicina Genómica 2009b.

68. Chan 2009.

69. International HapMap Consortium 2005.

70. Jimenez-Sanchez et al. 2008.

71. Silva-Zolezzi et al. 2009.

72. Cruz Martínez 2009.

73. Montoya 2007, 2011. For other examples and further analysis of the use of racial categories as proxies for genetic difference in scientific research and the molecularization of race, see Duster 2005; Fullwiley 2007; Kahn 2006; Reardon 2001.

74. Schwartz-Marín and Silva-Zolezzi 2010.

75. Rose 2001: 17.

76. Cruz Martínez 2009.

77. Instituto Nacional de Medicina Genómica 2009a.

78. Cruz Martínez 2009; Silva-Zolezzi et al. 2009.

79. López Beltrán and Vergara Silva 2011.

80. Choy 2011; Livingstone 2003; Messeri 2016; Redfield 2000.

81. Historian of science Robert Kohler (2002) has outlined the divide between lab and field, identifying them as distinct cultural domains with different languages, customs, material, and moral economies.

82. Braun 2007; Franklin 2005.

CHAPTER 1. FROM DEGENERATES TO REGENERATION, CONVICTS TO CONSERVATION

1. Aguirre-Muñoz et al. 2011a, 2011b, 2018.

2. Foucault 1994.

3. I identify the people I interviewed and did fieldwork with by pseudonyms in this text, with the exception of senior scientists and public figures who have agreed to be identified by name. Individuals I identify by first name only have been given pseudonyms.

4. Ensenada receives 33 percent of all cruise ship arrivals in Mexico (Padilla y Sotelo 2016).

5. See in particular his book El Otro México: Biografía de Baja California (Jordán 1951).

6. Zeiderman 2016.

7. Cabrera-Flores, López Leyva, and Serrano Santoyo 2017; Padilla y Sotelo 2016.

8. Comisión Nacional de Áreas Naturales Protegidas 2009: 1.

9. This rhetoric does reinforce the idea that Guadalupe is not valuable as "pristine" or untouched nature, but rather as an example of nature being used (Comisión Nacional de Áreas Naturales Protegidas 2009: 1).

10. Comisión Nacional de Áreas Naturales Protegidas 2009: 1.

11. Aguirre-Muñoz et al. 2011c.

12. Alonso 2004; Chorba 2007: 14.

13. Aguirre-Muñoz et al. 2011c: 387.

14. Aguirre-Muñoz et al. 2011c: 387.

15. Ferry 2005.

16. Gillis 2004: 123–24.

17. See Rosenberg 2016 for an analysis of multispecies biopolitics.

18. Aguirre-Muñoz et al. 2011c.

19. Comisión Nacional de Áreas Naturales Protegidas 2009; Jordán 1987.

20. Jordán 1987: 33.

21. Comisión Nacional de Áreas Naturales Protegidas 2009.

22. Cañizares-Esguerra 2005; Drayton 2000; Grove 1995; Iliffe 2003; Schiebinger 2004; Wulf 2015.

23. Pratt 1992: 152.

24. For more on what the vegetation of Guadalupe may have looked like before the arrival of humans, see Oberbauer 2005.

25. Comisión Nacional de Áreas Naturales Protegidas 2009; interview with Alfonso Aguirre-Muñoz, March 5, 2011.

26. These species were for a time believed to be extinct or nearly extinct. See Hanna 1925.

27. Banning 1925: 7–8.

28. Banning 1925: 6.

29. Banning 1925: 10–11.

30. Banning 1925: 22–24.

31. Hanna 1925: 227.

32. Hanna 1925; Anthony 1925.

33. Hanna 1925: 234.

34. Hanna 1925: 227

35. Hanna 1925: 232

36. Simonian 1995: 61.

37. Hanna 1925.

38. Gruel 2011: 77.

39. Gruel 2011: 73.

40. Gruel 2011: 67.

41. Gruel 2011: 84.

42. Gruel 2011: 61.

43. The penal colony represented in the movie was based on a prison established on the Islas Marías in 1905 under Porfirio Díaz.

44. Gruel 2011: 72.

45. Price 1973.

46. Ortega Ortiz 2008.

47. Emmanuel 1931.

48. The legitimacy of this decision continues to be disputed to this day (see, for example, González Avelar 2019).

49. Aguirre-Muñoz et al. 2012: 12.

50. Aguirre-Muñoz et al. 2012: 28.

51. Simonian 1995; Wakild 2009, 2012.

52. Hennessy 2018. Other examples and critiques of "fortress conservation," or efforts to protect biodiversity by excluding humans, are considered in Adams 2004, Brockington 2002, and Heatherington 2012.

53. Brockington 2002; Doolittle 2007; Pemunta 2019.

54. Secretaría de Medio Ambiente y Recursos Naturales 2013.

55. Benton 2010.

56. Aguirre-Muñoz et al. 2012: 8.

57. Discovery Channel 2016.

58. Beck 1992; Douglas (1966) 2002; Lentzos 2006.
59. Douglas (1966) 2002; Douglas and Wildavsky 1983; Luhmann 1993; Lupton 1999.

CHAPTER 2. THE CARE OF THE PEST AND ANIMAL BETRAYALS

1. Umland 1941.
2. For a classic account of the historic impact of ungulates on environment and social life in Mexico, see Melville 1994.
3. Helmreich 2005b; Woods 2017.
4. Bulmer 1967; Lowe 2006; Mansfield 2003; Takacs 1996.
5. Comaroff and Comaroff 2001; Tomes 1997.
6. For an example of global discourse on invasive species, see the United Nations 2030 Agenda for Sustainable Development (United Nations 2015).
7. Comisión Nacional para el Conocimiento y Uso de la Biodiversidad 2010.
8. Pisanty and Caso 2006: 299, Álvarez Romero et al. 2008.
9. Cruz 2011.
10. Álvarez-Romero et al. 2008: 5.
11. Chávez 2011; González Durand 2017; Guzmán Aguilar 2019.
12. Cruz 2011.
13. Moctezuma Barragán 2005.
14. Moctezuma Barragán 2005.
15. Comisión Nacional para el Conocimiento y Uso de la Biodiversidad 2012.
16. Kaiser 2001: 590.
17. Krajick 2005: 1410.
18. Krajick 2005, 1412.
19. Haraway 2008.
20. See, for example, Haraway 2008; Kirksey and Helmreich 2010.
21. Birke, Arluke, and Michael 2007.
22. Leopold 1999.
23. Hall 2001; Luna-Mendoza et al. 2019.
24. Sometimes the removal of invasive herbivores leads to "ecological kickback," the rapid growth of invasive vegetation. Prior to eradication, GECI conducted experiments to determine whether ecological kickback was likely to occur on Guadalupe, constructing fenced areas that goats could not enter and observing vegetation growth. They found that removing the goats would indeed allow native plants to flourish.
25. Kosek 2006: 23.
26. Kirksey and Helmreich 2010: 545.
27. Agamben 1998.
28. United States Fish & Wildlife Service 2016.
29. Jones 1919: 2.
30. The assertion that there were millions of goats on the island is an exaggeration. Jones 1919: 9.
31. Jones 1919: 24.
32. Cruz et al. 2009.
33. Sierra 1998.

34. León de la Luz, Rebman, and Oberbauer 2005.
35. Kohler 2002: 7.
36. Benson 2010.
37. Taylor and Katahira 1988: 298.
38. Keegan, Coblentz and Winchell 1994; Shackleton and Shank 1984.
39. Taylor and Katahira 1988: 298.
40. Taylor and Katahira 1988: 298.
41. Keegan, Coblentz, and Winchell 1994.
42. Nelson 2007: 299.
43. Campbell and Donlan 2005.
44. Krajick 2005: 1413.
45. Cruz et al. 2009.
46. McCann and Garcelon 2008.
47. Cruz et al. 2009.
48. Campos de Duffy and Cameron Duffy 1990.
49. Keegan, Coblentz, and Winchell 1994: 59.
50. Taylor and Katahira 1982: 299.
51. Taylor and Katahira 1982.
52. Keegan, Coblentz, and Winchell 1994: 59; Campbell and Donlan 2005: 1365.
53. Cruz et al. 2009.
54. Parkes 1990; Morrison et al. 2007; Russell et al. 2005; Cruz et al. 2009.
55. For more details, see the Grupo de Ecología y Conservación de Isla's website: www
.islas.org.mx/isla-guadalupe; Krajick 2005: 1411.
56. Lomnitz 2008: 454.
57. Lomnitz 2008: 463.
58. Lomnitz 2008: 58.
59. Salinas 2018; Raghu and Walton 2007.
60. Luna-Mendoza et al. 2011.
61. Rader 2004, 36.
62. Hayward 2010: 592.
63. Rader 2004.
64. Rader 2004.
65. Kohler 1994.
66. Friese and Clark 2012; Haraway 1997; Kohler 1994; Rader 2004; White 2006.
67. Kohler 1994: 127.
68. Lynch 1988: 266.
69. Birke, Arluke, and Michael 2007: 12.
70. On labs, see, for example, Knorr Cetina 1992.

CHAPTER 3. ACCLIMATIZING BIOSECURITY

1. AMEXBIO 2011: 5.

2. One of the many responses to the flu that provoked the ire of Mexican officials and diplomats by isolating Mexican citizens and limiting trade was the quarantine of Mexican citizens abroad, including ten in the Guomen Hotel in Beijing (Lacey and Jacobs 2009).

3. For the global turn in public health, see, for example, Katz et al. 2011; Yach and Bettcher 1998a, 1998b; Braun 2007.

4. World Health Organization 2005.

5. Sandia National Laboratory, in Albuquerque, New Mexico, is most famous for its role in the Manhattan Project, producing and testing the nonnuclear components of nuclear weapons. Today scientists at Sandia engage in research on a wide variety of national security issues (Scudellari 2011).

6. Scudellari 2011.

7. Scudellari 2011.

8. Cooper 2008: 83.

9. Cooper 2008: 89.

10. Caduff 2012; Foucault 2007; Lentzos and Rose 2009.

11. Foucault 2007; Caduff 2012.

12. Caduff 2012: 345.

13. Landecker 2011; Weiss 2005; Wynne 2005.

14. Nading 2012.

15. Lock 1993.

16. Anderson 1992; Livingstone 1999; Osborne 2000.

17. Ritvo 2012.

18. Roberts 2012: 3.

19. Livingston 2012: 8.

20. Alcántara 2009.

21. Secretaría de Salud 2006.

22. Román 2006a.

23. Román 2006b.

24. Notimex 2006.

25. The stories about the origin of H1N1 are part of what Nicholas King calls an "ontology of epidemic disease." They are discourses about disease that characterize "its causes and consequences, its patterns and prospects, the constellation of risks that it presents, and the most appropriate methods of preventing and managing those risks" (2002: 767).

26. Hernández Navarro 2009.

27. Jiménez Enviado 2009. Responses to the outbreak, including public displays of the ingestion of suspect meat, were reminiscent of earlier British responses to mad cow disease. See Lindenbaum 2001; Ritvo 1998.

28. These officials included the head of SAGARPA, Alberto Cárdenas Jiménez; Secretary of Labor Javier Lozano; Secretary of Agriculture Alberto Cárdenas; and the representative of the FAO in Mexico, Norman Bellino. They were documented in various states enthusiastically eating carnitas, chicharrones (pork rinds), and other pork products (La Jornada 2009).

29. Gobierno de los Estados Unidos Mexicanos 2007: 175.

30. Gobierno de los Estados Unidos Mexicanos 2007.

31. Gobierno de los Estados Unidos Mexicanos 2007.

32. Latour 1993a; King 2004.

33. Secretaría de Salud 2009; "Visita el Presidente Calderón instalaciones del INDRE" 2009.

34. Centro de Investigación en Enfermedades Infecciosas 2011.

35. For a timeline of the outbreak, including the emergence of cases in Mexico and the arrival of samples from Mexico to the CDC, see Centers for Disease Control and Prevention 2010.

36. Lacey 2009.

37. Alcántara 2009a, 2009b.

38. Flores 2009.

39. Alcántara 2009a, 2009b.

40. Loret de Mola 2009.

41. Livingston 2012.

42. Douglas (1966) 2002; Hodzic 2013.

43. See Lentzos 2008 for an analysis of the regulatory regimes in US biotech laboratories.

44. Hughes and Galán 2002.

45. For more on local immune systems, see, for example, Wilce 2003.

46. For details on the rate of diabetes in Mexico, see Jiménez-Cruz and Bacardi-Gascon 2004; Astudillo 2013; Rull et al. 2005.

47. For information on increased rates of infection among diabetic patients see Joshi et al. 1999; Muller et al. 2005.

48. "Meet Mr. Jenkins" (1960).

49. Joseph and Henderson 2002; Glaser 1971; Machado and Judge 1970.

50. Glaser 1971; Machado and Judge 1970.

51. Silbey 2009.

52. Stepan 1991.

53. Cueto 1994; Saldaña 2006.

CHAPTER 4. INVISIBLE BIOLOGIES, EMBODIED ENVIRONMENTS

1. Boyer 2007, 2015; Simonian 1995.

2. Farquhar 2010.

3. Roberts 2017.

4. Heather Paxson has theorized practices of microbiopolitics, describing the development of categories of microbial life-forms and the management and reorganization of human social practices to cultivate particular forms of microbial life. Incorporating the microbial into the political, she notes that "dissent over how to live with microorganisms reflects disagreement about how humans ought to live with one another" (2008: 16).

5. Landecker 2011.

6. Different understandings of the body produce different approaches to social life. See, for example, Emily Martin's work on representations of the immune system (1994) and Gregg Mitman's work on allergies (which have long been conditions that drew people's attention to the relationship between disease and place), in which he argues that "we have too narrowly focused our attention on the body within," calling for people to move beyond ideas of individual, well-defended bodies and even the belief that corporate capital and biomedical research can provide relief for illness (2008: 252). Eula Biss's recent work on vaccination treats health as a relationship. In it, she argues that the notion of communal or herd immunity dissolves individual boundaries and should push people to think about health as

a communal act. Attention to the ways our own immune systems both affect other people and are affected by other people and, more generally, the ways in which our bodies are porous and unbounded should transform our ideas of rights and obligations to one another (2014).

7. Anand 2011; Barnes and Alatout 2012; Orlove and Caton 2010; Walsh 2018.

8. Choy 2011.

9. Córdova Villalobos 2011.

10. Brizuela and Llerena 2013.

11. See, for example, Suárez Esquivel 2012.

12. Álvarez Laris 2009.

13. Bolaños Sánchez 2011.

14. Cárdenas de la Peña 1986, 8.

15. Mitman 2008.

16. Flores 2012.

17. For analysis of border pollution, its history, and environmental justice issues, see Di Chiro 2004; Johnson and Niemeyer 2008.

18. Buonaguro, Tornesello, and Buonaguro 2007.

19. Crane 2011.

20. Gorodezky et al. 2001.

21. Reardon 2001.

22. Montoya 2007, 2011.

23. Jimenez-Sanchez et al. 2008; Silva-Zolezzi et al. 2009.

24. Tsing 2005; Mansfield 2005; Mansfield and Hass 2006. Nicholas King (2004) looks at how biomedical scientists, mass media, and national security experts frame risks in terms that make particular interventions appear necessary, logical, and practical. King contrasts two approaches to global health: the "third public health revolution," which emphasized the provision of primary care, upstream determinants of health, and global capacity building as a way to protect global health (including in the United States), versus the "emerging diseases" rhetoric, which identified emerging disease as part of a complex global phenomenon but proposed solutions that reduced the scale of intervention to lab investigation and information management. Scale is also a key element in Bruno Latour's analysis of Pasteur's work and his argument for the social power of science in its ability to work at small scale and to convince others that this scale is simple, efficient, and effective (Latour 1993a).

25. Bautista-Arredondo et al. 2008.

26. Avila-Ríos et al. 2011.

27. Cruz Martínez 2010.

28. Fabian 1983: 2.

29. Suárez-Díaz, García-Deister, and Vasquez 2017; Dent and Ventura 2017; Suárez-Díaz 2017.

30. The comparison of DNA or RNA sequences to estimate their evolutionary history and relationships based on the degree to which the two sequences diverge.

31. Mendoza et al. 2014. Infection by HIV is generally the result of the transmission of a single variant of the virus, which is known as the founder strain. Extensive research has been done on the genotypic characteristics of founder strains (Parrish et al. 2013).

32. Mehta et al. 2015; Avila-Ríos and Reyes-Terán 2015.

33. For accounts of earlier Western understandings of the body that do incorporate landscape as an important actor and the shifting perceptions of the relationship between landscape and disease in Euro-American medical, lay practice, and colonial endeavors, see, for example, Anderson 2006; Kupperman 1984; Mitman 2008; Nash 2006; Valencius 2002.

34. Anderson and Mackay 2014.

35. Conklin 1996.

36. Conklin and Morgan 1996; Conklin 2001; Weismantel 2001.

37. See, for example, the articles in Suárez-Díaz, García-Deister, and Vazquez 2017.

38. Roberts 2017.

39. For examples of analyses of this turn in biological research, see Landecker and Panofsky 2013; Lock 2015; Meloni 2014; Singer 2016; Whitmarsh 2013.

40. Córdova Villalobos 2011.

41. Helmreich 2005a.

CHAPTER 5. THE BUREAUCRACY OF GENETIC MODIFICATION

1. At the time I conducted my fieldwork, the organization was officially named the Instituto Nacional de Ecología, although discussions had begun about changing the name to emphasize the increasing importance of climate change and to position the institute as Mexico's leading research and administrative center on climate change. The name has since been changed to the Instituto Nacional de Ecología y Cambio Climatico (INECC), or the National Institute for Ecology and Climate Change.

2. García 2010.

3. Boege 2008a, 2008b.

4. Malkin 2005; Pollan 2001.

5. See, for example, Fitting 2011; Gepts 2005; Pérez 2008; Ribeiro 2008; Soleri and Cleveland 2006; Soleri, Cleveland, and Cuevas 2006.

6. Álvarez-Buylla and Piñeyro 2009; Jasanoff 2005; Mann 2002.

7. Gusterson 2005.

8. Fitting 2011.

9. See, for example, Besky and Padwe 2016.

10. Braverman 2009; Head and Atchison 2009.

11. Ogden 2011; Raffles 2002.

12. The country's premier public university.

13. Hull 2012.

14. Thanks to Scott Freeman for this term.

15. Hetherington 2011; Heyman 1995; Hull 2012; Nelms 2015.

16. On the problem of ignorance in bureaucracies, see McGoey 2007. For a more general theorization of how science produces ignorance, see Proctor and Schiebinger 2008.

17. Enciso 2009.

18. For an ethnography of the life of maize in the laboratory and elsewhere, as well as an examination of the work of care in the laboratory, see Hartigan 2017.

19. See Anand 2015 for an analysis of the importance of producing textual artifacts in order to enable the operation of bureaucracy.

20. Benítez Díaz et al. 1998. These megadiverse countries contain almost 70 percent of the world's biodiversity. The other countries generally included in this group are: Colombia, Ecuador, Peru, Brazil, Zaire, Madagascar, China, India, Malaysia, Indonesia, and Australia (Comisión Nacional para el Conocimiento y Uso de la Biodiversidad 2018).

21. Benítez Díaz et al. 1998.

22. Hartigan 2017 analyzes the divergences and parallels between the use of race in humans and nonhumans, particularly maize.

23. Fitting 2011: 14.

24. Wilkes 2004.

25. Hayden 2003.

26. Soto Laveaga 2009.

27. Wilkes 2004.

28. Rockefeller Foundation 1959: 19.

29. For an analysis of concerns at the Rockefeller Foundation about the loss of maize genetic diversity, see Curry 2017.

30. Castillo 2011.

31. Centro de Ecodesarrollo 1980.

32. Rogers 1975.

33. Stone 2010.

34. Winerip 2013.

35. FAO 2012.

36. Stone 2010.

37. Pearson 2012.

38. Fitting 2011.

39. Comisión Intersecretarial de Bioseguridad de los Organismos Genéticamente Modificados 2011.

40. Mathews 2011.

41. "The Cartagena Protocol on Biosafety," Convention on Biological Diversity, last modified July 18, 2018. https://bch.cbd.int/protocol/default.shtml.

42. Specifically in the case of maize HX1, the genes are for Cry1F protein from *Bacillus thringiensis* (an insecticide that protects against certain moths and butterflies) and phosphinothricin acetyltransferase (*pat*) (which confers resistance to glufosinate ammonium herbicide) from the bacteria *Streptomyces viridochromogenes.*

43. The application reports that in studies for toxicity conducted on mice, the estimated median lethal dose (LD50, the dose required to kill half the test population) of the protein produced by the cry1F gene was 576 mg/kg, or 12,190 times more than a human would ingest if he or she ate corn with the cry1F gene. The application similarly dismisses the risk of the PAT protein based on oral toxicity studies with mice.

44. Bowker 2000; Waterton 2002.

45. Bowker 2000.

46. Quist and Chapela 2001; Jasanoff 2005; Mann 2002.

47. Various other groups have contested these findings, notably Dyer et al.'s 2009 report confirming Chapela and Quist's finding and disputing INE's inconclusive findings.

48. The EMA is a private organization that certifies the technical competency and reliability of laboratories.

49. Mathews 2011.

50. Mathews 2011, 4.

51. Rabasa 2015.

52. Genetic ID has subsequently been renamed FoodChain ID, and continues to offer GMO testing as well as certifying agricultural products for compliance with a variety of safety and sustainability standards. See their website at www.foodchainid.com for details.

53. Améndola, Castillo, and Martínez 2006.

54. Ortiz-Garcia et al. 2005.

55. Soleri and Cleveland 2006.

56. Dyer et al. 2009.

57. Despite this designation, in 2016 the government of Ecuador authorized field trials of genetically modified corn with the goal of improving food security and sovereignty.

CONCLUSION: VIVIR MEJOR AND THE BIODIVERSE NATION

1. Afraid of death, rather than be offered up as a sacrifice, Xolotl transformed first into a maize sprout, then a maguey or agave plant, and finally hid as an axolotl in Lake Xochimilco, a mythical transformation that ties these three life-forms and food sources together (Read and Gonzalez 2000).

2. Gould 1977: 322.

3. Gould 1977: 321

4. Peralta Flores 2012; Salles 1992.

5. Vance 2017.

6. For an account from Zambrano's lab on the development of the refuge see Valiente et al. 2010.

7. Salles 1992.

8. Valiente et al. 2010.

9. Koenig 2008. Recent noteworthy work on the axolotl includes a project that sequences its extremely large genome (its 32-gigabase pair genome is approximately ten times the length of the human genome). See Nowoshilow et al. 2018. Researchers hope that studies of the axolotl genome will allow them to better understand which genes related to regeneration have been conserved across species and how their regulation differs in mammals and salamanders (Farkas et al. 2016; Hutchins and Kusumi 2016; Koshiba et al. 1998).

10. Koenig 2008.

11. For examples of media coverage of the refuges, see "Ajolote podría extinguirse en cinco años: UNAM" (2011); Castello y Tickell 2012; Varela Huerta 2011; Walker 2009.

12. Lorimer 2015.

13. Narchi and Canabal 2015.

14. Paxson 2010; Weiss 2011.

15. An example is Pujol, Enrique Olvera's restaurant in Polanco, a neighborhood in Mexico City, which frequently appears on lists of the world's best restaurants and emphasizes local ingredients.

16. Olivares Alonso 2011.

17. Foucault 1978, 2008.

18. Bartra 1992. In 2011, Bartra also collaborated on the production of an anthropology of axolotl literature and imagery, produced with the Mexican Ministry of the Environment and intended to encourage the protection and restoration of the axolotl's habitat.

19. Bartra 1992.

20. De la Cadena 2010, 2015.

21. Latour 1993b.

22. Foucault 1978, 2008.

23. See, in particular, the work of environmental historian and political economist Jason Moore (2015), who suggests it would be better named the Capitolocene in an acknowledgement that it is not *human* activities in general that are reshaping the planet, but rather a particular economic system.

REFERENCES

Adams, William M. 2004. *Against Extinction: The Story of Conservation*. Sterling, VA: Earthscan.

Agamben, Giorgio. 1998. *Homo Sacer: Sovereign Power and Bare Life*. Translated by Daniel Heller-Roazen. Stanford, CA: Stanford University Press.

Agrawal, Arun. 2005. *Environmentality: Technologies of Government and the Making of Subjects*. Durham, NC: Duke University Press.

Aguilar-Rodríguez, Sandra. 2007. "Cooking Modernity: Nutrition Policies, Class, and Gender in 1940s and 1950s Mexico City." *The Americas* 64, no. 2: 177–205.

———. 2011. "Nutrition and Modernity: Milk Consumption in 1940s and 1950s Mexico." *Radical History Review* 110: 36–58.

Aguirre-Muñoz, A., A. Samaniego-Herrera, L. Luna-Mendoza, A. Ortiz-Alcaraz, M. Rodríguez-Malagón, M. Félix-Lizárraga, J.C. Hernández-Montoya, J.M. Barredo-Barberena, R. González-Gómez, F. Méndez-Sánchez, F. Torres-García and M. Latofski-Robles. 2011a. "Island Restoration in Mexico: Ecological Outcomes after a Decade of Eradications of Invasive Mammals." In *Island Invasives: Eradication and Management*, edited by C.R. Veitch, M.N. Clout, and D.R. Towns, 250–58. Gland, Switzerland: IUCN.

Aguirre-Muñoz, A., A. Samaniego-Herrera, L. Luna-Mendoza, A. Ortiz-Alcaraz, M. Rodríguez-Malagón, M. Félix-Lizárraga, J.C. Hernández-Montoya, R. González-Gómez, F. Méndez-Sánchez, F. Torres-García, and M. Latofski-Robles. 2011b. "The Conservation and Restoration of the Mexican Islands: An Overall Success Story with Some Failures, Lessons Learnt, and Policy Recommendations." In *Biodiversity Conservation in the Americas: Lessons and Policy Recommendations*, edited by E. Figueroa Benavides, 241–58. Santiago de Chile: Editorial FEN-Universidad de Chile.

Aguirre-Muñoz, A., A. Samaniego Herrera, L. Luna Mendoza, A. Ortiz Alcaraz, M. Rodríguez Malagón, M. Féliz Lizárraga, F. Méndez Sánchez, R. González Gómez,

F. Torres Garcia, J. C. Hernández Montoya, J. M. Barredo Barberena, and M. Latofski-Robles. 2011c. "Eradications of Invasive Mammals on Islands in Mexico: The Roles of History and the Collaboration between Government Agencies, Local Communities and a Non-Government Organisation." In *Island Invasives: Eradication and Management*, edited by C. R. Veitch, M. N. Clout, and D. R. Towns, 386–94. Gland, Switzerland: IUCN.

Aguirre-Muñoz, Alfonso, Karina Santos del Prado Gasca, Ana E. Marichal González, and Federico A. Méndez Sánchez, eds. 2012. "Estrategia nacional para la conservación y el desarrollo sustentable del territorio insular mexicano." Mexico City: Instituto Nacional de Ecología.

Aguirre-Muñoz, Alfonso, Yuliana Bedolla, J. C. Hernández-Montoya, Mariam Latofski Robles, Luciana Luna-Mendoza, Federico Méndez Sánchez, Antonio Ortiz-Alcaraz, Evaristo Rojas Mayoral, and Araceli Samaniego-Herrera. 2018. "The Conservation and Restoration of the Mexican Islands, a Successful Comprehensive and Collaborative Approach Relevant for Global Biodiversity." In *Mexican Natural Resources Management and Biodiversity Conservation: Recent Case Studies*, edited by Alfredo Ortega-Rubio, 177–92. Cham: Springer International Publishing.

"Ajolote podría extinguirse en cinco años: UNAM." 2011. *El Universal*, October 25, 2011. www.eluniversal.com.mx/articulos/66855.html.

Alcántara, Liliana. 2009a. "Cerca del diagnóstico, lejos de la vacuna." *El Universal*, April 16, 2009.

———. 2009b. "Evidencia virus rezagos en laboratorios." *El Universal*, May 16, 2009.

Alonso, Ana María. 2004. "Conforming Disconformity: 'Mestizaje,' Hybridity, and the Aesthetics of Mexican Nationalism." *Cultural Anthropology* 19, no. 4: 459–90.

———. 2005. "Territorializing the Nation and 'Integrating the Indian': Mestizaje in Mexican Official Discourses and Public Culture. In *Sovereign Bodies: Citizens, Migrants, and States in the Postcolonial World*, edited by Thomas Blom Hansen and Finn Stepputat, 39–60. Princeton, NJ: Princeton University Press.

Alvarez-Buylla, Elena, and Alma Piñeyro. 2009. "Urgencia de una política pública de bioseguridad." *La Jornada*, February 21, 2009. www.jornada.unam.mx/2009/02/21/opinion/014a1pol.

Álvarez Laris, Claudia. 2009. "Peligran zonas rurales del Ajusco 'por culpa del ex delegado Sánchez Torres.'" *La Jornada*, July 9, 2009. www.jornada.com.mx/2009/07/09/capital/040n1cap.

Álvarez Romero, Jorge, Rodrigo A. Medellin, Adán Oliveras de Ita, Héctor Gómez de Silva. and Óscar Sánchez. 2008. *Animales exóticos en México: Una amenaza para la biodiversidad*. Mexico City: Comisión Nacional para el Conocimiento y Uso de Biodiversidad.

Améndola, Ricardo, Epigmenio Castillo, and Pedro A. Martínez. 2006. *Country Pasture/Forage Resource Profiles*. Rome: UN Food and Agriculture Organization.

AMEXBIO. 2011. "Quiénes somos." *AMEXBIO Revista* (Mexico City).

Anand, Nikhil. 2011. "Pressure: The Polytechnics of Water Supply in Mumbai." *Cultural Anthropology* 26, no. 4: 542–63.

———. 2015. "Leaky States: Water Audits, Ignorance and the Politics of Infrastructure." *Public Culture* 27, no. 2: 305–30.

Anderson, Warwick. 1992. "Climates of Opinion: Acclimatization in Nineteenth-Century France and England." *Victorian Studies* 35, no. 2: 135–57.

————. 2006. *Colonial Pathologies: American Tropical Medicine, Race, and Hygiene.* Durham, NC: Duke University Press.

Anderson, Warwick, and Ian Mackay. 2014. *Intolerant Bodies: A Short History of Autoimmunity.* Baltimore, MD: Johns Hopkins University Press.

Anthony, A. W. 1925. "Expedition to Guadalupe Island, Mexico in 1922: The Birds and Mammals." *Proceedings of the California Academy of Sciences* 14, no. 12: 277–320.

Armenta Núñez, Antonio, and Julian Sánchez. 1999. "Salen toneladas de maíz transgénico de Veracruz." *El Universal*, December 9, 1999. www.eluniversal.com.mx/nacion/8792.html.

Astudillo, Olaya. 2014. "Country in Focus: Mexico's Growing Obesity Problem." *The Lancet: Diabetes and Endocrinology* 2: 15–16.

Avila-Ríos, Santiago, Claudia García-Morales, Daniela Garrido-Rodríguez, Christopher E. Ormsby, Ramón Hernández-Juan, Jaime Andrade-Villanueva, Luz A. González-Hernández, Indiana Torres-Escobar, Samuel Navarro-Álvarez, and Gustavo Reyes-Terán. 2011. "National Prevalence and Trends of HIV Transmitted Drug Resistance in Mexico." *PLoS One* 6, no. 11: e27812.

Avila-Ríos, Santiago, Christopher E. Ormsby, Jonathan M. Carlson, et al. 2009. "Unique Features of HLA-Mediated HIV Evolution in a Mexican Cohort: A Comparative Study." *Retrovirology* 6, no. 72.

Avila-Ríos, Santiago, and Gustavo Reyes-Terán. 2015. "HIV Phylogeographic Analyses and Their Application in Prevention and Early Detection Programmes: The Case of the Tijuana-San Diego Border Region." *EBioMedicine* 2, no. 10: 1296–97.

Banister, Jeffrey M., and Stacie G. Widdifield. 2014. "The Debut of 'Modern Water' in Early 20th Century Mexico City: the Xochimilco Potable Waterworks. *Journal of Historical Geography* 46: 36–52.

Banning, George Hugh. 1925. *In Mexican Waters.* Boston: Charles E. Lauriat.

Barnes, Jessica, and Samer Alatout. 2012. "Water Worlds: Introduction to the Special Issue of Social Studies of Science." *Social Studies of Science* 42, no. 4: 483–88.

Bartra, Roger. 1992. *The Cage of Melancholy: Identity and Metamorphosis in the Mexican Character.* Translated by Christopher J. Hall. New Brunswick, NJ: Rutgers University Press.

Bartra, Roger, ed. 2007. *Anatomía del Mexicano.* México, DF, Mexico: Delbolsillo.

Bartra, Roger, and Gerardo Villadelángel Viñas. 2011. *Axolotiada.* Mexico City: Fondo de Cultural Económica.

Bautista-Arredondo, Sergio, Tania Dmytraczenko, Gilbert Kombe, and Stefano Bertozzi. 2008. "Costing of Scaling up HIV/AIDS Treatment in Mexico." *Salud Pública de México* 50, supplement 4: S437–44.

Beck, Ulrich. 1992. *Risk Society: Towards a New Modernity.* London: Sage Publications.

Benítez Díaz, Hesiquio, Roberto Vega López, Arturo Peña Jiménez, and Ávila Foucat, eds. 1998. "Aspectos económicos sobre la biodiversidad de México." Mexico City: Instituto Nacional de Ecología.

Benson, Etienne. 2010. *Wired Wilderness: Technologies of Tracking and the Making of Modern Wildlife.* Baltimore: Johns Hopkins University Press.

Benton, Lauren. 2010. *A Search for Sovereignty: Law and Geography in European Empires, 1400–1900.* New York: Cambridge University Press.

Besky, Sarah, and Jonathan Padwe. 2016. "Placing Plants in Territory." *Environment and Society: Advances in Research* 7: 9–28.

Besser, Richard. 2009. "Press Briefing on Swine Influenza with Department of Homeland Security, Centers for Disease Control and Prevention, and White House," April 26, 2009. www.dhs.gov/ynews/releases/pr_1240773850207.shtm.

Birke, Lynda, Arnold Arluke, and Mike Michael. 2007. *The Sacrifice: How Scientific Experiments Transform Animals and People.* West Lafayette, IN: Purdue University Press.

Biss, Eula. 2014. *On Immunity: An Inoculation.* Minneapolis, MN: Graywolf.

Blanchette, Alex. 2015. "Herding Species: Biosecurity, Posthuman Labor, and the American Industrial Pig." *Cultural Anthropology* 30, no. 4: 640–69.

Boege, Eckart. 2008a. *El patrimonio biocultural de los pueblos indígenas de México.* México, DF: Instituto Nacional de Antropología e Historia.

———. 2008b. "Centros de Origen, Pueblos Indígenas y Diversificación del Maíz." *Ciencias* 92–93: 18–28.

Bolaños Sánchez, Ángel. 2011. "El bosque de Tlalpan, declarado zona ecológica y cultural." *La Jornada,* June 18, 2011.

Bonfil Batalla, Guillermo. 1996. *Mexico Profundo: Reclaiming a Civilization.* Austin: University of Texas Press.

Bordo, Susan. 1987. *The Flight to Objectivity: Essays on Cartesianism and Culture.* Albany: State University of New York Press.

Bowker, Geoffrey C. 2000. "Biodiversity Datadiversity." *Social Studies of Science* 30, no. 5: 643–83.

Boyer, Christopher. 2007. "Revolución y paternalismo ecológico: Miguel Ángel de Quevedo y la política forestal en México, 1926–1940." *Historia Mexicana* 57, no. 1: 91–138.

———. 2015. *Political Landscapes: Forests, Conservation, and Community in Mexico.* Durham, NC: Duke University Press.

Boyer, Christopher, ed. 2012. *A Land between Waters.* Tucson: University of Arizona Press.

Braun, Bruce. 2007. "Biopolitics and the Molecularization of Life." *Cultural Geographies* 14: 6–28.

Braverman, Irus. 2009. "Uprooting Identities: The Regulation of Olive Trees in the Occupied West Bank." *PoLAR* 32, no. 2: 237–63.

Brizuela, Bedilia, and Laura Llerena. 2013. "Los pulmones de la ciudad." *Excelsior,* March 31, 2013. www.excelsior.com.mx/comunidad/2013/03/31/891584.

Brockington, Dan. 2002. *Fortress Conservation: The Preservation of the Mkomazi Game Reserve, Tanzania.* Bloomington: Indiana University Press.

Brown, Theodore M., Marcos Cueto, and Elizabeth Fee. 2006. "The World Health Organization and the Transition from 'International' to 'Global' Public Health. *American Journal of Public Health* 96, no. 1: 62–72.

Bulmer, Ralph. 1967. "Why Is the Cassowary Not a Bird? A Problem of Zoological Taxonomy among the Karam of the New Guinea Highlands." *Man: The Journal of the Royal Anthropological Institute* 2, no. 1: 5–25.

Buonaguro, L., M.L. Tornesello, and F.M. Buonaguro. 2007. "Human Immunodeficiency Virus Type 1 Subtype Distribution in the Worldwide Epidemic: Pathogenetic and Therapeutic Implications." *Journal of Virology* 81, no. 19: 10209–19.

Cabrera-Flores, Mayer, Santos López Leyva, and Arturo Serrano Santoyo. 2017. "Relevancia, pertinencia y socialización del conocimiento, ¿cómo contribuyen los investigadores a la innovación de Ensenada, México? *Investigaciones Regionales* 37: 31–53.

Caduff, Carlo. 2012. "The Semiotics of Security: Infectious Disease Research and the Biopolitics of Informational Bodies in the United States." *Cultural Anthropology* 27, no. 2: 333–57.

Camacho Servín, Fernando. 2012. "Feminicidios en Juárez, peor que en los años 90." *La Jornada*, July 25, 2012, 15.

Campbell, Karl, and C. Josh Donlan. 2005. "Feral Goat Eradications on Islands." *Conservation Biology* 1362–74.

Campos de Duffy, Maria Jose, and David Cameron Duffy. 1990. Letter. *Conservation Biology* 4, no. 2: 117–18.

Cañizares-Esguerra, Jorge. 2000. "Iberian Colonial Science." *Isis* 96: 64–70.

Cárdenas de la Peña, Enrique. 1986. *Del Sanatorio de Huipulco, al Instituto Nacional de Enfermedades Respiratorias: Cincuenta años*. Mexico City: Secretaría de Salud.

Castello y Tickell, Sofia. 2012. "Mythic Salamander Faces Crucial Test: Survival in the Wild." *New York Times*, October 30, 2012. www.nytimes.com/2012/10/31/world/americas/struggle-of-axolotls-mexicos-mythical-salamander.html?pagewanted=all&_r=0.

Castillo, Miguel Ángel. 2011. "Peña Nieto: 'No Soy La Señora de La Casa.'" *Yahoo! Noticias*, December 13, 2011. https://es-us.noticias.yahoo.com/blogs/blognoticias/peña-nieto--no-soy-la-señora-de-la-casa.html.

Centers for Disease Control and Prevention. 2010. "The 2009 H1N1 Pandemic: Summary Highlights, April 2009-April 2010." www.cdc.gov/h1n1flu/cdcresponse.htm, accessed January 3, 2020.

Centro de Ecodesarrollo. 1982. *El cultivo del maiz en Mexico: Diversidad, limitaciones, y alternativas*. Mexico City: Centro de Ecodesarrollo.

Centro de Investigación en Enfermedades Infecciosas. 2011. www.cieni.org.mx, accessed April 14, 2011 (printout in author's possession).

Chan, Margaret. 2009. "Swine Influenza," statement by WHO director-general, April 25, 2009. www.who.int/mediacentre/news/statements/2009/h1n1_20090425/en/.

Chávez, Javier. 2011. "Invasión de pez león amenaza el Caribe; buscan control mediante procesamiento." *La Jornada*, April 17, 2011. www.jornada.com.mx/2011/04/17/estados/029n2est.

Chorba, Carrie C. 2007. *Mexico, from Mestizo to Multicultural: National Identity and Recent Representations of the Conquest*. Nashville: Vanderbilt University Press.

Choy, Timothy. 2011. *Ecologies of Comparison: An Ethnography of Endangerment in Hong Kong*. Durham, NC: Duke University Press.

Collier, George A., and Elizabeth Lowery Quaratiello. 2005. *Basta! Land and Zapatista Rebellion in Chiapas*. Oakland, CA: Food First.

Comaroff, Jean, and John L. Comaroff. 2001. "Naturing the Nation: Aliens, Apocalypse, and the Postcolonial State." *Journal of Southern African Studies* 27, no. 3: 627–51.

Comisión Intersecretarial de Bioseguridad de los Organismos Genéticamente Modificados. 2011. "Solicitudes de permisos de liberación 2011." www.conacyt.gob.mx/cibiogem/index.php/solicitudes/permisos-de-liberacion/solicitudes-de-permisos-de-liberacion-2011, accessed November 7, 2019.

Comisión Nacional de Áreas Naturales Protegidas. 2009. *Programa de manejo: Reserva de la Biosfera Isla Guadalupe*. Mexico City: Comisión Nacional de Áreas Naturales Protegidas.

172   REFERENCES

Comisión Nacional para el Conocimiento y Uso de la Biodiversidad. 2010. *Estrategia nacional sobre especies invasoras en México: Prevención, control y erradicación*. Mexico City: Comisión Nacional para el Conocimiento y Uso de la Biodiversidad.

———. 2012. "Palomilla del Nopal, *Cactoblastis cactorum*." www.conabio.gob.mx/conocimiento/cactoblastis/cacto/index.html, accessed November 7, 2019.

———. 2018. "¿Qué es un país megadiverso?" www.biodiversidad.gob.mx/pais/quees.html, accessed March 1, 2019.

Conklin, Beth. 1996. "Reflections on Amazonian Anthropologies of the Body." *Medical Anthropology Quarterly* 10, no. 3: 373–75.

———. 2001. *Consuming Grief: Compassionate Cannibalism in an Amazonian Society*. Austin: University of Texas Press.

Conklin, Beth, and Lynn Morgan. 1996. "Babies, Bodies, and the Production of Personhood in North American and a Native Amazonian Society." *Ethos* 24, no. 4: 657–94.

Cooper, Melinda. 2008. *Life as Surplus: Biotechnology and Capitalism*. Seattle: University of Washington Press.

Córdova Villalobos, José Ángel. 2011. "Secretario de Salud Del Gobierno Federal: Dr. José Ángel Córdova Villalobos" (interview). *AMEXBIO Revista* (Mexico City).

Crane, Johanna Tayloe. 2013. *Scrambling for Africa: AIDS, Expertise, and the Rise of American Global Health Science*. Ithaca, NY: Cornell University Press.

Cronon, William. 1996. "The Trouble with Wilderness: Or, Getting Back to the Wrong Nature." *Environmental History* 1, no. 1: 7–28.

Crosby, Alfred. 2003. *America's Forgotten Pandemic: The Influenza of 1918*. New York: Cambridge University Press.

Cruikshank, Julie. 2005. *Do Glaciers Listen? Local Knowledge, Colonial Encounters and Social Imagination*. Vancouver: University of British Columbia Press.

Cruz, Antimio. 2011. "Científicos documentan daños de peces invasores." *El Universal*, April 5, 2011. www.eluniversal.com.mx/cultura/65158.html.

Cruz Martínez, Ángeles. 2009. "Los Mexicanos, con 89 variaciones genéticas que provienen de indígenas." *La Jornada*, May 14, 2009.

———. 2010. "El sida que hay en México, más fuerte que el de otras naciones." *La Jornada*, June 16, 2010.

Cruz, Felipe, Victor Carrion, Karl J. Campbell, Christian Lavoie, and C. Josh Donlan. 2009. "Bio-Economics of Large-Scale Eradication of Feral Goats from Santiago Island, Galápagos." *Journal of Wildlife Management* 73, no. 2: 191–200.

Cueto, Marcos. 1994. "Laboratory Styles in Argentine Physiology." *Isis* 85, no. 2: 228–46.

Curry, Helen Anne. 2017. "From Working Collections to the World Germplasm Project: Agricultural Modernization and Genetic Conservation at the Rockefeller Foundation." *History and Philosophy of the Life Sciences* 39, no. 5b.

Dawson, Alexander. 1998. "From Models for the Nation to Model Citizens: Indigenismo and the 'Revindication' of the Mexican Indian, 1920–40." *Journal of Latin American Studies* 30, no. 2: 279–308.

De Alcántara, Cynthia Hewitt. 1984. *Anthropological Perspectives on Rural Mexico*. New York: Routledge.

De la Cadena, Marisol. 2000. *Indigenous Mestizos: The Politics of Race and Culture in Cuzco, Peru, 1919–1991*. Durham, NC: Duke University Press.

———. 2008. "Alternative Indigeneities: Conceptual Proposals." *Latin American and Caribbean Ethnic Studies* 33, no. 3: 341–50.

———. 2010. "Indigenous Cosmopolitics in the Andes: Conceptual Reflections beyond 'Politics.'" *Cultural Anthropology* 25, no. 2: 334–70.

———. 2015. *Earth Beings: Ecologies of Practice across Andean Worlds.* Durham, NC: Duke University Press.

Dent, Rosanna, and Ricardo Ventura Santos. 2017. "'An Unusual and Fast Disappearing Opportunity': Infectious Disease, Indigenous Populations, and New Biomedical Knowledge in Amazonia, 1960–1970." *Perspectives on Science* 25, no. 5: 585–605.

Diaz, Arturo. 1999. "A pesar de los logros no debemos bajar la guardia." *La Jornada.* April 8, 1999. www.jornada.unam.mx/1999/04/10/ls-soberon.html.

Di Chiro, Giovanna. 2004. "'Living Is for Everyone': Border Crossings for Community, Environment, and Health." *Osiris* 19: 112–29.

Discovery Channel. 2016. *Great Whites of Guadeloupe.* Video, 3:00. www.discovery.com/tv-shows/shark-week/videos/great-whites-of-guadeloupe, accessed October 11, 2016.

Doolittle, Amity. 2007. "Fortress Conservation." In *The Encyclopedia of Environment and Society,* edited by Paul Robbins, 705. Thousand Oaks, CA: SAGE Publications.

Douglas, Mary. (1966) 2002. *Purity and Danger: An Analysis of Concepts of Pollution and Taboo.* New York: Routledge.

Douglas, Mary, and Aaron Wildavsky. 1983. *Risk and Culture: An Essay on the Selection of Technological and Environmental Dangers.* Berkeley: University of California Press.

Drayton, Richard. 2000. *Nature's Government: Science, Imperial Britain and the "Improvement" of the World.* New Haven, CT: Yale University Press.

Duster, Troy. 2005. "Race and Reification in Science." *Science* 307, no. 5712: 1050–51.

Dyer, George A., J. Antonio Serratos-Hernández, Hugo R. Perales, Paul Gepts, Alma Piñeyro-Nelson, Angeles Chávez, Noé Salinas-Arreortua, Antonio Yúnez-Naude, J. Edward Taylor, Elena R. Alvarez-Buylla. 2009. "Dispersal of Transgenes through Maize Seed Systems in Mexico." *PLOS ONE* 4, no. 5: e5734.

Emmanuel, Victor. 1931. "Arbitral Award on the Subject of the Difference Relative to the Sovereignty over Clipperton Island." *American Journal of International Law* 26, no. 2: 390–94.

Enciso, Angélica L. 2009 "Estudio involucra a Sagarpa en la contaminación transgénica del maíz." *La Jornada,* July 1, 2009, 44.

Escobar, Arturo. 1997. "Cultural Politics and Biological Diversity: State, Capital and Social Movements in the Pacific Coast of Colombia." In *The Politics of Culture in the Shadow of Capital,* edited by David Lloyd and Lisa Lowe, 201–26. New York: Routledge.

Fabian, Johannes. 1983. *Time and the Other: How Anthropology Makes Its Object.* New York: Columbia University Press.

Fairhead, James, and Melissa Leach. 2003. *Science, Society and Power: Environmental Knowledge and Policy in West Africa and the Caribbean.* New York: Cambridge University Press.

Farkas, Johanna E., Piril Erler, Polina D. Freitas, Alexandra E. Sweeney, and James R. Monaghan. 2016. "Organ and Appendage Regeneration in the Axolotl." In *Regenerative Medicine—from Protocol to Patient,* edited by Gustav Steinhoff, 223–47. Switzerland: Springer.

Farquhar, Judith. 2010. "The Park Pass: Peopling and Civilizing a New Old Beijing." *Public Culture* 21, no. 3: 551–76.

Ferry, Elizabeth Emma. 2005. *Not Ours Alone: Patrimony, Value and Collectivity in Contemporary Mexico*. New York: Columbia University Press.

Fitting, Elizabeth. 2011. *The Struggle for Maize: Campesinos, Workers, and Transgenic Corn in the Mexican Countryside*. Durham, NC: Duke University Press.

Flores, Alejandro Cruz. 2012. "Al año, 4 mil muertes en el DF ligadas a la contaminación: OMS." *La Jornada*, August 3, 2012.

Flores, Javier. 2009. "Influenza y capacidades científicas." *La Jornada*, April 27, 2009.

FAO (Food and Agriculture Organization of the United Nations). 2012. *FAO Statistical Yearbook 2012: World Food and Agriculture*. www.fao.org/docrep/015/i2490e/i2490e00.htm.

Foucault, Michel. 1978. *The History of Sexuality*, vol. 1. Translated by Robert Hurley. New York: Vintage.

———. 1991. *The Foucault Effect: Studies in Governmentality; With Two Lectures by and an Interview with Michel Foucault*. Chicago: University of Chicago Press.

———. 1994. *Ethics: Subjectivity and Truth*. New York, NY: The New Press.

———. 2007. *Security, Territory, Population: Lectures at the College de France, 1977–1978*. New York: Palgrave MacMillan.

———. 2008. *The Birth of Biopolitics: Lectures at the College de France, 1978–1979*. New York: Palgrave MacMillan.

Franklin, Sarah. 2005. "Stem Cells R Us: Emergent Life Forms and the Global Biological." In *Global Assemblages: Technology, Politics, and Ethics as Anthropological Problems*, edited by Aihwa Ong and Stephen J. Collier, 59–78. Malden, MA: Blackwell Publishing.

Fraser, Christophe, Christl A. Donnelly, Simon Cauchemez, et al. 2009. "Pandemic Potential of a Strain of Influenza A (H1N1): Early Findings." *Science* 324, no. 5934: 1557–61.

Friese, Carrie, and Adele E. Clark. 2012. "Transposing Bodies of Knowledge and Technique: Animal Models at Work in Reproductive Sciences." *Social Studies of Science* 42, no. 1: 31–52.

Fuentes, Agustín. 2010. "Naturalcultural Encounters in Bali: Monkeys, Temples, Tourists, and Ethnoprimatology." *Cultural Anthropology* 25, no. 4: 600–624.

Fullwiley, Duana. 2007. "The Molecularization of Race: Institutionalizing Human Difference in Pharmacogenetics Practice." *Science as Culture* 16, no. 1: 1–30.

García, Patricia. 2010. "Jardín nativo de Pedregal en medio de la Ruta de la Amistad." *El Universal*, October 10, 2010. www.eluniversal.com.mx/cultura/63994.html.

Gepts, Paul. 2005. "Introduction of Transgenic Crops in Centers of Origin and Domestication." In *Controversies in Science and Technology: From Maize to Menopause*, edited by Daniel Lee Kleinman, Abby J. Kinch, and Jo Handelsman, 119–34. Madison, WI: University of Wisconsin Press.

Gillis, John R. 2004. *Islands of the Mind: How the Human Imagination Created the Atlantic World*. New York: Palgrave Macmillan.

Glaser, David. 1971. "1919: William Jenkins, Robert Lansing, and the Mexican Interlude." *Southwestern Historical Quarterly* 74, no. 3: 337–56.

Gobierno de los Estados Unidos Mexicanos. 2007. *El Plan Nacional de Desarrollo 2007–2012*. Mexico City: La Oficina de la Presidencia de la República Mexicana. www.diputados.gob.mx/LeyesBiblio/compila/pnd.htm, accessed December 10, 2019.

———. 2008. *Vivir Mejor: Política Social del Gobierno Federal*. Mexico City: Gobierno de los Estados Unidos Mexicanos.

Goldstein, Daniel. 2010. "Toward a Critical Anthropology of Security." *Current Anthropology* 51, no. 4: 487–517.

———. 2016. *Owners of the Sidewalk*. Durham, NC: Duke University Press.

González, Roberto J. 2001. *Zapotec Science*. Austin: University of Texas Press.

González Avelar, Miguel. 2019. "Clipperton, isla mexicana." *Revista de la Universidad de México* 73–84.

González Durand, Berenice. 2017. "Carismáticas, pero peligrosas: Especies invasoras." *El Universal*, November 12, 2017. www.eluniversal.com.mx/ciencia-y-salud/ciencia/carismaticas-pero-peligrosas-especies-invasoras.

Gorodezky, Clara, Carmen Alaez, Miriam N. Vázquez-García, Gabriela de la Rosa, Eduardo Infante, Sandra Balladares, Rosa Toribio, Elva Pérez-Luque, Linda Muñoz. 2001. "The Genetic Structure of Mexican Mestizos of Different Locations: Tracking Back Their Origins through MHC Genes, Blood Group Systems, and Microsatellites. *Human Immunology* 62, no. 9: 979–91.

Gould, Stephen Jay. 1977. *Ontogeny and Phylogeny*. Cambridge, MA: Harvard University Press.

Grove, Richard. 1995. *Green Imperialism: Colonial Expansion, Tropical Island Edens and the Origins of Environmentalism, 1600–1860*. New York: Cambridge University Press.

Gruel, Victor M. 2011. "Reos y cabras en Isla de Guadalupe: El proyecto de Agustín Olachea, 1931–1935." *Revista Meyibo* 3: 45–96.

Guillemin, Jeanne. 2005. "Inventing Bioterrorism: The Political Construction of Civilian Risk." In *Making Threats: Biofears and Environmental Anxieties*, edited by Betsy Hartmann, Bana Subramaniam, and Charles Zerner, 197–216. New York: Rowman & Littlefield.

Guillén, Guillermina. 1999a. "Viola la sagar leyes mexicanas, dice Greenpeace." *El Universal*, November 17, 1999. www.eluniversal.com.mx/nacion/5557.html.

———. 1999b. "Transgénicos, polémica mundial." *El Universal*, December 9, 1999. www .eluniversal.com.mx/nacion/8791.html.

Gusterson, Hugh. 2005. "Decoding the Debate on 'Frankenfood.'" In *Making Threats: Biofears and Environmental Anxieties*, edited by Betsy Hartmann, Bana Subramaniam, and Charles Zerner, 109–33. New York: Rowman & Littlefield.

Guzmán Aguilar, Fernando. 2019. "La voraz palomilla del nopal." *El Universal*, September 8, 2019. www.eluniversal.com.mx/ciencia-y-salud/ciencia/la-voraz-palomilla-del-nopal

Haenn, Nora. 2005. *Fields of Power, Forests of Discontent: Culture, Conservation, and the State in Mexico*. Tucson: University of Arizona Press.

Hall, Marcus. 2001. "Repairing Mountains: Restoration, Ecology, and Wilderness in Twentieth-Century Utah." *Environmental History* 6, no. 4: 584–610.

Hanna, Dallas G. 1925. "Expedition to Guadalupe Island, Mexico in 1922: General Report." *Proceedings of the California Academy of Sciences* 14, no. 12: 217–75.

Haraway, Donna. 1997. *Modest.Witness@Second_Millenium.FemaleMan_Meets_Onco-Mouse*. New York: Routledge.

———. 2003. *The Companion Species Manifesto*. Chicago: Prickly Paradigm Press.

———. 2008. *When Species Meet*. Minneapolis: University of Minnesota Press.

Hartigan, John. 2013. "Mexican Genomics and the Roots of Racial Thinking." *Cultural Anthropology* 28, no. 3: 372–95.

———. 2017. *Care of the Species: Races of Corn and the Science of Plant Biodiversity*. Minneapolis: University of Minnesota Press.

Hayden, Cori. 2003. *When Nature Goes Public: The Making and Unmaking of Bioprospecting in Mexico*. Princeton, NJ: Princeton University Press.

Hayward, Eva. 2010. "Fingeryeyes: Impressions of Cup Corals." *Cultural Anthropology* 25, no. 4: 577–99.

Head, Lesley, and Jennifer Atchison. 2009. "Cultural Ecology: Emerging Human-Plant Geographies." *Progress in Human Geography* 33, no. 2: 236–45.

Heatherington, Tracey. 2012. "Remodeling the Fortress of Conservation? Living Landscapes and the New Technologies of Environmental Governance." *Anthropological Forum* 22, no. 2: 165–85.

Helmreich, Stefan. 2005a. "Biosecurity: A Response to Collier, Lakoff, and Rabinow." *Anthropology Today* 21, no. 2: 21.

———. 2005b. "How Scientists Think; About 'Natives,' for Example: A Problem of Taxonomy among Biologists of Alien Species in Hawaii." *Journal of the Royal Anthropological Institute* 11, no. 1: 107–27.

———. 2009. *Alien Ocean: Anthropological Voyages in Microbial Seas*. Berkeley: University of California Press.

Hennessy, Elizabeth. 2018. "The Politics of a Natural Laboratory: Claiming Territory and Governing Life in the Galápagos Islands." *Social Studies of Science* 48, no. 4: 483–506.

Hernández, Rosalva Aída. 2001. *Histories and Stories from Chiapas: Border Identities in Southern Mexico*. Austin: University of Texas Press.

Hernández Navarro, Luis. 2009. "Las ciudades de Cerdos de Smithfield." *La Jornada*, May 12, 2009. www.jornada.unam.mx/2009/05/12/index.php?section=opinion&article=015a1pol.

Hetherington, Kregg. 2011. *Guerrilla Auditors: The Politics of Transparency in Neoliberal Paraguay*. Durham, NC: Duke University Press.

Heyman, Josiah. 1995. "Putting Power in the Anthropology of Bureaucracy: The Immigration and Naturalization Service at the Mexico-United States Border." *Current Anthropology* 36, no. 2: 261–87.

Hill, Sarah. 2003. "The Wasted Resources of Mexicanidad: Consumption and Disposal on Mexico's Northern Frontier." In *The Social Relations of Mexican Commodities*, edited by Casey Walsh et al., 157–85. La Jolla, CA: Center for U.S. Mexican Press.

Hodžić, Saida. 2013. "Ascertaining Deadly Harms: Aesthetics and Politics of Global Evidence." *Cultural Anthropology* 28, no. 1: 86–109.

Hull, Matthew. 2012. *Government of Paper: The Materiality of Bureaucracy in Urban Pakistan*. Berkeley: University of California Press.

Hughes, Eric A., and Jorge E. Galán. 2002. "Immune Response to Salmonella: Location, Location, Location?" *Immunity* 16: 325–28.

Humboldt, Alexander von. (1811) 1966. *Political Essay on the Kingdom of New Spain*. Translated by John Black. London: Longman, Hurst, Rees, Orme and Brown.

Hutchins, Elizabeth D., and Kenro Kusumi. 2016. "Genetics and Regeneration in Vertebrates." In *Regenerative Medicine—from Protocol to Patient*, edited by Gustav Steinhoff, 339–63. Switzerland: Springer.

Iliffe, Rob. 2003. "Science and Voyages of Discovery." In *The Cambridge History of Science*, edited by Roy Porter, 618–45. Cambridge: Cambridge University Press.

Instituto Nacional de Medicina Genómica. 2009a. "Landmark Mexican Study Reveals Significant Genetic Variation between Nation's Population and World's Other Known

Genetic Subgroups," press release, May 11, 2009. http://genomamexicanos.inmegen.gob
.mx/prensa/press%20release%20english.pdf.

———. 2009b. "Mapa Del Genoma de Poblaciones Mexicanas." http://genomamexicanos
.inmegen.gob.mx/index.html, accessed May 14, 2009.

International HapMap Consortium. 2005. "A Haplotype Map of the Human Genome.
Nature 437: 1299–1320.

Jacobs, Andrew. 2009. "Mexico Objects to Quarantines in China." *New York Times*, May 4,
2009.

Jasanoff, Sheila. ed. 2004. *States of Knowledge: The Co-Production of Science and Social
Order.* New York: Routledge.

Jasanoff, Sheila. 2005. *Designs on Nature: Science and Democracy in Europe and the United
States.* Princeton, NJ: Princeton University Press.

Jiménez-Cruz, Arturo, and Montserrat Bacardi-Gascon. 2004. "The Fattening Burden of
Type 2 Diabetes on Mexicans: Projections from Early Growth to Adulthood." *Diabetes
Care* 27, no. 5: 1213–15.

Jiménez Enviado, Sergio Javier. 2009. "Calderón reprocha trato injusto y hostil." *El Universal,* May 7, 2009.

Jimenez-Sanchez, Gerardo, Irma Silva-Zolezzi, Alfredo Hidalgo, and Santiago March. 2008.
"Genomic Medicine in Mexico: Initial Steps and the Road Ahead." *Genomic Research* 18:
1191–98.

Johnson, Melissa A., and Emily D. Niemeyer. 2008. "Ambivalent Landscapes: Environmental Justice in the US-Mexico Borderlands." *Human Ecology* 36, no. 3: 371–82.

Jones, Frederic W. 1919. *A Modern Monte Cristo and His Island: A Romantic Glimpse into
Goatology.* Beaumont, CA: Gateway.

Jordán, Fernando. 1987. *El otro México.* La Paz, México: Gobierno del Estado de Baja
California Sur.

Joseph, Gilbert M., and Timothy J. Henderson. 2002. *The Mexico Reader: History, Culture,
Politics.* Durham, NC: Duke University Press.

Joseph, Gilbert M., and Daniel Nugent. 1994. *Everyday Forms of State Formation: Knowledge
and the Negotiation of Rule in Modern Mexico.* Durham, NC: Duke University Press.

Joshi, Nirmal, Gregory Caputo, Michael Weitekamp and A. W. Karchmer. 1999. "Infections
in Patients with Diabetes Mellitus." *New England Journal of Medicine* 341, no. 25:
1906–12.

Kaiser, Jocelyn. 2001. "Galápagos Takes Aim at Alien Invaders." *Science* 293, no. 5530:
590–92.

Kaufert, Patricia, and Margaret Lock. 2001. "Menopause, Local Biologies, and Cultures of
Aging." *American Journal of Human Biology* 13: 494–504.

Katz, Rebecca, Sarah Kornblet, Grace Arnold, Eric Lief, and Julie E. Fischer. 2011. "Defining
Health Diplomacy: Changing Demands in the Era of Globalization." *Milbank Quarterly*
89, no. 3: 503–23.

Keegan, Dawn R., Bruce E. Coblentz, and Clark S. Winchell. 1994. "Feral Goat Eradication
on San Clemente Island, California." *Wildlife Society Bulletin* 22, no. 1: 56–61.

King, Nicholas. 2004. "The Scale Politics of Emerging Diseases." *Osiris* 19: 62–76.

Kirksey, S. Eben, and Stefan Helmreich. 2010. "The Emergence of Multispecies Ethnography."
Cultural Anthropology 25, no. 4: 545–76.

Knorr Cetina, Karin. 1992. "The Couch, the Cathedral, and the Laboratory: On the Relationship between Experiment and Laboratory in Science." In *Science as Practice and Culture*, edited by Andrew Pickering, 113–38. Chicago: University of Chicago Press.

Koenig, Robert. 2008. "Sanctuaries Aim to Preserve a Model Organism's Wild Type." *Science* 322, no. 5907: 1456–57.

Kohler, Robert. 1994. *Lords of the Fly: Drosophila Genetics and the Experimental Life.* Chicago: University of Chicago Press.

———. 2002. *Landscapes and Labscapes: Exploring the Lab-Field Border in Biology.* Chicago: University of Chicago Press.

Kosek, Jake. 2006. *Understories: The Political Life of Forests in Northern New Mexico.* Durham, NC: Duke University Press.

Koshiba, Kazuko, Atsushi Kuroiwa, Hiroaki Yamamoto, Koji Tamura, and Hiroyuki Ide. 1998. "Expression of Msx Genes in Regenerating and Developing Limbs of Axolotl." *Journal of Experimental Zoology* 282, no. 6: 703–14.

Krajick, Kevin. 2005. Winning the War against Island Invaders." *Science* 310, no. 5753: 1410–13.

Kraus, Arnoldo. 2010. "Ciudad Juárez." *La Jornada*, February 17, 2010. www.jornada.unam.mx/2010/02/17/opinion/021a2pol.

Kupperman, Karen O. 1984. "Fear of Hot Climates in the Anglo-American Colonial Experience." *William and Mary Quarterly* 41, no. 2: 213–40.

La Jornada. 2009. "Investigan si el nuevo virus de la gripe A/H1N1 fue producido en laboratorio," May 14, 2009. www.jornada.com.mx/2009/05/14/politica/014n1pol.

Lacey, Marc. 2009. "From Édgar, 5, Coughs Heard Round the World." *New York Times*, April 28, 2009.

Lacey, Marc, and Andrew Jacobs. 2009. "Even as Fears of Flu Ebb, Mexicans Feel Stigma." *New York Times*, May 4, 2009.

Lacey, Marc, and Donald G. McNeil Jr. 2009. "Fighting Deadly Flu, Mexico Shuts Schools." *New York Times*, April 24, 2009.

Lacey, Marc, and Elizabeth Malkin. 2009. "Mexico Takes Powers to Isolate Cases of Swine Flu." *New York Times*, April 25, 2009.

Lakoff, Andrew. 2008. "The Generic Biothreat, Or, How We Became Unprepared." *Cultural Anthropology* 23, no. 3: 399–428.

Lakoff, Andrew, and Stephen J. Collier, eds. 2008. *Biosecurity Interventions: Global Health and Security in Question.* New York: Columbia University Press.

Landecker, Hannah. 2011. "Food as Exposure: Nutritional Epigenetics and the New Metabolism." *BioSocieties* 6: 167–94.

Landecker, Hannah, and Aaron Panofsky. 2013. "From Social Structure to Gene Regulation, and Back: A Critical Introduction to Environmental Epigenetics for Sociology." *Annual Review of Sociology* 39: 333–57.

Lane, H. Clifford, and Anthony S. Fauci. 2001. "Bioterrorism on the Home Front: A New Challenge for American Medicine." *Journal of the American Medical Association* 286: 2595–97.

Latour, Bruno. 1993a. *The Pasteurization of France.* Cambridge, MA: Harvard University Press.

———. 1993b. *We Have Never Been Modern.* Cambridge, MA: Harvard University Press.

Lentzos, Filippa. 2006. "Rationality, Risk and Response: A Research Agenda for Biosecurity." *BioSocieties* 1, no. 4: 453–64.

————. 2008. "Countering Misuse of Life Sciences through Regulatory Multiplicity." *Science and Public Policy* 35, no. 1: 55–64.

Lentzos, Filippa, and Nikolas Rose. 2009. "Governing Insecurity: Contingency Planning, Protection, Resilience." *Economy and Society* 38, no. 2: 230–54.

León de la Luz, J. L., J. P. Rebman, and T. A. Oberbauer. 2005. "El estado actual de la flora y la vegetación de Isla Guadalupe." In *Isla Guadalupe: Restauración y conservación*, edited by Karina Santos del Prado and Eduardo Peters, 55–66. Mexico City: Instituto Nacional de Ecología.

Leopold, Aldo. 1999. *For the Health of the Land: Previously Unpublished Essays and Other Writings*. Washington, DC: Island Press.

Levinson, Brett. 1994. "The Other Origin: Cortázar and Identity Politics." *Latin American Literary Review* 22, no. 44: 5–19.

Lezaun, Javier, and Natalie Porter. 2015. "Containment and Competition: Transgenic Animals in the One Health Agenda." *Social Science & Medicine* 129: 96–105.

Lindenbaum, Shirley. 2001. "Kuru, Prions, and Human Affairs: Thinking about Epidemics." *Annual Review of Anthropology* 30: 363–85.

Livingston, Julie. 2012. *Improvising Medicine: An African Oncology Ward in an Emerging Cancer Epidemic*. Durham, NC: Duke University Press.

Livingstone, David. 1999. "Tropical Climate and Moral Hygiene: The Anatomy of a Victorian Debate." *British Journal for the History of Science* 32, no. 1: 93–110.

————. 2003. *Putting Science in Its Place: Geographies of Scientific Knowledge*. Chicago: University of Chicago Press.

Lock, Margaret. 1993. *Encounters with Aging*. Berkeley: University of California Press.

————. 2015. "Comprehending the Body in the Era of the Epigenome." *Current Anthropology* 56, no. 2: 151–77.

Lock, Margaret, and Vinh-Kim Nguyen. 2010. *An Anthropology of Biomedicine*. Malden, MA: Wiley-Blackwell.

Lomnitz, Claudio. 2008. *Death and the Idea of Mexico*. New York: Zone Books.

López Beltrán, Carlos. 2011. "Introducción." In *Genes (&) mestizos: Genómica y raza en la biomedicina mexicana*, edited by Carlos López Beltrán, 9–28. Mexico City: Ficticia.

López Beltrán, Carlos, and Francisco Vergara Silva. 2011. "Genómica nacional: El INMEGEN y el genoma del mestizo." *In genes (&) mestizos: Genómica y raza en la biomedicina mexicana*, edited by Carlos López Beltrán, 99–142. Mexico City: Ficticia.

Loret de Mola, Carlos. 2009. "Historias de Reportero." *El Universal*, April 30, 2009. www .eluniversal.com.mx/columnas/77951.html.

Lorimer, Jamie. 2015. *Wildlife in the Anthropocene*. Minneapolis: University of Minnesota Press.

Lowe, Celia. 2006. *Wild Profusion. Biodiversity Conservation in an Indonesian Archipelago*. Princeton, NJ: Princeton University Press.

————. 2010. "Viral Clouds: Becoming H5N1 in Indonesia." *Cultural Anthropology* 25, no. 4: 625–49.

Luhmann, Niklas. 1993. *Risk: A Sociological Theory*. New York: Walter de Gruyter.

Luna-Mendoza, L., A. Aguirre-Muñoz, J. C. Hernández-Montoya, M. Torres-Aguilar, J. S. García-Carreón, O. Puebla-Hernández, S. Luvianos-Colín, A. Cárdenas-Tapia and F. Méndez-Sánchez. 2019. "Ten Years after Feral Goat Eradication: The Active Restoration of Plant Communities on Guadalupe Island, Mexico." In *Island Invasives: Scaling Up to Meet the Challenge*, edited by C.R. Veitch, M.N. Clout, A.R. Martin, J.C. Russell, and C.J. West, 571–75. Gland, Switzerland: IUCN.

Luna-Mendoza, L., J.M. Barredo-Barberena, J.C. Hernández-Montoya, A. Aguirre-Muñoz, F.A. Méndez-Sánchez, A. Ortiz-Alcaraz, and M. Félix-Lizárraga. 2011. "Planning for the Eradication of Feral Cats on Guadalupe Island, México: Home Range, Diet, and Bait Acceptance." In *Island Invasives: Eradication and Management*, edited by C.R. Veitch, M.N. Clout, and D.R. Towns. 192–97. Gland, Switzerland: IUCN.

Lupton, Deborah. 1999. *Risk and Sociocultural Theory: New Directions and Perspectives.* New York: Cambridge University Press.

Lynch, Michael. 1988. "Sacrifice and the Transformation of the Animal Body into a Scientific Object: Laboratory Culture and Ritual Practice in the Neurosciences." *Social Studies of Science* 18, no. 2: 265–89.

Machado, Manuel A., and James T. Judge. 1970. "Tempest in a Teapot? The Mexican–United States Intervention Crisis of 1919." *Southwestern Historical Quarterly* 74, no. 1: 1–23.

Malkin, Elizabeth. 2005. "Science vs. Culture in Mexico's Corn Staple." *New York Times*, March 27, 2005. www.nytimes.com/2005/03/27/world/americas/science-vs-culture-in-mexicos-corn-staple.html.

Mallon, Florencia. 1995. *Peasant and Nation: The Making of Postcolonial Mexico and Peru.* Berkeley: University of California Press.

Mann, Charles C. 2002. "Has GM Corn 'Invaded' Mexico?" *Science* 295, no. 5560: 1617.

Mansfield, Becky. 2003. "From Catfish to Organic Fish: Making Distinctions about Nature as Cultural Economic Practice." *Geoforum* 34, no. 3: 329–42.

———. 2005. "Beyond Rescaling: Reintegrating the 'National' as a Dimension of Scalar Relations. *Progress in Human Geography* 29, no. 4: 458–73.

Mansfield, Becky, and Johanna Hass. 2006. "Scale Framing of Scientific Uncertainty in Controversy over the Endangered Steller Sea Lion." *Environmental Politics* 15, no. 1: 78–94.

Martin, Emily. 1994. *Flexible Bodies: Tracking Immunity in American Culture from the Days of Polio to the Age of AIDS.* Boston: Beacon Press.

Masco, Joseph. 2014. "Preempting Biosecurity: Threats, Fantasies, Futures. In *Bioinsecurity and Vulnerability*, edited by Nancy N. Chen and Lesley A. Sharp, 5–25. Santa Fe, NM: School for Advanced Research Press.

Mathews, Andrew S. 2011. *Instituting Nature: Authority, Expertise, and Power in Mexican Forests.* Cambridge, MA: MIT Press.

McCann, Blake E., and David K. Garcelon. 2008. "Eradication of Feral Pigs from Pinnacles National Monument." *The Journal of Wildlife Management* 72, no. 6: 1287–95.

McGoey, Linsey. 2007. "On the Will to Ignorance in Bureaucracy." *Economy and Society* 36, no. 2: 212–35.

McNeil, Donald G., Jr. 2009. "Other Illness May Precede Worst Cases of Swine Flu." *New York Times*, May 8, 2009.

McPherson, Coco. 2002. "The Year in Terror." *Village Voice*, September 10, 2002. www.villagevoice.com/2002/09/10/the-year-in-terror/.

"Meet Mr. Jenkins." 1960. *Time*, December 26, 1960.

Mehta, Sanjay R., Joel O. Wertheim, Kimberly C. Brouwer, Karla D. Wagner, Antoine Chaillon, Steffanie Strathdee, Thomas L. Patterson, Maria G. Rangel, Mlenka Vargas,

Ben Murrell, Richard Garfein, Susan J. Little, Davey M. Smith. 2015. "HIV Transmission Networks in the San Diego–Tijuana Border." *EBioMedicine* 2: 1456–63.

Melville, Elinor. 1994. *A Plague of Sheep: Environmental Consequences of the Conquest of Mexico*. New York: Cambridge University Press.

Meloni, Maurizio. 2014. "How Biology Became Social, and What It Means for Social Theory." *The Sociological Review* 62: 593–614.

Mendieta, Roberto. 2013. "The Death of Positivism and the Birth of Mexican Phenomenology." In *Latin American Positivism: New Historical and Philosophical Essays*, edited by Gregory D. Gilson and Irving W. Levinson, 1–12. Lanham, MD: Lexington Books.

Mendoza, Yaxelis, Alexander A. Martínez, Juan Castillo Mewa, Claudia González, Claudia García-Morales, Santiago Avila-Ríos, Gustavo Reyes-Terán, Blas Armién, Juan M. Pascale, and Gonzalo Bello. 2014. "Human Immunodeficiency Virus Type 1 (HIV-1) Subtype B Epidemic in Panama Is Mainly Driven by Dissemination of Country-Specific Clades." *PLOS ONE* 9, no. 4: e95360.

Merchant, Carolyn. 1980. *The Death of Nature: Women, Ecology, and the Scientific Revolution*. New York: HarperCollins Publishers.

Messeri, Lisa. 2016. *Placing Outer Space: An Earthly Ethnography of Other Worlds*. Durham, NC: Duke University Press.

Mitman, Gregg. 2008. *Breathing Space: How Allergies Shape Our Lives and Landscapes*. New Haven, CT: Yale University Press.

Moctezuma Barragán, Esteban. 2005. "México amenazado." *El Universal*, April 25, 2005. www.eluniversal.com.mx/editoriales/28132.html.

Montoya, Michael. 2007. "Bioethnic Conscription: Genes, Race, and Mexicana/o Ethnicity in Diabetes Research." *Cultural Anthropology* 22, no. 1: 94–128.

———. 2011. *Making the Mexican Diabetic: Race, Science, and the Genetics of Inequality*. Berkeley: University of California Press.

Moore, Jason. 2015. *Capitalism in the Web of Life: Ecology and the Accumulation of Capital*. New York: Verso.

Morrison, Scott A., Norman Macdonald, Kelvin Walker, Lynn Lozier, and M. Rebecca Shaw. 2007. "Facing the Dilemma at Eradication's End: Uncertainty of Absence and the Lazarus Effect." *Frontiers in Ecology and the Environment* 5: 271–76.

Muller, L. M., et al. 2005. "Increased Risk of Common Infections in Patients with Type 1 and Type 2 Diabetes Mellitus." *Clinical Infectious Diseases* 41: 281–88.

Murphy, Michelle. 2006. *Sick Building Syndrome and the Problem of Uncertainty: Environmental Politics, Technoscience, and Women Workers*. Durham, NC: Duke University Press.

Nading, Alex. 2012. "Dengue Mosquitoes Are Single Mothers: Biopolitics Meets Ecological Aesthetics in Nicaraguan Community Health Work." *Cultural Anthropology* 27, no. 4: 572–96.

Napolitano, Janet. 2009. "Press Briefing on Swine Influenza with Department of Homeland Security, Centers for Disease Control and Prevention, and White House," April 26, 2009. www.dhs.gov/ynews/releases/pr_1240773850207.shtm.

Narchi, Nemer E., and Beatriz Canabal Cristiani. 2015. "Subtle Tyranny: Divergent Constructions of Nature and the Erosion of Traditional Ecological Knowledge in Xochimilco." *Latin American Perspectives* 42, no. 5: 90–108.

Nash, Linda. 2006. *Inescapable Ecologies: A History of Environment, Disease, and Knowledge.* Berkeley: University of California Press.

National Research Council. 2009. *Countering Biological Threats: Challenges for the Department of Defense's Nonproliferation Program beyond the Former Soviet Union.* New York: National Academies Press.

Nelms, Taylor C. 2015. "'The Problem of Delimitation': Parataxis, Bureaucracy, and Ecuador's Popular and Solidarity Economy." *Journal of the Royal Anthropological Institute* 21, no. 1: 106–26.

Nelson, Bryn. 2007. "Tortoise Genes and Island Beings: Giant Galápagos Reptiles on Slow Road to Recovery." *Science News* 172, no. 19: 298–300.

Notimex. 2006. "Una pandemia de gripe aviar, catastrófica para AL: BID." *La Jornada*, January 30, 2006. www.jornada.unam.mx/2006/01/30/index.php?section=sociedad&article=045n1soc.

Nowoshilow, Sergej, Siegfried Schloissnig, Ji-Feng Fei, Andreas Dahl, Andy W.C. Pang, Martin Pippel, Sylke Winkler, et al. 2018. "The Axolotl Genome and the Evolution of Key Tissue Formation Regulators." *Nature* 554: 50–55.

Oberbauer, T.A. 2005. *La vegetación de Isla Guadalupe: Entonces y ahora.* Mexico City: Instituto Nacional de Ecología.

Ogden, Laura. 2011. *Swamplife: The Entangled Lives of Hunters, Gators and Mangroves in the Florida Everglades.* Minneapolis: University of Minnesota Press.

Ogden, Laura A., Billy Hall, and Kimiko Tanita. 2013. "Animals, Plants, People, and Things: A Review of Multispecies Ethnography." *Environment and Society: Advances in Research* 4: 5–24.

Olivares Alonso, Emir. 2011. "El ajolote se extinguirá en 10 años, alerta Luis Zambrano." *La Jornada*, May 4, 2011. www.jornada.unam.mx/2011/05/04/ciencias/a02n1cie.

Orisich, Shari. 2018. "'For the Creation of Strong Children, Beautiful and Intelligent': Eugenics, Youth, and the Nation in Post-Revolutionary Mexico City." *The Latin Americanist* 62, no. 3: 414–32.

Orlove, Ben, and Steven C. Caton. 2010. "Water Sustainability: Anthropological Approaches and Prospects." *Annual Review of Anthropology* 39: 401–15.

Ortega Ortiz, Reynaldo Yunuen. 2008. "Clipperton Island." In *Encyclopedia of Latin American History and Culture*, edited by Jay Kinsbruner and Erick D. Langer, 2nd ed., vol. 2. Detroit: Charles Scribner's Sons, 2008. 456–57.

Ortiz-Garcia, S., E. Ezcurra, B. Schoel, F. Acevedo, J. Soberón, A. Snow. 2005. "Absence of Detectable Transgenes in Local Landraces of Maize in Oaxaca, Mexico (2003–2004)." *Proceedings of the National Academy of Sciences of the United States of America* 102: 12338–43.

Osborne, Michael A. 2000. "Acclimatizing the World: A History of the Paradigmatic Colonial Science." *Osiris* 15: 135–51.

Ostherr, Kirsten. 2005. *Cinematic Prophylaxis: Globalization and Contagion in the Discourse of World Health.* Durham, NC: Duke University Press.

Padilla y Sotelo, Lilia Suana. 2016. "Diversificación sectorial y proyección internacional del municipio de Ensenada, Mexico." *Revista Transporte y Territorio* 15: 241–73.

Parkes, John P. 1990. "Eradication of Feral Goats on Islands and Habitat Islands." *Journal of the Royal Society of New Zealand* 20, no. 3: 297–304.

Parrish, Nicholas F., et al. 2013. "Phenotypic Properties of Transmitted Founder HIV-1." *PNAS* 110, no. 17: 6626–33.

Paxson, Heather. 2008. "Post-Pasteurian Cultures: The Microbiopolitics of Raw-Milk Cheese in the United States." *Cultural Anthropology* 23, no. 1: 15–47.

———. 2010. "Locating Value in Artisan Cheese: Reverse Engineering Terroir for New World Landscapes." *American Anthropologist* 112, no. 3: 444–57.

Paz, Octavio. 1994. *The Labyrinth of Solitude: The Other Mexico, Return to the Labyrinth of Solitude, Mexico and the United States, the Philanthropic Ogre*. New York: Grove Press.

Pearson, Thomas. 2012. "Transgenic-Free Territories in Costa Rica." *American Ethnologist* 39, no. 1: 90–105.

Pemunta, Ngambouk Vitalis. 2019. "Fortress Conservation, Wildlife Legislation and the Baka Pygmies of Southeast Cameroon." *GeoJournal* 84, no. 4: 1035–55.

Peralta Flores, Araceli. 2012. *Xochimilco y su patrimonio cultural*. DF, México: Instituto Nacional de Antropología e Historia.

Pérez, Matilde. 2008. "Interponen una controversia contra la ley de bioseguridad." *La Jornada*, August 4, 2008. www.jornada.unam.mx/2008/08/04/index.php?section=socieda d&article=046n1soc.

Pisanty, Irene, and Margarita Caso, eds. 2006. *Especies, espacios y riesgos*. Mexico City: Secretaría de Medio Ambiente y Recursos Naturales.

Pollan, Michael. 2001. "The Year in Ideas: A to Z; Genetic Pollution." *New York Times*, December 9, 2001.

Pratt, Mary Louise. 1992. *Imperial Eyes: Travel Writing and Transculturation*. New York: Routledge.

Price, John A. 1973. *Tijuana: Urbanization in a Border Culture*. Notre Dame: University of Notre Dame Press.

Proctor, Robert N., and Londa Schiebinger, eds. 2008. *Agnotology: The Making and Unmaking of Ignorance*. Stanford, CA: Stanford University Press.

Quist, David, and Ignacio H. Chapela. 2001. "Transgenic DNA Introgressed into Traditional Maize Landraces in Oaxaca, Mexico." *Nature* 414: 541–43.

Rabasa, Diego. 2015. "Hope in the Heart of Apache Territory: Mexico City's Deportivo Chavos Banda." *The Guardian*, November 10, 2015. www.theguardian.com/cities/2015 /nov/10/hope-in-the-heart-of-apache-territory-mexico-citys-deportivo-chavos-banda.

Rader, Karen. 2004. *Making Mice: Standardizing Animals for American Biomedical Research, 1900–1955*. Princeton: Princeton University Press.

Raffles, Hugh. 2002. *In Amazonia: A Natural History*. Princeton: Princeton University Press.

Raghu, S., and Craig Walton. 2007. "Understanding the Ghost of *Cactoblastis* Past: Historical Clarifications on a Poster Child of Classical Biological Control." *BioScience* 57, no. 8: 699–705.

Read, Kay Almere, and Jason J. Gonzalez. 2000. *Mesoamerican Mythology: A Guide to the Gods, Heroes, Rituals, and Beliefs of Mexico and Central America*. New York: Oxford University Press.

Reardon, Jenny. 2001. "The Human Genome Diversity Project: A Case Study in Coproduction." *Social Studies of Science* 31, no. 3: 357–88.

Redfield, Peter. 2000. *Space in the Tropics: From Convicts to Rockets in French Guiana*. Berkeley: University of California Press.

Ribeiro, Silvia. 2008. "La bioseguridad según Monsanto." *La Jornada*, March 29, 2008. www .jornada.unam.mx/2008/03/29/index.php?section=opinion&article=023a1eco.

Ritvo, Harriet. 1998. "Mad Cow Mysteries." *American Scholar* 67, no. 2: 113–22.

———. 2012. "Going Forth and Multiplying: Animal Acclimatization and Invasion." *Environmental History* 17: 404–14.

Roberts, Elizabeth. 2012. *God's Laboratory: Assisted Reproduction in the Andes.* Berkeley: University of California Press.

———. 2017. "What Gets Inside: Violent Entanglements and Toxic Boundaries in Mexico City." *Cultural Anthropology* 32, no. 4: 592–619.

Rockefeller Foundation. 1959. Annual Report. New York: Rockefeller Foundation.

Rogers, Michael. 1975. "The Pandora's Box Congress." *Rolling Stone*, June 19, 1975, 37–42, 74–82.

Román, José Antonio. 2006a. "México, listo ante cualquier foco de gripe aviar, afirma Julio Frenk." *La Jornada*, February 21, 2006. www.jornada.unam.mx/2006/02/21/index.php?s ection=sociedad&article=045n1soc.

———. 2006b. "Pide la FAO a AL no descuidar la lucha contra la gripe aviar." *La Jornada*, December 13, 2006. www.jornada.unam.mx/2006/12/13/index.php?section=sociedad&a rticle=048n2so.

Rose, Nikolas. 2001. "The Politics of Life Itself." *Theory, Culture & Society* 18, no. 6: 1–30.

Rosenberg, Gabriel. 2016. "A Race Suicide among the Hogs: The Biopolitics of Pork in the United States, 1865–1930." *American Quarterly* 68, no. 1: 49–73.

Rull, Juan A., Carlos A. Aguilar-Salinas, Rosalba Rojas, Juan Manuel Rios-Torres, Francisco J. Gómez-Pérez, and Gustavo Olaiz. "Epidemiology of Type 2 Diabetes in Mexico." *Archives of Medical Research* 36, no. 3: 188–96.

Russell, James C., David R. Towns, Sandra H. Anderson, and Mick N. Clout. 2005. "Intercepting the First Rat Ashore." *Nature* 437: 1107.

Saade Granados, Marta. 2011. "México mestizo: De la incomodidad a la certidumbre; Ciencia y política pública posrevolucionarias." In *Genes (&) mestizos: Genómica y raza en la biomedicina mexicana*, edited by Carlos López Beltrán, 29–64. Mexico City: Ficticia.

Saldaña, J. J., ed. 2006. *Science in Latin America: A History.* Austin: University of Texas Press.

Salinas, Carlos Marichal. 2018. "Mexican Cochineal, Local Technologies and the Rise of Global Trade from the Sixteenth to the Nineteenth Centuries." In *Global History and New Polycentric Approaches: Europe, Asia, and the Americas in a World Network System*, edited by Manuel Perez Gracia and Lucio De Sousa, 255–74. Singapore: Palgrave Macmillan.

Salles, Vania. 1992. "Xochimilco: Perdurabilidad de la tradición en un contexto de cambio." *Estudios Sociológicos* 10, no. 29: 341–62.

Sanburn, Josh. 2014. "Murders in U.S. Cities Reach Record Lows Again." *Time*, January 2, 2014. http://nation.time.com/2014/01/02/murders-in-u-s-cities-again-at-record-lows/.

Schiebinger, Londa. 2004. *Plants and Empire: Colonial Bioprospecting in the Atlantic World.* Cambridge, MA: Harvard University Press.

Schwartz-Marín, Ernesto, and Irma Silva-Zolezzi. 2010. "The Map of the Mexican's Genome: Overlapping National Identity, and Population Genomics." *Identity in the Information Society* 3, no. 3: 489–514.

Scudellari, Megan. 2011. "Can Biosecurity Go Global?" *Pacific Standard*, April 27, 2011. www.psmag.com/politics/can-biosecurity-go-global-29848/.

Secretaría de Medio Ambiente y Recursos Naturales. 2013. *Programa de manejo reserva de la biosfera Isla Guadalupe*. Mexico City: Secretaría de Medio Ambiente y Recursos Naturales.

Secretaría de Salud. 2006. *Plan Nacional de Preparación Y Respuesta Ante Una Pandemia de Influenza*. Mexico City: Secretaría de Salud.

———. 2009. "Esta mañana el presidente Calderón visitó las instalaciones del Instituto de Diagnóstico Y Referencia Epidemiológicos." www.prevencioninfluenza.gob.mx/2009/04/esta-manana-el-presidente-calderon-visito-las-instalaciones-del-instituto-de-diagnostico-y-referencia-epidemiologicos-indre/, accessed April 30, 2009.

Shackleton, D.M., and C.C. Shank. 1984. "A Review of the Social Behavior of Feral and Wild Sheep and Goats." *Journal of Animal Science* 58, no. 2: 500–509.

Shah, Nayan. 2001. *Contagious Divides: Epidemics and Race in San Francisco's Chinatown*. Berkeley: University of California Press.

Sharp, Lesley A., and Nancy N. Chen. 2014. Introduction to *Bioinsecurity and Vulnerability*, edited by Nancy N. Chen and Lesley A. Sharp, xi–xxxiii. Santa Fe, NM: School for Advanced Research Press.

Shukin, Nicole. 2009. *Animal Capital: Rendering Life in Biopolitical Times*. Minneapolis: University of Minnesota Press.

Sierra, A.C. 1998. "La conservación de los recursos genéticos animales en México." *Archivos de Zootecnia* 47: 149–52.

Silbey, Susan S. 2009. "Taming Prometheus: Talk about Safety and Culture." *Annual Review of Sociology* 35: 341–69.

Silva-Zolezzi, Irma, et al. 2009. "Analysis of Genomic Diversity in Mexican Mestizo Populations to Develop Genomic Medicine in Mexico." *Proceedings of the National Academy of Sciences* 106, no. 21: 8611–16.

Simonian, Lane. 1995. *Defending the Land of the Jaguar: A History of Conservation in Mexico*. Austin: University of Texas Press.

Soleri, Daniela, and David A. Cleveland. 2006. "Transgenic Maize and Mexican Maize Diversity: Risky Synergy?" *Agriculture and Human Values* 23: 27–31.

Soleri, Daniela, David A. Cleveland, and Flavio Aragón Cuevas. 2006. "Transgenic Crops and Crop Varietal Diversity: The Case of Maize in Mexico." *BioScience* 56: 503–13.

Soto Laveaga, Gabriela. 2009. *Jungle Laboratories: Mexican Peasants, National Projects, and the Making of the Pill*. Durham, NC: Duke University Press.

———. 2013. "Bringing the Revolution to Medical Schools: Social Service and a Rural Health Emphasis in 1930s Mexico." *Mexican Studies/Estudios Mexicanos* 29, no. 2: 397–427.

Stepan, Nancy Leys. 1991. *The Hour of Eugenics: Race, Gender, and Nation in Latin America*. Ithaca, NY: Cornell University Press.

Stephen, Lynn. 2002. *Zapata Lives: Histories and Cultural Politics in Southern Mexico*. Berkeley: University of California Press.

Stern, Alexandra Minna. 1999. "Responsible Mothers and Normal Children: Eugenics, Nationalism, and Welfare in Post-Revolutionary Mexico, 1920–1940." *Journal of Historical Sociology* 12, no. 4: 369–97.

Stone, Glenn. 2010. "The Anthropology of Genetically Modified Crops." *Annual Review of Anthropology* 39: 381–400.

Strathern, Marilyn. 1992. *After Nature: English Kinship in the Late Twentieth Century*. New York: Cambridge University Press.

Suárez-Díaz, Edna, Vivette García-Deister, Emily E. Vasquez. 2017. "Populations of Cognition: Practices of Inquiry into Human Populations in Latin America." *Perspectives on Science* 25, no. 5: 551–63.

Suárez-Díaz, Edna. 2017. "Blood Diseases in the Backyard: Mexican 'indígenas' as a Population of Cognition in the Mid-1960s." *Perspectives on Science* 25, no. 5: 606–30.

Suárez Esquivel, Mariana. 2012. "Urgente, rescatar el bosque de Tlalpan." *La Jornada*, November 4, 2012.

Takacs, David. 1996. *The Idea of Biodiversity: Philosophies of Paradise*. Baltimore: Johns Hopkins University Press.

Tate, Carolyn E. 2010. "The Axolotl as Food and Symbol in the Basin of Mexico, from 1200 BC to Today." In *Pre-Columbian Foodways: Interdisciplinary Approaches to Food, Culture, and Markets in Ancient Mesoamerica*, edited by John E. Staller and Michael D. Carrasco, 511–52. New York: Springer.

Taubenberger, Jeffery K., and David M. Morens. 2006. "1918 Influenza: The Mother of All Pandemics." *Emerging Infectious Diseases* 12, no. 1: 16–22.

Taylor, Dan, and Larry Katahira. 1988. "Radio Telemetry as an Aid in Eradicating Remnant Feral Goats." *Wildlife Society Bulletin* 16, no. 3: 297–99.

Todd, Zoe. 2016. "An Indigenous Feminist's Take on the Ontological Turn: 'Ontology' Is Just Another Word for Colonialism." *Journal of Historical Sociology* 29, no. 1: 4–22.

Tomes, Nancy. 1997. *The Gospel of Germs: Men, Women, and the Microbe in Modern Life*. Cambridge: Harvard University Press.

Tsing, Anna Lowenhaupt. 2005. *Friction: An Ethnography of Global Connection*. Princeton, NJ: Princeton University Press.

Umland, Rudolph. 1941. "Words from South Omaha." *American Speech* 16, no. 3: 235–36.

United Nations. 2015. General Assembly Resolution 70/1, "Transforming Our World: The 2030 Agenda for Sustainable Development," September 25, 2015. www.un.org/ga/search/view_doc.asp?symbol=A/RES/70/1&Lang=E.

United States Fish & Wildlife Service. 2016. "Wisdom, The Laysan Albatross." www.fws.gov/refuge/Midway_Atoll/wildlife_and_habitat/Wisdom_Profile.html, updated September 13, 2016, accessed October 11, 2016.

"U.S. Buying 100 Million Doses of Anthrax Antibiotic." 2001. *CNN.com*, October 24, 2001. www.cnn.com/2001/HEALTH/conditions/10/24/anthrax/index.html.

Valencius, Conevery Bolton. 2002. *The Health of the Country: How American Settlers Understood Themselves and Their Land*. New York: Basic Books.

Valiente, Elsa, Armando Tovar, Homán González, Dionisio Eslava-Sandoval, and Luis Zambrano. 2010. "Creating Refuges for the Axolotl (*Ambystoma mexicanum*)." *Ecological Restoration* 28, no. 3: 257–59.

Vance, Erik. 2017. "Biology's Beloved Amphibian—the Axolotl—Is Racing Towards Extinction." *Nature* 551: 286–89.

Varela Huerta, Itza. 2011. "En riesgo, plan de conservación del ajolote en canales de Xochimilco." *La Jornada*. December 29, 2011. www.jornada.unam.mx/2011/12/29/sociedad/031n1soc

Vasconcelos, José. (1925) 1997. *The Cosmic Race*. Baltimore: Johns Hopkins University Press.

"Visita el Presidente Calderón instalaciones del INDRE." 2009. *Tijuana Noticias*, April 2009. https://tijuananoticias.blogspot.com/2009/04/visita-el-presidente-calderon.html.

Viveiros de Castro, Eduardo. 1998. "Cosmological Deixis and Amerindian Perspectivism." *Journal of the Royal Anthropological Institute* 4, no. 3: 469–88.

Villalpando, Rubén. 2010. "Entre 14 mil y 18 mil viviendas de Ciudad Juárez, abandonadas." *La Jornada*, July 28, 2010.

Vogel, Kathleen. 2008. "Framing Biosecurity: An Alternative to the Biotech Revolution Model?" *Science and Public Policy* 35, no. 1: 45–54.

Wakild, Emily. 2007. "Naturalizing Modernity: Urban Parks, Public Gardens and Drainage Projects in Porfirian Mexico City." *Mexican Studies/Estudios Mexicanos* 23, no. 1: 101–23.

———. 2009. "International Boundary Parks and Mexican Conservation, 1935–1945." *Environmental History* 14, no. 3: 453–75.

———. 2012. "National Parks, Transnational Exchanges and the Construction of Modern Mexico." In *Civilizing Nature: National Parks in Global Historical Perspective*. New York: Berghahn Books.

Walker, Matt. 2009. "Axolotl Verges on Wild Extinction." *BBC Earth News*, August 26, 2009. http://news.bbc.co.uk/earth/hi/earth_news/newsid_8220000/8220636.stm.

Wallace, K. 2001. "Gephardt Thinks Anthrax, Terror Attack Linked." *CNN.com*, October 23, 2001. www.cnn.com/2001/HEALTH/conditions/10/23/anthrax.gephardt/index.html.

Walsh, Casey. 2003. "'A Rosy Future': Cotton and Regional Development in Mexico's Northern Borderlands, 1920–1965." In *The Social Relations of Mexican Commodities*, edited by Casey Walsh et al., 19–54. La Jolla, CA: Center for U.S. Mexican Studies Press.

———. 2018. *Virtuous Waters: Mineral Springs, Bathing, and Infrastructure in Mexico*. Oakland: University of California Press.

Waterton, Claire. 2002. "From Field to Fantasy: Classifying Nature, Constructing Europe." *Social Studies of Science* 32, no. 2: 177–204.

Watts, Vanessa. 2013. "Indigenous Place-Thought & Agency amongst Humans and Non-Humans (First Woman and Sky Woman Go on a European World Tour!)." *Decolonization: Indigeneity, Education & Society* 2, no. 1: 20–34.

Weismantel, Mary. 1995. "Making Kin: Kinship Theory and Zumbagua Adoptions." *American Ethnologist* 22, no. 4: 685–704.

———. 2001. *Cholas and Pishtacos: Stories of Race and Sex in the Andes*. Chicago: University of Chicago Press.

Weiss, Brad. 2011. "Making Pigs Local: Discerning the Sensory Character of Place." *Cultural Anthropology* 26, no. 3: 438–61.

Weiss, Kenneth. 2005. "The Phenogenetic Logic of Life." *Nature Reviews: Genetics* 6, no. 1: 36–45.

White, Paul S. 2006. "The Experimental Animal in Victorian Britain." In *Thinking with Animals*, edited by Gregg Mitman and Lorraine Daston, 59–82. New York: Columbia University Press.

Whitmarsh, Ian. 2013. "Troubling "Environments": Postgenomics, Bajan Wheezing, and Lévi-Strauss." *Medical Anthropology Quarterly* 27, no. 4: 489–509.

Widdifield, Stacie G., and Jeffrey M. Banister. 2015. "Seeing Water in Early Twentieth-Century Mexico City: Henry Wellge's *Perspective Plan of the City and Valley of Mexico, D. F., 1906*." *Anales del Instituto de Investigaciones Estéticas* 37, no. 107: 9–37.

Wilce, James M., Jr. 2003. *Social and Cultural Lives of Immune Systems*. New York: Routledge.

Wilkes, Garrison. 2004. "Corn, Strange and Marvelous: But Is a Definitive Origin Known?" In *Corn: Origin, History, Technology, and Production*, edited by C. Wayne Smith, Javier Betrán, and E. C. A. Runge, 3–64. Hoboken, NJ: John Wiley & Sons.

Winerip, Michael. 2013. "You Call That a Tomato?" *New York Times*, June 24, 2013. www .nytimes.com/2013/06/24/booming/you-call-that-a-tomato.html?_r=0.

Woods, Rebecca J. H. 2017. *The Herds Shot Round the World: Native Breeds and the British Empire: 1800–1900*. Chapel Hill: University of North Carolina Press.

World Health Organization. 2005. "International Health Regulations 2005." www.who.int /ihr/publications/9789241580496/en/, accessed November 6, 2019.

———. 2009. "Influenza A (H1N1)—Update 17." May 6, 2009. www.who.int/csr/don /2009_05_06/en/index.html.

Worster, Donald. 2008. *A Passion for Nature: The Life of John Muir*. New York: Oxford University Press.

Wulf, Andrea. 2015. *The Invention of Nature: Alexander von Humboldt's New World*. New York: Alfred A. Knopf.

Wynne, Brian. 2005. "Reflexing Complexity: Post-Genomic Knowledge and Reductionist Returns in Public Science." *Theory Culture Society* 22, no. 5: 67–94.

Yach, Derek, and Douglas Bettcher. 1998a. "The Globalization of Public Health, I: Threats and Opportunities." *American Journal of Public Health* 88: 735–38.

———. 1998b. "The Globalization of Public Health, II: The Convergence of Self-Interest and Altruism." *American Journal of Public Health* 88: 738–41.

Zambrano, Luis. 2011. "La Extinción del Axolote en Xochimilco." In *Axolotiada*, edited by Gerardo Villadelángel Viñas and Roger Bartra, 230–50. Mexico City: Fondo de Cultural Económica.

Zeiderman, Austin. 2013. "Living Dangerously: Biopolitics and Urban Citizenship in Bogotá, Colombia." *American Ethnologist* 40, no. 1: 71–87.

———. 2016. *Endangered City: The Politics of Security and Risk in Bogotá.* Durham, NC: Duke University Press.

INDEX

acclimatization, of biosecurity programs, 74–75
aerosols, 81
Africa: biomedicine practices in, 75; HIV
   infections in, 107
agriculture: canals in Xochimilco, 144, 146–47,
   147*fig*, 149; chinampa, 146–47, 147*fig*, 149;
   corn exports, 127; effect on biodiversity, 133;
   ejido system, 10–11, 155n47; GMO labels and
   actual farming practices, 142–43; hog farms,
   78–79; industrial agriculture, criticisms of,
   78; livestock, 5, 28–29, 129, 154n16; milpa
   system, 133; terroir, 149, 151; Zapotec maize
   cultivation, 10–11. *See also* genetically
   modified organisms (GMOs); maize
Aguirre-Muñoz, Alfonso, 19, 24, 26; on
   collaboration with navy on Guadalupe, 34;
   on considering humans and biodiversity, 37;
   on goat eradication program, 58
AIDS, opportunistic infections, 112–13. *See also*
   HIV
air: control of in research facilities, 100–104,
   103*fig*; relationship of body and environment,
   105–6
airborne pathogens, biosafety practices for, 81,
   100–104, 103*fig*
air pollution, 5, 97; as biosecurity concern,
   98–100, 106; in Mexico City, 104–6
albatross, 48–49
Alcántara, Liliana, 83–84
Álvarez, Victoriano, 31

AMEXBIO (Asociación Mexicana de Bioseguridad), 5; conference in Puebla Mexico,
   88–91; founding of, 71, 71*fig*; H1N1 influenza
   response, 78; U.S. concerns about biosecurity
   standards, 72–76
Análisis de Riesgos para la Liberación de
   Organismos Genéticamente Modificados en
   al Medio Ambiente (AROMMA), 130–32
Anderson, Warwick, 114
*Animales exóticos en México: Una amenaza para
   la biodiversidad,* 45
animals: axolotl, 144–50, 145*fig*, 147*fig*; biosecurity
   and, 18, 71; desirable organism, use of term,
   135; ecological kickback, 158n24; on Guadalupe, 23–24, 48–49, 52, 60, 67; human management of nonhuman life, 11, 46–48, 52–53,
   65, 71, 73, 149–52; killing of invasive species,
   37–38; in laboratory settings, 67–68; shifting
   values about species roles in ecosystems,
   41–42, 45–46, 67–68; variation in value associated with animals, 65. *See also* biodiversity;
   goats; invasive species; native species
Anthropocene, 69, 151–52, 166n23
antiretroviral therapy (ART), 111
AROMMA (Risk Analysis for the Release of
   Genetically Modified Organisms in the
   Environment), 130–32
Asociación Mexicana de Bioseguridad.
   See AMEXBIO (Asociación Mexicana de
   Bioseguridad)

Founded in 1893,
UNIVERSITY OF CALIFORNIA PRESS
publishes bold, progressive books and journals
on topics in the arts, humanities, social sciences,
and natural sciences—with a focus on social
justice issues—that inspire thought and action
among readers worldwide.

The UC PRESS FOUNDATION
raises funds to uphold the press's vital role
as an independent, nonprofit publisher, and
receives philanthropic support from a wide
range of individuals and institutions—and from
committed readers like you. To learn more, visit
ucpress.edu/supportus.